Praise for *Murder at Shandy Hall*
and
Game, Set, M

"An absolutely extraordinary tale . . ."

"This is a scholarly and meticulous piece of historical journalism that will be sought out by aficionados of true crime" –
Irish Independent

"When Sheridan gives full rein to his imagination . . . the result is truly spine chilling" – *The Irish Examiner*

"This intriguing story is well told by Sheridan" –
The Sunday Business Post

"Michael Sheridan has unearthed another absorbing scandal . . . meticulously researched . . . forensically fashioned" –
The Sunday Times

"All the elements you need for a compelling mystery . . . an interesting read" – *Hot Press*

"A cracking good yarn" – *Ireland AM, TV3*

"What more could you ask for? . . . Thoroughly researched and engagingly written, this book is sure to send a shiver up your spine" –
Woman's Way 'Book of the Fortnight'

"Beautifully put together" – *Sunshine Radio*

"Fantastic . . ." – THE TOM DUNNE SHOW, *Newstalk*

"An intriguing story" – *Irish Independent*

"A riveting read" – *Evening Echo*

Also by Michael Sheridan

Game, Set, Murder

Murder at Shandy Hall

Published by Poolbeg

MURDER
AT
IRELAND'S EYE

MICHAEL SHERIDAN

POOLBEG

Published 2012
by Poolbeg Press Ltd
123 Grange Hill, Baldoyle
Dublin 13, Ireland
E-mail: poolbeg@poolbeg.com
www.poolbeg.com

1

A catalogue record for this book is available from the British Library.

ISBN 978-1-84223-528-7

Typeset by Patricia Hope in Sabon 11/15

Printed and bound by CPI Group (UK) Ltd, Croydon, CR0 4YY

www.poolbeg.com

ABOUT THE AUTHOR

Michael Sheridan is the bestselling true crime author of *Death in December*, an investigation into the murder of French film producer Sophie Toscan du Plantier; *Frozen Blood: Serial Killers in Ireland*; *A Letter to Veronica*; *Tears of Blood* and *Bloody Evidence*. He is co-author and ghostwriter of *Don't Ever Tell: Kathy's Story*, an account of Kathy O'Beirne's traumatic childhood, which spent 22 weeks in the UK Top Ten and was a *Sunday Times* bestseller.

His bestselling *Murder at Shandy Hall (The Coachford Poisoning Case)* was published by Poolbeg in 2010, followed by *Game, Set, Murder in 2011* (previously published by Poolbeg as *Murder in Monte Carlo*).

Michael has worked for the *Irish Press* and the *Sunday Independent* as a freelance journalist.

ACKNOWLEDGEMENTS

Firstly my thanks, as always, to family – Ger, Cian, Fionn, Marty, Sarah, mother Patsy, sister Christine and brother Dave – for continuing support and encouragement. Also to the staff of Poolbeg – Paula, Kieran, Dave, Sarah and Ailbhe. And special mention, as always, to the brilliant editorial eye of Gaye Shortland and her immense contribution to the finishing and polishing of the manuscript.

To the staff of the National Library, patient and extremely helpful, the same which can be said of Royal College of Physicians librarian Robert Mills and archivist Harriet Wheelock, and Mary O'Doherty of the library of the Royal College of Surgeons.

Thanks to the staff of Higgins of Clonskeagh – Niall, John, Debby and the rest – for their tolerance and patience.

Finally to my friend Pascal Conroy, a friend in need and a friend indeed.

Dedicated to the memory of
Sarah Maria Louisa Kirwan (1824–1852).
In the matter of murder, the victim is
all too soon forgotten.

CONTENTS

INTRODUCTION

The great observer of criminal legal process and chronicler of Victorian murders and trials, William Roughead, made these comments in an essay on the Ireland's Eye case in 1924:

> It presents a puzzle sufficient in perplexity to intrigue even a blasé taste and to stimulate the Sherlockian spirit that sleeps in the bosom of the most blameless of Watsons. It is, in the first place, a trial for murder, if crime there was; it was unprecedented at the time: the drowning of a wife by her husband.

There are two key features in his assessment: first, the correct observation that the fulcrum of the event was the courtroom and, second, the element of doubt expressed in "if crime there was". That doubt has persisted for 160 years and even after seven decades, while examining the circumstances, Roughead trod carefully and declared he was not taking any risks. In the matter of this extraordinary event which took place on Ireland's Eye on Monday, September 6th, 1852, few writers wanted to take a minority view on the credibility of the outcome.

The popular view was that it was a clear instance of miscarriage of justice founded on a mixture of moral prejudice and the reliance on purely circumstantial evidence at trial. On the surface, it may have appeared to fit the category but, in this as in many mysteries, much that emerged was not as it seemed. Any clarity which might have been hoped for was made less achievable by the burial of some vital circumstances of crucial evidential value. The consequence of this was that any definitive judgement by observers, whether independent or not, was both tainted and limited.

For any writer delving into the circumstances, in any depth, the role of literary detective would have to be adopted. Roughead recognised this – it was a role he constantly adopted – and titled his essay "The Secret of Ireland's Eye" with the subtitle "A Detective Story". It is, of course, anything but a tale of detection as another unusual aspect of this story is that the normal leading light – the detective – is barely evident in the unfolding of the narrative. It is a story in which the figures of lawyers and forensic pathologists loom larger by far, and it was a member of the latter profession I found to be the only player capable of lifting the veil of mystery which had shrouded the event for over a century and a half, the elucidation of the truth consigned to a long unthumbed medical journal.

Roughead instances an infamous case which went to trial in 1915, featuring one George Joseph Smith, an Englishman who was responsible for the deaths of three wives in succession. The killer was considered by the Scottish chronicler as a mere mechanic, a capable craftsman who, instead of profiting by his escape from detection for the first murder, was so stupid as to become his own copycat, doubling the odds in favour of his capture. What he lacked, according to the writer, was imagination and style; instead of using his first success as a base for moving on to higher and more complex acts, he went for the lazy and dangerous option of repetition. Smith's choice of location could not have been more confined: the cramped bathrooms of drab lodging houses in dank and depressing streets. He could have hung a banner outside those peeling brick dumps: *Motive – Murder For Money*. The location of Ireland's Eye provided a stark contrast: an island off the coast of Howth, hauntingly picturesque, with the artefacts of history still standing on its rocky hump and the tides which washed its strands, creeks and cliffs echoing the human drama that would be forever associated with the location. The crime, "if crime there was", was in a category far beyond the reach of the Smith types; great subtlety and invention might be a description, if justified at all, which would immediately spring to mind.

2

Apart from the central mystery and the unanswered questions the case presented, there are two other issues worthy of elucidation.

The first is the adversarial system used in British and Irish courts. In Victorian times the murder trial was given huge media coverage; it was more popular than the theatre with a huge demand for tickets of admission – and little wonder. The accused's life was at stake, which intensified the drama at the centre of which two opposing counsel strutted and fretted on the courtroom stage, indulging in withering examination of witnesses and delivering sometimes brilliant soliloquies to sway the jury to their contradictory points of view.

The adversary by definition is an opponent and this is the stance adopted by prosecution and defence counsel. They present evidence through the medium of witnesses, police and experts such as pathologists and engineers, and by skilful questioning serve the interests of their respective clients. Along the way, by the nature of this exercise, there are efforts made to suppress certain facts that might be perceived to be prejudicial to either of the clients.

As Roughead puts the matter: "In hearing, reading, or writing about these cases, I always feel how much there is behind the scenes that one ought to know in order to arrive at a fully informed judgement. How much that, by reason of sundry rules of the game played by counsel, with the prisoner's life at stake, is never allowed to come out in court." This observation is entirely relevant to the case in question.

Unlike the inquisitorial system operated in some European countries, the purpose of which is to find out the truth of a criminal event, the adversarial system is designed and aided by rules of evidence to make the discovery of truth a very difficult exercise. In 18th century France the *juge d'instruction* sifted out the prosecution witnesses by a process of examination and elimination. By contrast, in England, the appearance in court of all sorts of self-serving witnesses – holding grudges, seeking rewards or accomplices turning witness – became such a hazard that a defence counsel was introduced to represent the interests of the accused. The pendulum literally swung in the other direction with the accused being granted a right of silence, and strict and limiting rules being imposed on police interrogation. The accused did not have to account for any action and could not be cross-examined by the prosecution counsel.

The purpose of the exercise of cross-examination was to destroy the credibility of the witness. Questioning by either side would attempt to reduce the importance of certain witness evidence. Important witnesses were often not called because it was decided that they might not say the right thing or become flustered under examination. Such a system and practices, improperly or even efficiently used, inevitably led to the conviction of the innocent and the setting free of the guilty.

The adversarial system was perfectly designed for miscarriage of justice.

The trial became one of conflict as opposed to one of discovery. This legal process, as will be seen, was particularly pertinent to the tragedy on Ireland's Eye.

Within this framework the second issue arose and that was the matter of circumstantial evidence. Testimony can be direct evidence or it can be circumstantial. If the witness claims he or she saw a crime take place, this is considered direct evidence. For instance, a witness saying that he saw the defendant stabbing the victim is giving direct evidence. By contrast, a witness who says that he saw the defendant enter a house and that screaming was heard and then he saw the defendant leave the house with a bloody knife gives circumstantial evidence. It is the necessity for inference that determines that evidence is circumstantial.

Direct evidence is popularly, but mistakenly, considered more powerful. In fact, many successful criminal prosecutions down through the years have relied largely on circumstantial evidence.

In practice, circumstantial evidence can have an advantage over direct evidence, in that it can come from multiple sources that check and re-enforce each other. The law makes no distinction between the weight or importance given either to direct or circumstantial evidence. It is up to the prosecutors to show, through a set of circumstances, that their theory of what took place is the only logical deduction – that the circumstances can be explained by no other theory. Conversely, it is the job of the defence to show that the same set of circumstances could be explained by an alternative theory.

Much has been made of the role of circumstantial evidence in the Kirwan case, contributing largely to the view that it had little but the capacity to lead to a miscarriage of justice. It is thus of importance to hear the view of a famous Irish judge on the matter of circumstantial evidence.

Judge Kenneth Deale outlines his opinion in the preface to his book *Memorable Irish Trials*, published in 1960, as follows:

> A friend once said to me, I would never convict a man on circumstantial evidence, showing that like many people he misunderstood the nature of this kind of evidence. Now, the criminal usually takes good care not to be seen committing his crime, and so criminal trials nearly always depend on circumstantial evidence.
>
> Circumstantial evidence is contrasted with direct evidence. If you see A putting his hand into B's pocket, taking out B's wallet and running away with it, and you so swear at A's trial, you will be giving direct evidence. You have seen the event and no inference is needed to show that A is the thief. But, suppose you only see A standing beside B and, having looked away for a moment, you look again and see A running away, you pursue and catch him and find B's wallet in his hand. If all this is sworn to at A's trial, it will be circumstantial evidence that A picked B's pocket. Nobody saw him do it, but the only rational inference from the circumstances is that he is the thief.
>
> So far, so good. But the circumstances may point to more than one inference. Suppose that this time A and B, strangers to each other, are staying at the same hotel. On Monday B's wallet is stolen, the thief being unknown. On Wednesday the wallet is found in a drawer in A's room and that is the only evidence against A. It cannot be safely inferred that A is the

thief, for the presence of the wallet in his bedroom may equally mean that someone else stole it, and either gave it to A, who put it in the drawer, or hid it there unknown to A – a reasonable probability since a hotel room may be accessible to several people besides the occupier. A cannot be convicted of the theft.

The foregoing are simple examples designed to show the nature of circumstantial evidence, but of course in a trial the facts are far more numerous and, because of contradictions, difficult to determine.

Circumstantial evidence has its limits, but is frequently more reliable than direct evidence, for it is not subject to human frailty. If a witness swears that he saw the accused, a stranger to him, at the scene of a crime fifty yards away on a dark night, he may be convinced that he is right, yet he may be wrong. The bad light, a defect in his vision may vitiate his testimony.

Suppose though that no one sees the accused, but a footprint identifiable with one of his shoes is found at the scene, or some threads, which match a tear in his coat or even a personal belonging such as a ring or cigarette case – that evidence may be much safer proof that he was in fact there.

It is said that circumstantial evidence cannot lie, and in one sense this is true. Its weakness is not in its nature, but in the inference which the tribunal chooses to draw from it. If more than one inference is open, the rule of law is that the accused may not be convicted unless the inferences point conclusively to his guilt, and to no other rational conclusion.

When this rule is properly applied, circumstantial evidence is by far the most reliable evidence.

Many of the foregoing issues and observations are highly pertinent to the tragic event that occurred on Ireland's Eye and in particular to the dramatic aftermath.

CHAPTER 1

PROLOGUE

*"Some beat on, boats against the current, borne back
ceaselessly into the past."*
SCOTT FITZGERALD

He was on his way back to the island, having spent almost two
and a half decades on another one, over two hundred miles
removed. In that time he had ceaselessly been haunted by the
tragedy that had robbed him of life when he was in his prime, at
the height of his artistic and physical power. What had become
of the glories of his youth, his innocent dreams and ambitions?
He was swallowed into a tomb of stone on a harsh rock
surrounded by water; the tides which controlled his fate those of
the sea and the fortune that comes with them.

Constantly moving water, driven by the moon, endlessly
attacking and retreating, calm and still like a sleeping lion and
then crashing and roaring like a marauding elephant. Every day,
nature at a small remove lashed and whipped by either its
crushing indifference or angry punishment. The sea was the cruel
master of his memory. She, at least, was at peace in her watery
grave on land. No need to haunt him like the waves. For twenty-

four years he had never been free from the salt water in his eyes, nose and deep in his heart.

He was ceaselessly brought back on that ghost boat and the phantom rowers to the island, now and for all those interminable years in his imagination. The once love of his life lay there with the scratches on her face and her body and he woke every early dawn screaming at the sight and pleading for forgiveness and she would tell him that it wasn't for him to ask and she was trying her hardest to protect him. But was she, and for what reason? It was another fantasy of misguided consolation.

The hell of his suffering was made all the worse by the fact that in his youth Fortune had smiled on him. Thus favoured, the more fastidiously sensitive he had become, and unless all things answered to his whim he was overwhelmed by the most trifling misfortunes, because he was so utterly unschooled in adversity. So petty he realised, too late, are the trifles which rob the most fortunate of happiness.

How manifestly he had absorbed the trappings of status, monetary values and the pursuit of fame. Beset by the anxieties that accompany such ambition, he failed to take the true path and strip away his ego-driven obsessions and his myriad vanities. How easy it was, he would bitterly realise, to be seduced by one's imagined power. How could he have ever imagined that happiness could consist of things that are the sport of chance?

He deluded himself into thinking that his success was a result of his talent and application and not the lottery of birth. The memory of past happiness burned in his brain, those days before the storm clouds gathered and poured their wrath upon him. His monstrous ego had convinced him that he could live by tenets contrary to the laws of God and man. As if there was something unique in his method of handling his affairs. Man's capacity for self-delusion is infinite.

The island in his mind had been his undoing, as if an inanimate force of nature had guided his hand. Over the interminable decades that day had been replayed in his mind over and over and over again. His imagination may have given him the momentary privilege of a different outcome but soon the sound of the waves brought him back to reality. Once effected, a deed can never be changed, no more than a moment of life retrieved.

As an artist, he had with an image attempted to freeze the moment – to last, according to his vanity, forever. Little did he realise that the march of time consigns every moment to the past. One looks at the image and remembers. It was then, and the now made no difference to the passage of the interim. Nothing can stop the hands of the clock. Like the tide it moves in, stays and retreats, in constant and eternal movement. There is but a pause and then on and on and back and back. His minutes were now hastening to their end, as the waves to the pebbled shore. The breath of man echoes it and then ceases, forever. The tide and time move on and on.

The years had not been generous – his once strong body had been reduced to a creaking, painful wreck. He was physically and mentally spent. The lack of air, of exercise, the paralysis of his artistic ambition had turned his muscle and bone to withering and twitching nothingness. His mind was a pit of decomposing regret for every molecule of his being. His skin flaccid, eyes sunken below the grey brows, every line of his face a testament to the grim, intolerable, burden of his incarceration and the twist of fate that had brought him to the second island, the endless, painful crawl to grim and crooked maturity.

The physical deprivation had taken its toll but that was little compared to the unrelenting mental and emotional anguish that is an inevitable consequence of a reality whose harshness not even repentance, which he eschewed, could have alleviated. Worst of all the fading of hope, whose light diminished more and more over the years until it was the flickering, smoking wick of a burnt-out candle.

Thousands of miles away across that vast Atlantic Ocean, progeny of his had moved from childhood to adulthood, becoming potential strangers to him with the passing of every day. His vanity had cast his children to the streets and the wind and robbed them of a deserving place in society, which he had also wanted for them. But even from the start when the earth orbited the sun of his ego, he had already sacrificed them to the prejudice of society in spite of providing them with material comfort and his part-time presence. How his brain had been beguiled by the selfish tentacles of his desire and belief in his omnipotence!

He considered himself a man of new ideas, who did not like many of his contemporaries who were conservative in temperament, law-abiding and willing subjects to the control of the authorities. He was an artistic man of creative mind and not a slave to the narrow moral confines of the arch-conservative Victorian society. He thought of himself as extraordinary and as such did not have to adhere to the rules embraced by the ordinary upon whom he looked down from his perch of artistic snobbery. He had the foolish notion that this modus vivendi was a form of freedom. It would take him until the long years of reflection to understand that it was nothing of the sort, but a form of despotism.

He had imposed his view of a new order on those closest to him without the faintest suspicion that his regime was as capable of imposing damage on the subjects in the long-term as any other built on a more solid moral foundation. More damage, in fact, as it was built on a base of deception, illicit moral behaviour and ultimately hypocrisy. But he was a man then so tightly pinioned by the serpent of his total self-belief that he could not anticipate a release of fatal venom.

And then he was released from the years of torture into more pain of adjustment. The rope he had hoped to avoid all those years ago now appeared like the greatest mercy he might have wished. For then there would have been an end, now none but what yawned at a stage of his time on earth when he had no energy left. There was a large boat waiting for the new land but his appetite was gone for any sort of adventure. It was more a matter of whiling out the years that were left to him and some form of limited redemption. And it was the least responsibility he could assume for another action of his past vanity.

He floated through the streets of Dublin – a ghost looking backwards at the images of the past. The inescapable past. Down

Merrion Row and left into Upper Merrion Street he drifted until, hugging the darkness, he stopped right opposite his former home now occupied by the eminent Lombe Atthill, a plethora of medical letters after his name, the master of the Rotunda Hospital. A sickening pain stabbed his weakened heart. His footprints may have faded from the floorboards but now another occupier obliterated them beyond trace.

A conference of ghosts assembled, the two beautiful women that had occupied the left and right side of his heart, divided as it was by nature. The shadows and sounds of children, laughing, crying, sleeping. How painfully had he learnt the lesson that a man who thinks that he can live on his own terms on this earth is a fool. Not even nature brooks the union of contraries. That contradiction, which he refused to recognise, would be the source of his undoing. Divided affection forges a divided self and no man can live in two minds for long. He ignored the affliction and tried to set aside the burden but his tangled thoughts became too much in the end and sent him into the depths of depression. He had entered a mental tunnel and had to find a way out even if it meant shunting his conscience into a siding.

He stopped again outside Number 23, the house of the man that supervised his descent into Hades, George Smyly Q.C., who ironically had been his neighbour.

And a further irony was that it would be himself who would be remembered as a resident of this Georgian enclave for generations to come, long after the eminent men of the law and medicine had disappeared into the vaults of the past. But not for the legacy of the artist he had long dreamed of but for something entirely different. And when he hoped that he might finally be forgotten, somebody would resurrect him in a book or newspaper article, his reputation there for all to see. And he had little doubt that his paintings would gain a certain currency for all the wrong reasons.

There was one last journey he had to make before he left his native land forever.

The boat slipped out of the harbour and the island appeared like a low-lying, sleeping stone whale. The sea was calm, the blue sky speckled with puffy cloud formations drifting in slow motion away from the mainland. The boatman was young, silent and respectful, too intent on the powerful rhythm of the oars to indulge in small talk. The boat cut through the silky sea and made the journey in just over fifteen minutes.

The landing place and strand near the Martello Tower was the same as he had sketched with a couple of boats anchored.

The high bank where he had stood that day was now bathed in sunlight, not enveloped as then in darkness, but a shiver still ran down his stiff spine. It was akin to adding salt to his wounded pride but he had to see the scene that determined his fate one last time. It all seemed so innocent, so natural after all those years. He wished he had that time again – he would have seen that it all turned out so differently. But such is the nature of both human and divine retribution. The curse of the irrational mind, which could for even one moment contemplate the impossible notion of turning the clock back. The boatmen were most likely long dead but for a moment he heard their calls echoing through the tunnel of time, and his stilted, nervy reactions of false composure as he tried to bury the emotion which does not adhere to any rule book of human conduct. He heard the dunk of their oars in the calm sea waters. If only nature had allowed him the benefit of the slightest inclemency of high wind or water, then all would have been changed, utterly.

But then, he had not paid attention in his rehearsal to the most obvious and clear signs of the element of nature that might have guided more propitiously his plan of action. That tide and the totally predictable movement in both height and direction. More constant and reliable than the thoughts that had been affecting his mind. Those had similar motion but emotion has no foundation of constancy. He heard the sounds of a new generation of birds and their cries mocked him, as they could never have done then, when he was invulnerable. His present condition mocked him even more, just as the boatmen had then but now they were no more and he envied them the comfort of oblivion.

He would not be staying for long as his stiff legs would not allow him the privilege of retracing his steps on that fateful evening and night. He would with difficulty make the bank and the tower. But to go to the strands and the creek would defeat his best efforts. Even had he been physically able, he would have been constrained by the prospect of an emotional reaction. Time increases rather than alleviates the potential for depression.

The minute that the young boatman helped him, now an old and feeble man, onto the strand, the sluice gates of memory opened and it all came flooding back.

CHAPTER 2

THE ISLAND

On the fine calm morning of Monday, September 6th, 1852, a strikingly handsome man and his beautiful wife stepped on to a hired boat in Howth Harbour to set out on a day trip. The destination was Ireland's Eye, a small uninhabited island less than a mile to the north of the harbour, which because of its picturesque character and setting was frequented by parties for the purposes of picnicking, bathing and enjoying the views.

The nearest point to the mainland is a spot called the Broad Patch at the extreme south-eastern end of the island and running along the island to the west on the landward side are two strands, one much longer than the other, and divided by a group of rocks called the John Winter Rocks. The strand at the western end leads to a Martello tower (*c*.1805), and the usual landing place for boats.

About 500 yards from the tower are the ruins of an old church. The island was the site of an early Christian monastery, founded by St Nessan in the 6th century. The name of the island in Irish is *Inis Mac Neasáin* ['*the island of Nessan*'], while the present-day name derives its "Eye" from the old Norse word "ey" meaning "island".

14

Some 280 yards from the church towards the south-eastern end of the island is an inlet called the Long Hole which would play a pivotal role in the events that would unfold that day. It is about 360 feet in length, narrow at the entrance and wider towards the head, with precipitous cliffs on each side. A little beyond the middle of the creek, it is divided into two channels by a large and elevated rock. Just beyond that rock on the seaward side is a barrier of scattered rocks stretching across the channel about 12 feet above the watermark. The channel at this part, the two channels again being joined, is 28 feet in breadth. At this point the bottom of the sea is rocky, while on the landward side the bottom is composed of coarse gravel. By location, the Long Hole is hidden from the mainland, being on the seaward side of the island; it is distant from Howth by 1,250 yards (0.7 miles) in a straight line.

Like all picturesque places, the island can glitter and glow like a gem under a reflective sun and blue sky, but when the shadows lengthen and the veil of darkness falls, the rocks, cliffs, tower and church ruins can take on a more sinister aspect.

On this Monday, full tide was at 4.37 p.m., low water at 10.15 p.m. and half ebb at 7.25 p.m.. At the tide's limits, the creek is either full of seawater or empty.

As the boatmen rowed closer to the island on the fifteen to twenty-minute journey the couple could observe several bunches of razorbills, guillemots and cormorants sunning themselves on the rocks, and titlarks and a few oystercatchers crossed the boat, their piping cries perhaps a mild protest at intrusion. Somewhere further off was the whirr of a falcon's wings.

Sometime shortly before 10.30 a.m., Patrick Nangle and his cousin Michael (later described as "elderly men", Michael apparently being the elder) guided the boat into the landing spot on a small strand near the Martello tower at the north-western tip of the island. This was the usual, though not the only, spot for dropping and collecting visitors. The couple were not of the mould of the usual day-trippers; they were a class apart from most pleasure-seekers. They were immaculately dressed and carried a leather bag and a reticule basket, containing sketch-books, drawing and painting utensils, bathing apparel and food provisions. The gentleman carried a long cane.

The instruction given to the Nangles was that they should return to collect them at 8 p.m. that evening. It might have seemed a strange hour to the boatmen as it would be dark at eight but they had ferried the couple twice to the island the previous week with collection times of 6 p.m. and 7 p.m. and it may therefore not have caused much comment among them.

The couple had been residing at a lodging house in Howth since the middle of June and, though somewhat distant and private in their behaviour, were familiar to the local community and particularly to the landlady, a widow Mrs. Margaret Campbell.

The man, 38 years of age, was William Burke Kirwan, an artist of some standing, and his wife, 29-year-old Sarah Maria Louisa, a strong swimmer and an avid reader. She was one of eight children, the daughter of James Crowe, who had been a lieutenant in the 2nd West India Regiment, and they had been married twelve years. They lived at 11 Upper Merrion Street in the fashionable Georgian enclave which included the square favoured by the top legal and medical professionals of the city of Dublin. Kirwan made a living by providing anatomical drawings to surgeons as well as mapmaking for clients and cleaning and restoring paintings. He was a hardworking man and earned a very good income.

The boatmen then returned to Howth to ferry another party, a family by the name of Brew, to the island. They arrived back at 12 noon and the Kirwans, still in the vicinity, engaged the Nangles in conversation. During the period the Brew family remained on the island they encountered the couple a number of times, including once at the ruined church where Kirwan was sketching while his wife was walking about and reading a book. When the time arrived for their departure at 4 p.m. Mr. Brew saw Mrs. Kirwan on the strand and offered her passage back with the family. She declined but reminded the boatmen to collect her and her husband at the arranged time.

The Kirwans were now alone on the island as the last of the visitors had departed. At about twenty minutes to seven the sun began to set and shadows lengthened.

One hour later the Nangles, accompanied by two other men, set out for the island and reached the landing place at about 8 p.m.. It was an unusually calm night with hardly a ripple on the water, prompting Michael Nangle to later reflect that a candle could have been lit without fear of it being extinguished. Nonetheless, the crew were anxious to complete their task as quickly as possible. They were totally unprepared for what would become for them and many others a long and painful nightmare.

When the boat pulled in at the strand there was no sign of the couple. They called out and Kirwan answered from a high bank overlooking the strand. He required help to bring down his bag and Patrick Nangle obliged, taking it and a sketch book in hand. Kirwan then began to descend and was met by Michael Nangle who enquired about his wife. He said that he had not seen her for an hour and a half.

What immediately struck Patrick Nangle, an observant man, was that until his cousin's enquiry Kirwan had made no mention of his wife nor expressed any concern that she had not arrived at the landing place. Michael suggested that he go look for his wife and asked what direction she had gone. The artist pointed and the boatman, clearly annoyed, told him that he should have had his wife at the landing place and they should not have to search for her at this hour of night.

Kirwan and Michael Nangle went off to look for Mrs. Kirwan, leaving Patrick and the other men at the boat in case she turned up in the interim. Kirwan told Michael that she had left after the last shower (around 6 p.m.) to bathe while he was sketching. As they moved through the darkness they called out her name but there was no reply. They walked along the strand beyond the John Winter Rocks and then turned inland towards the old church and onwards south-east to the Long Hole where they began to search.

Meanwhile, back at the landing stage near the Martello tower, where the artist would later say he had been sketching after his wife left to bathe, Patrick Nangle decided to join the search and called out the men's names. His cousin Michael, then beside the creek, heard him and he and Kirwan retraced their steps and met with Patrick at the John Winter Rocks. Michael Nangle's frustration had reached boiling point and once more he berated Kirwan for leaving his wife to make her own way back and lead them on to a dark and dangerous search. This must have rankled deeply with Kirwan, to be dressed down by a person of more humble social status, an insolent boatman more used to obeying the orders of his superiors. For one reason or another, he bit his tongue.

Since there was no sign of Mrs. Kirwan, they decided to split up and retrace their steps. Michael went along the strand and on to the Broad Patch at the south-eastern end of the island and doubled back towards the Long Hole while Kirwan and Patrick went by a more direct route to the creek. They kept calling her name while Kirwan in a low voice repeated "Oh, Maria, oh, Maria!". As if to emphasise the folly of apparently leaving his wife to her own devices, Kirwan stumbled on the edge of the cliff above the Long Hole and was saved by the quick reaction of Patrick Nangle.

They assembled at the Long Hole with its two channels divided by the elevated rock. Michael and the artist took the left channel while Patrick took the right side. With about an hour to low water, the tide had receded considerably towards the sea.

As Patrick moved towards the barrier of scattered rocks on the seaward side of the elevated rock, he spotted something white in the gloom. He called out to his fellow searchers: "I see something here!"

As he walked closer he saw the prone body of Mrs. Kirwan, on her back, on a low rock less than a foot high, with the head falling downwards over the seaward end and her legs and feet at the other. She had on bathing boots which rested in a small pool but no bathing cap. Her bathing shift was gathered under her outstretched arms exposing her breasts and lower body. There was a wet sheet on the rock underneath. Her face was covered in blood, there were scratches around the eyes and an effusion of blood from the ears and vagina.

Suppressing his shock, the boatman quickly pulled down the bathing shift and tied the wet sheet around the neck and legs. At that moment Michael and Kirwan arrived and the artist threw himself on the body of his wife and cried. When he composed himself he asked the cousins to get her clothes. Michael later testified that he looked for them along the strand while Patrick climbed the elevated rock, while Patrick testified that Kirwan pointed at once towards the rock.

At this juncture it might be noted, as it was later, that witnesses of a tragic or traumatic event are wont to differ in the detail of what they saw or thought they saw. It is a common and much-chronicled phenomenon. The darkness of the creek would not have helped. And it must be remembered that it was Patrick, the more intelligent and observant of the cousins, who actually discovered the body.

The cousins returned empty-handed. Kirwan then climbed the elevated rock himself. After a few minutes he returned, carrying what Michael saw as something white, "like a sheet", and a shawl. He told Patrick he would now find the clothes there. Patrick climbed up again and, at a spot which he had previously searched and found nothing, he found the clothes. This was as mystifying to him as Kirwan being able to find the clothes in the first place. While making no deep impact at the time, considering the exigencies of the event, such details would have cause to be etched deeply in the boatman's mind and memory. But for now there was the pressing matter of transporting the body back to Howth.

William Burke Kirwan declined the invitation to go back to the landing spot with the men, preferring to spend the time in solitary grief with the earthly remains of his wife. A worthy, understandable, and laudable gesture in the circumstances.

The Nangles trekked again across the half mile of rough terrain to the landing place and with the waiting men rowed around the island to the creek. There was likely during the journey to be much complaining on the part of Michael and a more strained but stoic attitude from his cousin. But even Patrick, the more placid of the two, had been angered by his perception of Kirwan's neglect that had contributed to the tragedy. And the simple task of their day had been transformed into a most affecting and stressful act of duty. Elderly men, the cousins must have been in a state of exhaustion even before the journey from the Martello tower around the jagged coast and on to the creek, a trip that would take an hour. They manoeuvred the vessel into the narrow mouth of the creek and to within 20 feet of what would be known as the "Body Rock".

The body of Mrs. Kirwan was removed from the rock, placed in the bottom of the boat and wrapped in a sail. The landside of the rock barrier was practically completely dry and only one of the other boatmen got wet as he helped move the body into the boat. Neither the Nangles nor Kirwan stepped in water at any time during the operation.

Kirwan sat at the head of the body but was told by Patrick, who lost his patience, to move as he was interfering with the oars and that he ought to have taken more care of his wife while she was alive. The implication being that if he had done so, none of them would be performing this sad task. Kirwan once again did not respond and did what he was told. The oarsmen got to work and sometime between 11.00 and 11.30 p.m. finally arrived back at Howth Harbour.

The Nangles ordered a dray horse and car to bring the deceased back to the lodging house. The local police sergeant Joseph Sherwood was informed and came also to the harbour. Then a most curious incident ensued. The Nangles asked Kirwan for the sum of £2 to recompense them for their efforts on the evening. The original fee for the arranged trip was three shillings. It was not an inconsiderable sum (£2 was worth about £169 in present-day money – three shillings £12.70) but when divided in whatever proportion among the men reasonable enough. Kirwan refused to pay; perhaps it was his way of getting back at the men for their insolence. Patrick Nangle, somewhat out of character and enraged by the attitude of the artist, held the head of the dray horse and refused to let it go until they were paid. Kirwan then agreed to pay one pound and the balance was promised by Sergeant Sherwood on the simple basis that the men had performed a task that would have had to be commissioned had the body remained on the island.

However, the unseemly confrontation did nothing to endear William Burke Kirwan to the local community, and his parsimony, in the face of the boatmen's justified claim for what could only be described as heroic efforts on the awful night, told against him.

It wasn't just a question of money – it was clear that Kirwan, who had just lost a wife in tragic circumstances whose body would not have been found without the Nangles, had little or no appreciation of the exhausting and traumatic work performed on his behalf. Grief could explain many an oversight but would hardly account for the presence of mind to refuse a reasonable financial request.

There was more to come. When the improvised cortège reached the house, the body was removed from the cart and placed in a bed in one of the lodging-house rooms. Kirwan ordered Mrs. Campbell to have the body washed and she procured the help of three women to perform the task. The woman in charge was Anne Lacey, a "nurse tender" of forty years' experience, who had during her career attended to the bodies of many drowning victims.

One of the helpers, Catherine McGarr, pointed out to Kirwan that the body should be left in its present state for a police inquiry and medical examination at inquest. He replied that he did not give a damn about the police and the job was to be done. It appeared, after all the trauma of the evening, he had regained his composure. There had been a previous incident indicative of either artistic temperament or downright rudeness. One day he was passing the house of a servant girl who worked for Mrs. Campbell and the dog barked at him. He warned the girl if it happened again she would receive a summons.

Kirwan's response to McGarr's legitimate concern could also lead to an interpretation most unfavourable to him in the proper inquiry which would inevitably follow. One way or another, good manners would have helped.

Sometime after midnight, with the aid of a candle held by another woman, Lacey and McGarr commenced the clean-up of the body. The nurse tender noted a number of wounds and scratches on the face and breast, that the lips were swollen with froth emanating from the mouth, that one eye was closed and the open one bloodshot. There was considerable bleeding from the ears and vagina; from the latter site she observed that this was not as a result of menstruation as the colour and thickness of the blood was entirely different. There were clots on the sheet that had been around the body. She had never seen such appearances on the body of a drowning victim.

Both she and Mrs. Campbell saw Kirwan drying out his trousers which were very wet in front of an open fire.

Unaccountably the sergeant, Sherwood, was not present at the time and no doubt had he been he would have prevented the washing of the wounds on the body. It is likely that he was making his preliminary report on the death which would be sent to the county coroner Henry Davis first thing in the morning. Poignantly, that was also the day when the Kirwans were due to return to Dublin.

While the constabulary man's report would of necessity be brief, there would be a lot of questions to be answered in the coroner's inquiry.

First of all, given that William Burke Kirwan was the only other person on the island at the time of the death, if there were any doubt cast about the circumstances of his wife's death, as with all spouses he would be first in line of suspicion.

It would also be important, as in all such inquiries, not to take a fixed or premature position in relation to the cause of death. A thorough and professional medical assessment of the appearances of the body would be the first step, followed by an investigation into all the circumstances surrounding the incident.

At this early stage the general assumption was that Mrs. Kirwan had been a victim of accidental drowning. However, even a good medical examination of the appearances of a body without the aid of a post mortem can prove problematic. The problem is further exacerbated if there is a long time interval before the post mortem. There may also be few definitive signs on external examination. In cases of drowning, for instance, there may be a visible amount of froth on the mouth or nose, perhaps tinged with blood that has come from the lungs – but this is not always present and should not be relied on as a positive indication of drowning. If the coroner encountered any doubt in this regard or in the circumstances that led to death, it would be incumbent on him to order an immediate post mortem.

To establish those circumstances the coroner would need to take depositions from all the people involved in the progress of the event, from the discovery of the body to the return to the lodging house, and those who in some way or another handled the body along the way.

There were some other matters to be explored. The body of a drowning victim normally floats face downwards. How then did the body of Mrs. Kirwan end up on its back on a rock with a wet sheet underneath? Was this position consistent with the wounds and bleeding sites noted by Patrick Nangle and Anne Lacey and what caused the effusion of blood from the vagina in a victim of apparent drowning? In relation to the wounds and bleeding, were they an indication of injuries which had been sustained before or after death?

The women who had laid out and washed the corpse stayed in the room all night, a more than adequate confirmation of devotion to their duty. Without any direct knowledge of, or connection to the victim, they maintained a respectful vigil. They were clearly decent human beings and utterly caring of the needs of the deceased, in spite of being misdirected by her husband.

CHAPTER 3

THE INVESTIGATION

On the morning of the 7th of September the Dublin county coroner Henry Davis received a report of the death of Mrs. Kirwan from Sergeant Sherwood of Howth where he stated that the previous morning Mr. and Mrs. Kirwan went to Ireland's Eye by boat and, at eight o'clock that night, when the boatmen arrived to collect them, Kirwan said that Mrs. Kirwan had gone to bathe at six o'clock and that he had gone in search of her; that the boatmen with Kirwan went in search of her and found her drowned at the east side of the Eye with marks of violence on her face etc. "This case appears strange, as there was a sheet about the woman. Please come as soon as you can." Presumably the sergeant was referring to the fact that the sheet was under her when she was found, not to the fact that Patrick Nangle had tied the bathing sheet about her.

Armed with the constable's information and suspicion about the circumstances, Davis went to Howth from his home in Donnycarney. He met with Craddock, the sub-inspector of the Howth constabulary, and summoned a jury. As he knew that there was no doctor residing in Howth, he despatched a policeman to Baldoyle (about 4 miles from Howth) where the nearest medical practitioner lived. On his return the policeman informed him that the doctor was away in Dublin and would not be home until the evening. There was no other doctor nearer than Clontarf or Malahide (each roughly 8 miles from Howth). He was informed that there was a medical man lodging in Howth by the name of Hamilton, and sent for him, not knowing that he was in fact an unqualified medical student.

Davis had examined the body himself previously and claimed that, although he had no qualification, ten years of dealing with cases of drowning gave him some insight. He came to the conclusion that there were no marks of violence on the body. What he saw, of course, was the washed body, the marks on which he attributed to crabs. He said the stomach was full, though it is doubtful he could have told this from an external examination – unless of course he was referring to the abdomen. He had clearly overstepped the boundaries of his job and was acting as medical examiner as well as coroner.

The medical student Hamilton, from his cursory and ill-informed examination, agreed with the coroner's equally unprofessional assessment.

The coroner claimed that there were no suspicious circumstances, despite having been told of Sergeant Sherwood's initial concern. There would be no possibility of any police investigation until after the coroner had completed the inquest. He also decided that a medical student was competent to perform the hugely important task of the physical examination. And his inquiries did not stretch beyond the superficial. He did not know the body had been washed, knew nothing of a bloody sheet or sail or any previous ill-treatment of the victim by her husband or bleeding from the ears or other parts. If he had called the women who had washed the body he would have been well informed, but he never bothered. It appears his attitude was that the information must come to him; he was not going to look for it. The Kirwans had been in Howth for months and Davis made absolutely no inquiry to establish if that stay had been an entirely peaceful one.

From his "medical" examination he reached a conclusion, with which the inquest jury agreed, of accidental drowning –

with no evidence, expert or witnesses other than the Nangles who had noted the physical appearances of the body. And he obviously found it far from suspicious that a man would consent to his wife bathing in a remote creek in the island and then agree to an arrangement that involved her returning over rough and at places dangerous terrain in the dark.

There were half a dozen valid reasons why an open verdict should have been recorded and a post mortem ordered but Henry Davis was more concerned with the mechanics of the inquiry than its substance. But even within the limited scope of the inquest, he also proved inadequate for that task. His incompetence would come back to haunt him later when he would be targeted for much criticism.

Patrick Nangle was the first to be examined and when it came to the part where he said she was lying with the sheet partly under her, he was interrupted by Michael who said that the gentleman had brought down the sheet.

Kirwan, unaccountably and illegally, then added his voice, saying: "That man [*i.e. Pat*] is wrong, the other man tells the truth."

The coroner urged Michael Nangle to be quiet and when his turn came he would be examined. Pat's examination continued but he would say later that the interruption and the coroner's conducting of the proceedings prevented him from giving the most important evidence about what he had seen at the Long Hole: the blood, the wounds, the manner in which he tied the body up in the sheet, Kirwan pointing to where the clothes lay – matters which the experienced sailor knew even at this early stage were unusual. The coroner asked him had he anything more to say and he said that he had not.

Michael Nangle was next up, adding little to the understanding of the event at that particular time. He did say that Kirwan had found the deceased's clothes because he had climbed higher on the rock to look for them. It struck neither the coroner nor the foreman of the jury, Alexander Boyd, as odd that while claiming that he was not with her at the time, Kirwan happened to know where she had put her clothes.

Worse still, when Kirwan was called, his account of the event was of alarming brevity but was neither questioned in any fashion nor urged to be magnified in any way by the coroner.

This was his statement as recorded at the time:

> Saith: I am an artist, residing at No. II, Upper Merrion Street, Dublin; the deceased lady Maria Kirwan was my wife; I was married to her about nine or ten years [12 *years, in fact*]; I have been living with Mrs. Kirwan in Howth for five or six weeks [*closer to 10 weeks, in fact*]; I was in the habit of going over to Ireland's Eye as an artist; Mrs. Kirwan used to accompany me; she was very fond of bathing, and while I would be sketching she would amuse herself roaming around or bathing; yesterday we went over as usual; she bathed at the Martello Tower on going over, but could not stay long in the water as the boatmen were to bring another party to the island; she left me in the latter part of the day, about six o'clock to bathe again; she told me she would walk around the hill after bathing, and meet me at the boat; I did not see her alive afterwards, and only found the body as described by the sailors.

Mr. Henry Davis could and should have had a number of questions to ask Kirwan about his cursory account of this tragic event. Instead it conformed to his view, later expressed, a view not informed by an inquiring mind but more in character of a man wishing to get the formalities over and done with as quickly as possible. Kirwan's examination was equally brief and he told the inquest what he had been sketching and he was asked to produce it. The picture was a representation of the evening appearance of the Dublin Mountains, and must in their opinion have been taken near the Martello tower on the island, where he had told them he had been.

His bag was produced which contained the remains of the meal taken on the island and knives, forks and plates.

Here are the coroner Davis's own words recalling what he observed, in a statement made well after the event:

A gentleman and his wife, whose characters are unimpeached, living happily together (and we had no reason to believe that Kirwan and his wife were otherwise), the wife a remarkably handsome woman, lodging for six weeks at Howth during the summer months, going frequently to Ireland's Eye to spend the day, taking with them their dinner; he with his sketch book, she with her bathing dress; she tells the boatmen, as she did on other occasions, to return for them at eight o'clock in the evening; they do so and are told by the husband that his wife had gone to bathe about six o'clock, that she had not returned, that he was uneasy about her, and had been looking for her; and finding her dead near the place where ladies are in the habit of bathing on the Eye (it was sworn before me) without marks of violence – the scratch on the forehead, and the marks left by fish on the eyes and ears excepted; you have the case presented before me and the jury at the inquest.

The naivety of the statement is breathtaking, verging in parts on the romantic, in others resembling a schoolboy's essay. He states that Mrs. Kirwan told the boatmen, as she did on other occasions, to return for them at eight o'clock. Even with the benefit of hindsight the coroner cannot get his facts right. Mrs. Kirwan had never before asked the boatmen to come at eight o'clock, the previous occasions being an hour and two hours earlier than eight.

Davis's capacity for self-delusion was only matched by that of the foreman of the inquest jury, Alexander Boyd, who in 1853 made a statement to John Knight Boswell for the defence document published after Kirwan's trial and sentencing. He too played the role of an amateur pathologist by judging the cause of Mrs. Kirwan's death by surface appearances.

His statement was as follows:

There were no marks whatsoever that might have been caused by blows or pressure; the body was white and fair; the skin was not hurt or bruised in any way except that

the eyelids and the tender flesh under the eyes were raw
as if the skin had been caught bit by bit between the nails
and plucked away, leaving here and there small pieces
untouched; the coroner said those were crab marks and I
agreed; the face was pale and placid and did not exhibit
the appearance of violence; the forehead on the right
side had a slight scratch, as if it had been rubbed on a
rock; the nose was not swollen or bruised or bent over on
the side of the face; the lips did not appear to be swollen,
there was a little foam over them; the tongue did not
protrude from the mouth; the ears were marked in the
same manner as the eyes, but they were not torn, nor was
there a piece of the lobe hanging on only; the earrings
were in the ears.

Boyd's oddly worded reference to the earlobe and earrings was
in reaction to the evidence of the medical student Hamilton at
the trial ("the earring was held on by a slight strip of integument")
and Dr. Hatchell's remarks on his findings a month after the
inquest ("the lobe of the right ear was wanting").

He went on to say the stomach was full and firm; one
wonders whether this is a confused echo of testimony from other
examiners who stated that the abdomen was "full and firm".

He said that the hair was short, save a small portion at the front
– a curious statement considering women's hair was always long at
the period, worn twisted into a chignon at the back of the head,
sometimes with ringlets arranged on each side of the face – unless,
of course, he was clumsily attempting to describe such a hairstyle.

He then referred to not being told about the body being
washed and remarked that they [*i.e. Lacey and McGarr*] were
present and did not mention anything. Of course, it was not
their place to do so; that was his superior's responsibility which
he failed to discharge.

Mrs. Kirwan's clothes were produced and the reticule basket
found beside them which contained her shawl-pin, her garters,
and on the top her stockings one drawn inside the other. The

items had been placed high on the large rock that divides the tide into two channels in the Long Hole. He and Davis came to the conclusion from the arrangement of the items that Mrs. Kirwan must have quietly and deliberately undressed herself, have taken off her boots and put on her bathing dress and bathing boots. Her bonnet was beside the clothes and later other items were found on the same rock including a black lace cap, a small looking-glass and a rack comb.

There was one item missing which escaped their attention: the bathing cap. For as sure as she dressed for bathing, she would put it on. It was not found among the items. Why was it not on the head of the deceased when the body was discovered? That no inference was drawn from this indicated that it had, like a lot more important facts about the death, escaped their attention and duly the jury was directed to a conclusion of accidental death: "Found Drowned."

A vital and most desirable opportunity to order an immediate post mortem to properly account for the death of Maria Kirwan was missed.

It appeared that as a result of the verdict of the coroner's inquest, however extreme the breadth and depth of its failure to properly examine the cause and circumstances surrounding the death of Sarah Maria Louisa Kirwan, the case was closed and the file would gather dust in the offices of the Dublin County Coroner. It would be some time before the inquest proceedings would be subject to intense critical scrutiny, summed up by one commentator writing to a newspaper, thus:

> What can the judges and law officers do if coroners so grossly neglect their duties or are ignorant of the use of those powers put at their disposal and of the great responsibility of their office; if proceedings slovenly devised and carelessly conducted are suffered to go on in the old track?

In the interim, the body of the deceased was released to her husband and four days later was interred in Glasnevin Cemetery in a grave which, with a supreme sense of irony, was watery.

It seemed as if William Burke Kirwan would reside alone at his stately abode in Upper Merrion Street, continue his lucrative trade in providing anatomical drawings to the medical profession among whom he was well respected for his skills, and further establish his reputation as an artist. In all probability, his grief having diminished, he would marry again. After all, he was a strong handsome man of some means and such an outcome would provide a happy resolution to this short unhappy tale.

As it transpired, it was but the beginning of a long and complicated saga which would not take long to get underway and would make the character of Kirwan and the event on Ireland's Eye a subject of intense public scrutiny and debate.

Contrary to what he stated at the inquest, the artist had married Sarah Maria Louisa Crowe not nine or ten but twelve years before. For some years the couple resided at 6 Lower Merrion Street, the house of his art-dealer father Patrick. Then, in 1850, the Kirwans, who had no children, moved into 11 Upper Merrion Street, to their own well-appointed marital home.

While at the former address they had been subjected to the attentions of a next-door neighbour, Mrs. Maria Byrne, whose interfering behaviour caused friction between the couple and resulted in Mrs. Kirwan having to show her the door and forbid her to return again. Whether this was at the instruction of the husband is debatable but more than likely, as from that time on Mrs. Byrne harboured intense feelings bordering on hatred for the artist. Her perceived humiliation would not be easily forgotten and she probably kept the man under the radar of her malice, awaiting the opportunity for some measure of revenge, and she was not alone is such a questionable ambition. The tragic event at Ireland's Eye provided Mrs. Byrne and another woman, Mrs. Bowyer, with a good platform for their malice. At one stage Mrs. Byrne spread a rumour that Kirwan had not only murdered his brother-in-law Mr. Crowe and Mr. Bowyer but also her own husband.

The aforementioned Mrs. Bowyer claimed that Kirwan had robbed her husband of a collection of valuable books and paintings.

Even the most outrageous rumours have some sticking power. Under certain conditions the fact that Mrs. Bowyer had spent some time in a lunatic asylum might not diminish the credibility of the accusations. The death of Mrs. Kirwan offered those conditions.

On the 8th of September, the day after the reports of the inquest appeared in the newspapers, a "person" made a visit to the county coroner Henry Davis with some information. The "person" provided a sworn statement that there were good reasons to believe that Kirwan had made away with his wife, based on acts that the artist was alleged to have committed years before.

The coroner, perhaps harbouring some fear about the shortcomings of his inquiry, felt that the information excited sufficient suspicion to warrant contacting and passing on the information to the sub-inspector of police, James Craddock, that very same evening. An educated guess can be made in relation to the identity of the informant.

On the 21st of September, Mrs. Byrne went to the police and made a sworn statement in respect of her opinion of the events on Ireland's Eye. She said that, having found out that Mr. and Mrs. Kirwan had left the residence at 11 Upper Merrion Street about three weeks previously, she suspected that Kirwan had taken his wife to some strange place to destroy her. She made an enquiry as to where they had gone and she had no doubt in her mind that Mrs. Kirwan was wilfully drowned by her husband and she had reason to believe that he had made away with other members of his family under suspicious circumstances.

Mrs. Byrne could do her worst but worse was to come, which both tellingly and astoundingly had somehow escaped the attention of the malicious amateur sleuth.

Quite apart from the bushfire of rumour, there had been enough disquiet about the circumstances of the death of Mrs. Kirwan brought to the attention of the police to warrant an investigation. How seriously that course of action was taken was evidenced by the fact that it was under the direct supervision of Major Brownrigg, second in command of the constabulary at Dublin Castle.

Enquiries conducted in Howth resulted in statements being given to the investigating constabulary by five people who had separately heard screams coming from Ireland's Eye around 7 p.m. on the 6th of September. Four of the people had been in the vicinity of Howth Harbour at the time but, even more tellingly, one had been a fisherman aboard a vessel which had been passing close to the island on the way back to the harbour at the time. The screams seemed to the man to have come from the direction of the Long Hole.

The landlady of the lodging house, Mrs. Campbell, was interviewed and recounted a disturbing argument she had overheard in which Kirwan had threatened his wife and apparently subjected her to a beating. There had been other arguments of a less vicious nature. It appeared that they then ceased for a period leading up to the fateful day.

The statement of Anne Lacey was even more disturbing as the medical appearances of the body described by her were at total variance with that elicited by the medical student Hamilton at the inquest. Added to this, Catherine McGarr's account of the artist's reaction to her advice about the washing of the body could not have impressed Major Brownrigg as other than suppression of medical evidence.

What the major and his team lacked was a motive but they were not long in finding one that might fit. Sometime after the funeral and burial a woman and some children were seen visiting and staying for a time at Kirwan's marital home. Whether the woman stayed overnight would be later disputed but her presence was noted. She resided at an address in Sandymount Avenue and a perusal of Thom's Directory did not name her as the occupier. The resident recorded in the Dublin Street Directory was William Kirwan. Further enquiries established that another house in the area, in a terrace called Spafield off Sandymount Avenue, had been occupied by Teresa Kenny and a number of children for some years.

The house was a rented one and the team tracked down and interviewed the landlord, Mr. Bridgeford, who revealed the tenant was indeed William Kirwan but the house was mainly the home of a Miss Teresa Kenny and her seven children. He said the couple were known as Mr. and Mrs. Kirwan.

It appeared Kirwan had been conducting a liaison as long as he had been married and it could be confirmed that he had stayed over and slept with Miss Kenny at the house in Spafield Terrace during a four-year period. Latterly, since July of that year Kirwan had been staying at the house in Sandymount Avenue during his trips from Howth to Dublin, a fact confirmed to the investigating team by a young servant girl who lived in at the house.

Given the tragic event on Ireland's Eye, this must have come as a shocking revelation, especially in the moral climate of Victorian times where the family was sacrosanct. However, adultery was not a criminal offence – nor was suspicion of murder. So proof would have to be found.

In the matter of the long-term sexual liaison, it would have to be established whether either or both women had knowledge of the other's existence. The basic tenets of human behaviour and emotion would tend to suggest not. One witness was dead and the other, given her relationship and dependence on the man under suspicion, would tend to serve his interests as they coincided with her own.

However, ultimately any case against Kirwan would depend on the medical evidence to attempt to prove that the cause of death was by violent means and not accidental death by drowning. There was not a trace of proof linking the husband to the scene of his wife's death at the time of her demise which had now been established was sometime around seven o'clock. Was it possible that she had a fainting fit and while falling sustained the injuries witnessed on the body?

An order was secured for the exhumation of the body which took place at Glasnevin Cemetery on the 6th of October, thirty-one days after the date of the death. The grave was located in a particularly damp part of the burial ground which usually has a negative effect on the state of preservation of the corpse.

After being taken out of the grave, the coffin containing the remains of Mrs. Kirwan was taken to a nearby shed for examination by Dr. Hatchell, the police surgeon, a fellow of the Royal College of Surgeons in Ireland with a reputation as a highly accomplished anatomist.

This is what he found:

Exterior

The body had been buried at a depth of about 7 feet; the grave was found to have contained much water, which had freely penetrated the interior coffin. The surface of the body presented the appearances of one that had been at least partially surrounded by water. The face was covered with a greenish film of soapy consistency. The right eye was prominent and the left protruded on the cheek. The conjunctive vessels of both were much injected.

The upper lip was swollen. The tongue projected between the teeth, and was marked by the latter. The lining membrane of the mouth and gums was livid [*in common parlance, black and blue*]. The abdomen was much distended with gas. The labia pudenda were livid, very much swollen and everted but not emphysematous [*i.e. distended with air*]; their inner surface was very vascular. The whole of the right side from the axilla to the knee was of a purplish red colour.

There were no signs of injury on or beneath the scalp. The margins of both ears were scratched and the lobe of the right ear was wanting. There were also scratches above the right eyebrow and over the right malar bone [*i.e. cheekbone*]. The neck was greenish but presented no marks of ecchymosis [*i.e. subcutaneous bruising*] or abrasion.

Interior

Dura mater [*i.e. membrane covering brain and spinal cord*] flaccid. Brain semi-fluid and of a pink colour. No trace of fracture or extravasation [*i.e. leakage of fluid, as for instance blood into tissues*]. There was nothing remarkable in the mouth, larynx or pharynx. The lungs were collapsed and greatly engorged with blood but otherwise healthy. The bronchial tubes were empty. The heart was quite healthy, and its cavities and adjacent veins

35

were empty. The diaphragm was pushed high into the chest by the pressures of gas in the intestines. The stomach was empty and contracted. Urinary bladder was in a similar state. The uterus was small, and its cavity contained no bloody or other fluid. An ulcer covered with yellow pus was observed in the uteri, extending into the cervix. Ovaries small and flattened. The vagina was purplish and much congested, its mucous membranes smeared with a thin bloody fluid. The genital organs presented no trace of wounding. Rectum natural. The blood was generally fluid and flowed copiously on division of the great veins of the neck, and from the superior vena cava. The cavities of the chest and abdomen showed scarcely any traces of decay.

Dr. Hatchell concluded that the cause of death was not drowning but asphyxia due to some form of constriction or compression, possibly in tandem with forcible drowning. Sarah Maria Louisa Kirwan had not died accidentally.

While Dr. Hatchell was writing his report, Major Brownrigg was interviewing Teresa Kenny in Dublin Castle. As there were rumours of bigamy, she confirmed that she had not been married to Kirwan although they were known as Mr. and Mrs. Kirwan. She had been aware of Mrs. Kirwan for ten years and, to her knowledge, the wife was aware of her relationship with Mr. Kirwan. That was tantamount to saying "as far as I know", which suggests that Kirwan told her that this was so without his wife being aware of the fact. Or perhaps he told her nothing.

Brownrigg knew of a relatively recent incident in which Mrs. Kirwan had called to the house in Sandymount and some form of unpleasant altercation ensued. Perhaps either Teresa or Maria's mother, who had also been interviewed, informed him of this event, unwittingly providing the prosecution with serious ammunition – because, if Maria Kirwan had not learnt of her husband's relationship with Teresa Kenny until a matter of months before her death, it certainly presented a motive for murder. Whoever the informant, the source of the information was sound enough for Brownrigg to proceed on the assumption that the discovery of the long-term relationship with Teresa Kenny some months before had caused a very serious falling-out between Mrs. Kirwan and her husband, causing the intense friction evidenced by the incident in the lodging house in Howth.

It would be safe to assume that Mrs. Kirwan, herself childless, would not tolerate any further deception on her husband's part and had issued an ultimatum which would preclude him from continuing the relationship with his mistress. The Major had gathered from his enquiries that Kirwan was extremely fond of his children and would suffer greatly by their absence. It was also obvious to the constabulary that William Burke Kirwan was not a very popular man, or rather had made himself not popular by his pompous and arrogant behaviour.

On the evening of October 6th William Burke Kirwan was arrested, charged with the murder of his wife and remanded to Kilmainham jail.

But it was the moral compass of the artist's behaviour that would dominate the public consciousness and media in the months after his arrest and foment a tide of revulsion against the prisoner. This had its provenance in the fact that he had not only kept and cohabited with his mistress but also fathered seven children with her. It was a ménage scarcely imaginable in an era of such moral probity. The resulting revulsion towards Kirwan contained an irony in that the much more serious charge of murdering his wife was somewhat lost in the avalanche of controversy brought on by his moral behaviour.

The victim was almost forgotten in the concentration on the sixth as opposed to seventh commandment. This would subsume for some time the more serious facts of what occurred on Ireland's Eye in early September. The rumour factory in Dublin was at full capacity in a manner rarely if ever experienced before. It was not just the dangerous liaison that occupied the public mind but the sheer daring of the deceit. The mistress had not been housed in some country location but in a house somewhere over a mile from the marital abode.

The central character in the perfidious triangle was a man of substance living in an area of splendour, the vast majority of the inhabitants of which were pillars of society. In addition the circumstances of the event were strange and striking, the setting hauntingly picturesque and the character of the main players curiously beautiful and damned. There were in addition, classical elements: a society scandal; a sexual triangle; moral outrage; a death; an exhumation; a police investigation; and, to follow, a sensational trial which would become steeped in controversy.

After his arrest the tide of public opinion flowed against William Burke Kirwan but tides by the law of nature move in two directions and that is precisely what would happen on this occasion. The trial and the legal privilege attached to the proceedings was a vehicle to lift the veil on the mysterious life of the prisoner and the other participants in the events surrounding the tragedy, to ventilate the truth of what happened within the strictures of criminal law and to decide the fate of the accused.

But there would be some things of vital importance in this trial that would, by the rules of evidence, be perceived to be too prejudicial to the interests of the prisoner and that would be omitted, to the detriment of justice.

The trial of William Burke Kirwan for the murder of his wife was eagerly awaited. For some strange reason in this strange case remand proceedings were conducted in secret, excluding the press, which prompted the leader writer in *The Freeman's Journal* of Saturday, October 16th, 1852, to tackle the subject in the following uncompromising fashion:

THE MYSTERIOUS DROWNING AT IRELAND'S EYE

Elsewhere will be found the report, or rather the attempt to obtain a report of the proceedings in this strange case. It will be seen that the adjourned investigation was as strictly private as was the former one, but we can scarcely credit the concluding paragraph: "that Mr. Kirwan was accordingly committed for trial."

There may be cogent reasons shown for carrying on an investigation privately through even several adjournments but we can admit none for the conclusion of a secret examination and the committal of a prisoner for trial without publication of the grounds on which he has been committed. Were such a course tolerated by the public or slurred over by the press, it would lead us back to the dark ages of the Star Chamber, the black dungeon of the torturer. It seems that the reason assigned for this unusual and most mischievous proceeding was that the publication of evidence might lead to a public pre-judgement of the case. If there were any weight in such arguments the immediate result should be the closing of all our inferior courts of criminal jurisdiction against the intrusion of the public and the press.

But the allegation is valueless. Publicity is the very life of justice. Wide publicity opens the gates of her court to evidence; not one-sided evidence, but evidence on both sides.

Were there no coroner's inquest in existence, how many a murder would be kept secret? Even as it is, how many cases of foul assassination would escape both coroner and his jury, either through their carelessness, their stupidity, their over-tender care about the feelings of relatives, or the difficulty of obtaining proper evidence, but for the watchful care of the press and its pertinacity in bearing deadly mysteries to the public view?

And finally, in this matter of pre-judgement, how often has the innocent man, against whom prejudice and circumstances were united, been furnished with the proof of his innocence through the means of publicity which has been given, and given in time, to the evidence against him?

We protest against a man being put upon his trial for a crime, the first public proof of which will be adduced before judge and jury who are to hear and to pronounce finally on his guilt or innocence. It would be a death blow to justice. It would be the opening of a door to murder under the garb of law, or to the escape of miscreants under the pretence of fairness. As to the case under consideration, the prisoner has already been pre-judged from the mere fact of his committal, nay, from the preliminary fact of his arrest, so long after the admittedly unsatisfactory results of the coroner's inquest.

There is not a single strange or unaccountable circumstance connected with the death of the poor lady, the finding of her body and the previous and subsequent conduct of her husband that has not been canvassed during the last week, whenever three persons assembled, and that has not been set down to his disadvantage, for the obvious reason that no explanation of them has been offered to the public.

Rumours are in circulation so universally that it would be ridiculous to pretend ignorance of their existence, about shrieks of distress and cries for mercy having been heard by fishermen who were proceeding home to Wicklow, and those cries seem to have come from Ireland's Eye about the time Mrs. Kirwan is supposed to have perished; yet who can now inform the public whether such rumours were founded in the truth, or are merely some of those wicked inventions that people afflicted with a morbid desire to circulate tales of wonder delight in fabricating?

View it in what light we may, we can see nothing but evil arising out of secrecy in such a case. Publicity tends alike to find evidence that will acquit or convict. We demand that justice shall be forwarded and her ends promoted and her work is not to be done in the dark. We have no paling sympathy for the guilty, and we have no fear of light for the cause of the innocent. Above all things, we protest against the risk of the criminal being allowed to escape through want of evidence, still more against the awful chance of an innocent man being brought to a felon's doom through lack of means to rebut the charges against him.

This, despite the forthright plea for the lifting of the reporting restriction imposed on the remand proceedings, is also an argument for trial by press which it seems is the very reason why the authorities decided to hold them in camera. That all such proceedings should be allowed to be reported is, as the writer argues, true, but the reasons given – that the press should be in a position to provide evidence of guilt or innocence – is going too far. It was also a fact that the press had already printed unfounded rumours, without one bit of evidence, that the accused had been involved in previous criminal activity – no doubt the work of gossipmonger Mrs. Byrne.

The writer unfortunately then demolishes his own argument by citing the story of the cries "for mercy" heard by fishermen travelling to Wicklow which is not only highly inaccurate but clearly prejudicial to the prisoner.

The press seized on everything they could. They even published a story that, around 1836, Kirwan had seduced and abandoned the servant girl of his landlord, whereupon her brother posted placards all over Dublin attacking Kirwan's character. When Kirwan's family pulled them down, the brother retaliated by horsewhipping him.

In any case, there would be no restriction on the reporting of the trial which, after the Grand Jury finding in October, a false start and an adjournment, would start at the beginning of December.

CHAPTER 4

THE TRIAL: FIRST DAY

COMMISSION OF OYER AND TERMINER

Held at Green Street, Dublin, December, 1852

Presiding Judges:
The Honourable Phillip C. Crampton
The Right Honourable Richard W. Greene
(Baron of the Exchequer)

Counsel for the Prosecution:
George Smyly Q.C.; Edmund Hayes L.L.D. Q.C.;
John Pennefather, Esqr.

Counsel for the Prisoner:
Isaac Butt Q.C. M.P.; Walter Burke Q.C.;
William Brereton, Q.C.; John A. Curran, Esqr.

THE QUEEN against WILLIAM BURKE KIRWAN

A true bill had been found against the prisoner by the Grand
Jury, at the previous October Commission, for the murder of
his wife Maria Louisa Kirwan, on the 6th of September, 1852,

42

and on indictment the prisoner was arraigned and having pleaded "Not Guilty," on the application of the Counsel for the Crown, the trial was postponed until the present Commission.

—<o>—

FIRST DAY
Wednesday, December 8th, 1852

Long before the arrival of the judges, the avenues leading to the court were thronged with a vast number of gentry seeking admission. However, as a result of the excellent arrangements made by the Sheriff, ample accommodation was secured by the bar and the public press area. The galleries and the seats in the body of the court were densely crowded with an assembly which included a number of ladies.

At a quarter past ten o'clock the judges took their seats upon the bench and the Clerk of the Crown then proceeded to call over the long panel for the County of Dublin, and forty-eight jurors having answered their names, William Burke Kirwan was placed at the bar and on being asked was he ready for his trial, he replied in the affirmative. He was then asked to look to his challenges and, the prisoner having challenged three, the following jury was sworn, no juror having been set aside on the part of the Crown.

John Dennis	Charles F. Goodwin
David Drummond	James Halpin
Edward Evans	Charles B. Johnson
Edward J. Figgis	Richard Johnson
Christopher Flanagan	James Kerr
Maurice Flanagan	Patrick Langan

Intense anxiety prevailed among the crowd to catch a view of the prisoner whose demeanour was firm and collected. He was a good-looking man in his thirties with dark hair and eyes, dressed

43

with evident care in a close-fitting paletot of fine black cloth. He also wore a black satin stock and black kidskin gloves. He was obviously a person who devoted considerable attention to his clothes and general appearance.

The prisoner was then given in charge to the jury by the Clerk of the Crown, on the following indictment:

> The Jurors for Our Lady The Queen upon their oath do say and present that William Burke Kirwan late of Howth in the county of Dublin, gentleman, not having the fear of God before his eyes but being moved and seduced by the instigation of the devil on the sixth day of September, in the sixteenth year of the reign of our sovereign Queen Victoria, with force and arms at Ireland's Eye in the county of Dublin aforesaid did wilfully, feloniously and of his malice prepense, kill and murder one Maria Louisa Kirwan against the peace of our said Lady The Queen, her crown and dignity.

To this indictment the prisoner pleaded "Not Guilty" and the issue for the jury was to try to determine whether or not he was guilty.

On the application of Mr. Isaac Butt Q.C. M.P., Counsel for the Prisoner, the witnesses on both sides with the exception of the medical gentlemen were directed to leave the court.

Mr. George Smyly Q.C., Counsel for the Prosecution, rose to begin his case for the Crown. There was a hush in the court only barely interrupted by the shuffling of papers on the table of the prosecutor and all eyes from the gallery to the body of the court and including the prisoner at the bar were focused on the man who had taken on the task for the Crown after the Attorney General became indisposed. And by a strange irony the counsel was a neighbour of Kirwan's who lived in 23 Upper Merrion Street.

Smyly cleared his throat and broke the silence. There was a relaxation of the very tense atmosphere that builds at the beginning of every criminal trial, amplified all the more by the fact that the life of a man depended on the outcome. The higher the stakes, the higher the tension – in this instance, heightened also by the spark of scandal, the flames of which had been fanned by the bellows of the press, a sexual triangle and an alleged murder on an island committed by a man of the privileged classes.

If, of course, murder it was.

There would be no direct evidence in this trial, as there had been no witness to the death of the victim, so the prosecution case would be built on the chain of circumstance that was attached to what had happened on the island on the evening of the 6th of September, 1852.

Whatever the salacious detail of the private life of the prisoner which would be eagerly awaited by the spectators and the press, Mr. Smyly and his team knew that it would not be for his moral behaviour that Kirwan would be successfully prosecuted.

What was of vital importance was the medical evidence, which for the prosecution was fraught with difficulty. The exhumation of the body of Maria Kirwan revealed that she had been buried in a wet grave and the seepage of water into the coffin had accelerated the decomposition of the surface of the body. This diminished considerably the possibility of establishing external marks of violence on the body.

While Dr. Hatchell was a police surgeon and medical witness for the Crown, his medico-legal role demanded that he should objectively rely on scientific evidence and not take a view one way or another. However, an art of that role would be to stick steadfastly to the scientific findings in the face of withering cross-examination while the defence attempted with their own medical witnesses to propose an accidental cause of death and if at all possible to throw as much doubt into the minds of the jury members as possible.

In that regard, Smyly and the prosecution had an ace card up their sleeve but it was one that they chose not to use. Given the tenuous nature of the medical evidence, it was a decision that could prove fatal to their case.

Also Smyly was at a disadvantage. Stepping into the role of Chief Prosecuting Counsel for the Attorney General at the last minute, however able he was, he would not have had the time to familiarise himself completely with the details of the case. He would be forgiven for making a few mistakes, and make them he would. However, he had an excellent and well-briefed team to pick up the slack.

In his defence, the prisoner had the services of the trenchant and brilliant Isaac Butt who would go on to greater things in the nationalist political arena, and John Adye Curran who would achieve the same in the legal world. Butt, certainly, quite apart from his legal acumen, was the perfect defence counsel for Kirwan with whom he shared an appetite for philandering and producing progeny outside marriage. The moral aspect of the case would be of no consequence to the leading defence counsel and correctly so.

This case, by any manner or means, was poised on a knife edge and the outcome would depend on the level of credible performance by all participants, including the witnesses and the counsel. Listed among the former was Teresa Kenny, the mistress of the accused, and it would not be idle to speculate that her evidence and cross-examination would provide the highlight of the proceedings for the spectators, gentry, gossipmongers and most of all the slavering hounds of the press.

There was complete silence in the room of the famous courthouse as the Chief Prosecuting Counsel, George Smyly Q.C., addressed the jury and it must be noted at this juncture that this opening address contained quite a few inaccuracies and errors.

My lords, ladies and gentlemen of the jury, up to within the last hour I expected that my honourable and learned friend, The Attorney General, would be present in court in order to open to you the case for the prosecution on this trial. However, in the absence of my Right Honourable friend, I am called upon to perform that duty, and to put you in possession of the principal facts and leading circumstances of this case, so as to enable you the more clearly to understand the evidence when submitted to you in detail by several witnesses.

You have heard from the Clerk of the Crown, that the prisoner at the bar, William Burke Kirwan, stands indicted for the murder of his wife, Maria Louisa Kirwan. The prisoner and the deceased lady were married about twelve years ago but no children have resulted from that marriage. The prisoner and his wife resided together in the house No. 11, Upper Merrion Street, in this city. That has been for some time the usual dwelling place of the prisoner.

In the opening facts to you, I believe I shall convince you that this case is one of no ordinary importance; that it is a case of deep and serious moment, not only as regards the consideration of the possible consequences to the prisoner himself, but also as regards the due administration of justice, and, as affects the protective power of the law, in defending the lives of Her Majesty's subjects.

I am fully convinced, gentlemen of the jury, that you are well aware of the importance of this case which you have to try; yet it is my duty to urge upon you the obligation which is imposed on you, as jurors, of giving all the facts of this case your best and fullest consideration. I must add that it is not alone in the nature and character of the case in this instance which must demand your attention. It will be equally your duty, to consider, maturely, the peculiar nature of the evidence upon which the charge has been founded, and by which it is sought to be maintained.

The evidence which the Crown is about to adduce in support of the charge against the prisoner, is not what is styled in legal language "direct evidence". It is that species of testimony known by the designation of "circumstantial evidence".

Gentlemen of the jury, you, of course, fully recognise the distinction between these two species of evidence; you are, of course, aware, that what is called "direct evidence" is, from its very designation, the evidence of parties who have themselves witnessed the perpetration of the act, who have been present when the crime was committed, who have heard the shot fired, who have seen the blow struck, or other injury inflicted, by which the death of the victim was caused and the murder effected.

But, gentlemen, the other description of evidence is that wherein witnesses are brought forward, each and every one of whom gives a relation of certain circumstances coming within his or her own cognizance and observation, and relates a series of facts distinct and independent of all other statements, and which facts, thus stated, when collected and compared, constitute an aggregate assemblage of circumstances which tend naturally and forcibly to impress the mind with a conviction of the guilt of the accused party. Then you have a case sustained upon what is properly termed "circumstantial evidence".

And, gentlemen, I now tell you (under correction of the court) that, upon that species of evidence, a jury may be as safely justified in acting, and may form its conclusions as decisively and securely, as if the evidence before it were altogether "direct", and sworn to by actual witnesses of the act.

Gentlemen of the jury, I have said that this case is one of deep importance as regards the heinous nature and dreadful character of the crime charged against the prisoner. I have told you that the crime is alleged to have been committed by the prisoner at the bar upon his wife, the being of all others whom it was his bounden duty to cherish and protect. However, I much fear in this sad case, affection and kind regard on the part of the husband have not gone hand in hand with duty.

I say this, because I believe there can be no doubt thrown on one portion of the case, which will, I think, be proved to your satisfaction in the course of this trial, namely, that the prisoner, although he was married during a period of twelve years to the unfortunate lady who has met, as alleged, an untimely death at his hands, had been during nearly the whole of that period living and cohabiting with another woman by whom he had a numerous family of children. It should be observed that this double connexion of the prisoner, the one with his lawful married wife, and the other woman of an illicit and immoral nature, went on through this long period of years undiscovered by the prisoner's wife, and what is more strange, undetected (as it would appear) by the woman with whom he kept this private and illicit intercourse.

Gentlemen, the prisoner is an artist; and his time, during the greater portion of each day, used to be occupied in the pursuit of his profession, his occupation being principally as an anatomical draftsman, as an artist employed to make anatomical drawings. The prisoner was also engaged in furnishing certain coloured maps, having been employed for that purpose by a gentleman of respectability, resident of this city.

Such, gentlemen of the jury, was the prisoner's daily employment, a reputable and respectable occupation; but it becomes my duty to tell you, that the greater portion of his time, not devoted to his business, was spent, not in the society of his wife, but in the company of the woman Maria Teresa Kenny, the woman to whom I have already alluded. And I must repeat this strange fact that, although the prisoner, during the twelve years of his married life, had been cohabiting with the said Maria Teresa Kenny, and had by her a family of no less than seven children, it so happened and was so managed, that neither Maria Kirwan nor Teresa Kenny had, either of them, the least notion or idea of each other's existence as regarded the prisoner, or his of having intercourse with any other person, save themselves, respectively, until a comparatively recent period.

Mrs. Kirwan believed that she was the sole possessor of her husband's affections, whilst, on the other hand, the woman Teresa Kenny was assured of his undivided regard until some months back. These facts, gentlemen will appear in the evidence; nay, more with such consummate art was his system of double deception carried on, that it was only within the last six months that either of these two women became aware of the fact that each had a rival in the prisoner's affections, or that he was associating with any female but herself. However, gentlemen, the discovery was made by both women in or about the period I have mentioned.

The ordinary residence of Mr. Kirwan in Dublin was, as I have stated, the house, No. 11, Upper Merrion Street. His wife resided there, and there was his specified address. But, in the month of June last, Mr. Kirwan took lodgings at Howth for himself and his wife Maria Kirwan, for the benefit of sea bathing and fresh air. Whilst sojourning at Howth, it was the habit of Mr. Kirwan to occupy himself in sketching scenery in the vicinity. It was arranged by Mr. Kirwan that he and his wife were to remain until the 7th of September, the day following the evening on which the death of the ill-fated wife of the prisoner took place.

Gentlemen, I presume that you are tolerably well acquainted with a small island in the immediate vicinity of Howth Harbour, known as "Ireland's Eye". To this little island, the prisoner, Mr. Kirwan, accompanied by his wife, made two excursions previous to that on 6th of September from which the unfortunate lady never returned alive. On the Wednesday, and also on the Friday, previous to the fatal event, Mrs. Kirwan accompanied her husband to this island. They were conveyed thither in a boat, manned by boatmen, inhabitants of the neighbourhood.

The 5th of September, the day before the death of Mrs. Kirwan, was the Sabbath. On the evening of that day, Mr. Kirwan, accompanied by his wife, went down to the pier, and arranged with the crew of one of the boats to convey them across from Howth to the island on the following morning.

Gentlemen, I should have observed that Mr. Kirwan and his wife were at this time residing in the lodging which they had occupied since the month of June, and of which their tenure according to the previous agreement was to expire on the next day. The person who owned the house and who had received the prisoner and his wife as lodgers is a woman named Campbell who occupied a portion of the house herself. On the Monday forenoon, in accordance with the previous day's arrangement, the prisoner and his wife embarked at Howth Harbour, at about ten o'clock, and proceeded across towards the island. It will be stated to you, on embarking, Mr. Kirwan and his wife had with them a basket, carpet bag and two bottles. There was also a portfolio or sketch book.

After landing the prisoner and his wife on the island, the boat returned to Howth, and subsequently about twelve o'clock, the same boat and crew conveyed another party across to the island – Mr. Brew, his lady and family – who remained on the island for recreation until about four o'clock, when the same boat came for them by appointment, and they crossed over to Howth.

During the four hours that Mr. Brew and his family remained on the island, they met Mrs. Kirwan several times, and when they were about to leave, she was near the strand where the boat was. Mr. Brew and his lady offered to convey Mrs. Kirwan back to Howth, if she so desired, but Mrs. Kirwan replied that she had directed a boat to come over for herself and her husband at eight o'clock. There was, besides, another visitor to Ireland's Eye on that day. A boatman named Doyle had taken over in his boat a gentleman named Hamilton. But that gentleman did not remain on the island beyond an hour, and was taken back in Doyle's boat.

Now, gentlemen, I believe that it will be clearly and satisfactorily proved that after the hour of four o'clock in the afternoon, no person, whatever, remained on the island, save and except the prisoner William Burke Kirwan and his wife. I have told you that the orders to the boatmen were to call for Mr. and Mrs. Kirwan at eight o'clock in the evening. A man named Hugh Campbell will tell you that he was leaning on the pier wall at Howth Harbour at about half past seven o'clock, or a little after, when he saw a boat belonging to a man named Nangle leave the harbour, and then proceed to the island.

But, gentlemen, previous to this, the attention of this man Campbell was attracted by a circumstance of considerable importance. In or about an hour before the departure of Nangle's boat from the harbour, Campbell heard a loud cry from the direction of the island; that cry he heard repeated more than once; that circumstance occurred at about seven o'clock, possibly a little later; Campbell was not the only one who heard those cries at the same period of the evening from the same quarter.

Gentlemen, it will be one of the questions which you will have to consider, whether the cries which reached the ear of Campbell were the same as those which were heard by the other parties who will be produced, and also, whether the cries heard by these different persons came from the same exact direction, from the same place, and whether the cries were of the same nature as heard in each instance.

I do not desire to express what have been my own deductions from this portion of the evidence; but this I may state, that I believe you will find that those cries or screams, both as to the time of their alleged occurrence, as to the nature and character of their tone and intensity, and as to the direction in which they were heard, are characterised by a strong coincidence, tending to establish their identity as being the same cries which were heard by the several different witnesses. The man Campbell will tell you that he heard those cries about three quarters of an hour before he saw Nangle's boat leaving the harbour. Another witness who lives near the ladies' bathing place, at the east side of Howth Harbour, named Alicia Abernethy, will testify to having heard similar cries, at about the same period of the evening specified by the man Campbell. Another witness, Catherine Flood, whilst standing at the door of the house of a gentleman named Singleton, will prove to you that she also heard similar cries, and she will describe to you the nature and character of those cries, as they were heard by her. Another witness, John Barrett, will depose that he heard similar cries, and that he went down to the harbour in order to learn the cause of them. He will tell you his impressions as to the nature of those cries.

At the same period of the evening in question, a sailboat was returning, and of the crew of this boat, eight in number, only one man, Thomas Larkin, was on deck. This man will tell you that his boat came around the island, and passed near one part of it, and whilst thus passing he heard loud cries, cries which I believe you will find to be stated to be of the same character as those heard by the other parties. Now, gentlemen, it may be well to put you in possession of information as accurate as possible with reference to the bearings and distance of this small island of Ireland's Eye, in relation to Howth Harbour, and also as to the peculiar features of the island itself.

The learned counsel here produced and referred to a map of the island, and of the adjacent vicinity. A map was also produced showing the aspect and character of the part of the island where the body of the deceased was found. Counsel then continued his address.

The island lies opposite the harbour of Howth, the nearest point being a spot called the Broad Patch, at the extreme eastern end of the island. Verging towards the west from this point are two strands, one much larger than the other. The strand at the west end leads towards the ruins of a Martello tower, and this is one of the usual landing places for boats. It was at this spot that the prisoner and his wife landed from the boat on the morning of the 6th of September.

Between this strand and the Broad Patch there is a level spot whereon there are the ruins of an ancient church. At the back of the Broad Patch and hidden from Howth Harbour, is a creek or gulley, called the Long Hole. The tide flows into this creek, and it is filled with water at high tide, but when the tide is out the Long Hole is entirely dry. Now, gentlemen, all the witnesses who will give evidence as to the cries which they heard, will all be found to concur in stating that those cries came from the direction of the Long Hole; and it will be shown to your satisfaction that cries issuing from that spot could be heard from the various places at which the witnesses happened to be at the time.

Shortly before eight o'clock the boat which had been directed to call at the island for Mr. and Mrs. Kirwan left Howth Harbour. That boat contained four boatmen, namely Patrick Nangle, Michael Nangle, Thomas Giles and Edward Cavanagh. It was nearly dark when they reached the island. The men, on reaching the landing place, hailed Mr. Kirwan. They could not see him at first, but after a short time he came down to the boat, on reaching which he desired one of the men to go up the strand and bring down his bag.

At this juncture, a conversation occurred between Mr. Kirwan and the men. The details of that conversation will be furnished in evidence. After some time one of the men asked Mr. Kirwan, "Where is the mistress?" In reply to this Mr. Kirwan said he had not seen her since the shower of rain (meaning the shower which had fallen at six o'clock) at which time she had left him to go and bathe. Two of the men suggested a search should be made for the lady.

The prisoner consented and he proceeded, accompanied by the man Michael Nangle, towards the direction of the

Long Hole. They did not succeed in finding Mrs. Kirwan, and they returned to the boat and apprised the other men of their unsuccessful search. Another boatman, Patrick Nangle, then proposed to renew the search, to which the prisoner consented, and he, accompanied by Patrick and Michael Nangle, proceeded through a large portion of the island. At length they approached the Long Hole. Patrick Nangle led the way, and called out to his comrade and the prisoner "to make a good search this time". Patrick Nangle took the east side and Michael Nangle and the prisoner the west side.

Now, gentlemen, it is necessary to recollect that on the 6th of September last, the time of the high water was half past three o'clock. At the hour of seven o'clock when the cries were heard, at 8 o'clock when the boat passed over, and at nine o'clock when the first search began, the tide was receding. At ten o'clock when the body was found, the tide was quite out. In the centre of the Long Hole there is a small rock and lying across this rock, the body was found. When the body was found that rock was dry and the tide had receded six feet from it. The deceased lady was found lying on her back on the rock, with her bathing dress gathered up under her arms, and partly under the body was found a bathing sheet. The bathing cap was missing. The body, when found, was certainly warm.

Gentlemen, your attention must be especially directed to the position in which the body was found. The exact position and aspect of the body, the position of the bathing dress and the sheet, constitute matters of the deepest importance. When Patrick Nangle discovered the body, he called out to his comrade; but it appeared that he spent some brief time in arranging the dress more decently on the remains. When the prisoner came to the spot, he rushed forward and threw himself on the body, exclaiming. "Oh, Maria, Maria!" exclamations which I trust were the sincere and genuine ejaculations of sorrow.

But then the prisoner turned around and said to the men, "Go and fetch her clothes." Patrick and Michael Nangle then went to search for the clothes, but being unable to find them, they returned to where they had left the prisoner beside the body. On learning that their search had been fruitless, the prisoner said "Come, I will go with you myself to look for the clothes." The prisoner then went up the rock by himself, and after a short time came back and said if the men went up the rock, they would find the clothes. Patrick Nangle then went up and did find the clothes, but he found them in a spot which he had searched on the previous occasion, and where the clothes had not been then. This would be sworn to.

The two boatmen then went to their boat, leaving the prisoner alone with the body. It took nearly an hour to bring the boat around from the landing place to the Long Hole where the body lay. The men enveloped the body in a sail, and placed it in the boat, and rowed back to Howth.

Some time after [*i.e. after that day*] a party visiting the island discovered a bathing cap, which would be proved to have been Mrs. Kirwan's.

Gentlemen, I repeat that the state in which the body was discovered will constitute a most important subject for your consideration. The body was found lying on the back. There were marks of scratches on the face; blood was flowing from the breast, from the ears and from another part of the body. On the body being removed from the boat at Howth, the sail in which it was wrapped was saturated with blood. The body was conveyed on a dray to Mrs. Campbell's house, where the prisoner and his wife had lodged, and there washed and laid out by three women. A coroner's inquest was held the next day on the body. The principal witness at the inquest was the prisoner himself. The two Nangles were examined, also a medical student named Hamilton. However, the investigation was speedily concluded, the verdict being

56

that the deceased lady had been drowned while bathing at Ireland's Eye.

I have already observed, when the body was found there was no water around the rock where it lay, but I am enabled to give you the depths of water at this spot, at different periods of the day in question: at high water at half past three o'clock, there were 8 feet of water above the small rock where the body was found; at half past six o'clock when the prisoner said Mrs. Kirwan went to bathe, there were but 2 feet 6 inches of water over that rock; at seven o'clock, when the cries were heard, there was but 1 foot 9 inches of water on it; at eight o'clock when the boat left to go over to the island, there were but 3 inches of water on that rock; and at half past nine o'clock, in or about the time the body was found, the tide had receded two feet below the rock in question.

Thus far, gentlemen, I have laid before you a brief outline of the evidence which will be submitted to you, sufficient to enable you to put together the various concurrent facts of the case. But before I conclude, I should inform you that about a month after the inquest an investigation of the case had been held and the facts which transpired then led to the present proceedings.

The body was buried in Glasnevin Cemetery; it was buried in, perhaps, the wettest part of it. When measures were taken to exhume the body, the coffin was found plunged in 2 feet of water, and thus, from the state of the body, it was found impossible to arrive at any determinate conclusion as to the nature of the injuries, or as to the cause of the lady's death.

But you will have the evidence of an intelligent man who examined the body, and who has also inspected the locality where the death took place. He will be able to give you information, which, I trust, will be sufficiently important and decisive to satisfy your minds, in one way or another, as to the truth of the matter.

The death of this lady must have occurred in either of three ways: by accident, by suicide or by homicide. It will be, for you, gentlemen, to ascertain whether that death was accidental; whether it was the result of the deceased's own act; or whether it was caused by another person – such latter act constituting the crime of murder.

You will consider whether, if the act appears to you to have been committed by another person, could that act have been committed by another hand besides that of the prisoner? As to suicide, the ascertained state of mind of the lady on the day in question, the position of the body, and, in fact, all the circumstances, put suicide out of the question. Could accident, then, have an influence on the matter?

If the tide had been rising instead of ebbing, and if the body were found outside, instead of inside the rock [*i.e. the barrier of rocks*], we might, perhaps, be led to infer a case of accidental drowning. But there was no rising tide; there was no wind, no swell. Also the hour at which we are told that the lady went to bathe precludes all idea of drowning having taken place at the small rock. The neck of the bathing dress was found untied; the arms were stiffened out from the body; the face was scratched, and the aspect of the body was not like that of a drowned person. If it were accidental drowning, would the sheet have been found partly under the body?

Could any imaginable accident have put that sheet in such a position? What accident had removed the bathing cap from the head of the lady, supposing she had been drowned? If the drowning were accidental, how came the clothes to be found in a place where they were not at the time it was first examined?

In considering the evidence you will be greatly assisted by the testimony of the medical gentlemen; but if all the facts deposed to by the whole of the witnesses form a chain of circumstances which though trifling in themselves when viewed independently of one another, yet taken altogether are calculated to convince you that the death of Mrs. Kirwan could not possibly have been either suicidal or accidental, can you then believe it to be consistent with the innocence of the prisoner, that her body could have been found in the position where it was, when discovered by the boatmen on the night of the 6th of September last?

Unless you are satisfied, on the whole of the evidence, that such might be the case, you ought not convict the prisoner; but if all the circumstances of the case, taken together, force on you the conviction that it would be impossible to account for the death of this woman except by the agency of the prisoner himself, then, however shocking it may be to your feelings to do so, it will be your duty to bring in a verdict according to your convictions.

Now, gentlemen, I believe I have detailed sufficient of this case, to enable you to understand the nature and bearing of the evidence which will be laid before you, on the part of the prosecution. I will now proceed to call those witnesses, and it will be for you to weigh, well and maturely, the facts which will be comprised in their testimony.

─◇─

Here follows an edited account of the trial as recorded at the time, constituting a compact account of the testimony without the counsel's questions intervening, and interspersed with commentary on the proceedings.

First Witness: Alfred Jones
Examined by Mr. Hayes

Witness: I am a surveyor and draftsman; I reside at Rathgar; I was at Ireland's Eye on the 5th of October last, and also on the 13th and 20th of that month; I was accompanied on all those occasions by Major Brownrigg, Mr. Dunne [*i.e. one of Brownrigg's team*] and Patrick and Michael Nangle; Patrick Nangle, in particular, pointed out to me certain localities in connection with the death of Mrs. Kirwan. [Two maps were handed to the witness] I constructed these maps; one I believe to be a correct map of the island; the tracing attached to it is from the Ordnance Survey, and represents, truly, the position of the island in reference to Howth Harbour; the other map truly represents the Long Hole; the direction of the Long Hole is about north-east and south-west; from low to high watermark at the Long Hole is 163 feet; a large rock in the middle of it is about 22 feet at the highest part, and on either side of it is a strand passage.

The sides of the rock are rough, and slope upwards to a sharp point; its surface is rather broken and rugged at the land end of the rock. The water rises about a foot upon the rock at high water; I make these observations from measurements; Patrick Nangle pointed out to me where the deceased lady's clothes were found; the spot pointed out to me was about the middle of the rock. [Witness showed the spot on the map] It was about 5 feet 6 inches above the gravel, and at high tide it would be one foot 6 inches out of the water.

Pat Nangle showed me where the body was found; it was on a rock in the Long Hole, about 3 feet long, 12 inches high on one end, one foot at the centre and 5 or 6 inches at the other end; it lies transversely in the Long Hole; there is another rock adjacent to this which is about 3 feet 4 inches above the surface of the strand; on the 6th of September there was an ordinary tide, high water at half past 3 p.m. on the bar of Dublin; at that hour the tide would have been about 7 feet above the rock on which the body was discovered; at 6.30 p.m. in the evening, 2 feet 6 inches above it; at 7 p.m. 1 foot 9 inches; at quarter past, 1 foot 4 and a half inches; at 7.30 p.m. one foot; and at 8 p.m. 3 inches.

At 9.30 p.m. the tide would have been 2 feet vertically below the rock; the tidal mark would have been 11 feet 6 inches distant from it; the water passes out of the Long Hole and leaves a bare strand around the rock, inclined towards the sea on both sides of it; the inclination was about one in eighteen in one place and one in ten at another; there are small rocks across the entrance to the Long Hole; it was rather difficult to get to where the clothes were from the water; you would have had to scramble.

Then the place to which the boat came to take away the body was pointed out to me by Patrick Nangle. [Showed the place on the map] At the mouth of the Long Hole there is a flat rock about 16 feet from where the body was found, and at low water a person could get into a boat without being wet.

The place where the boat landed for Mr. and Mrs. Kirwan in the evening was pointed out to me by Patrick Nangle; it is at the north-west or tower end of the island; it is about 792 yards from the Long Hole in a straight line. I remember an old ruin on the island; it is 280 yards from the land entrance to the Long Hole; it is nearly on the direct route from where the prisoner was standing to the Long Hole. The Martello Tower is 43 yards from where the prisoner was standing and 835 yards from the Long Hole. There are two strands on the island, separated from each other by the John Winter Rocks; that on the eastern side is 280 yards in length; the one on the west 160 yards in length.

Cross-examined by Mr. Butt

Witness: The two strands are on the Howth side of the island, near Baldoyle; the Long Hole points out in a direction to the seaward side of Lambay; the highest point of the Broad Patch, which is on one side of the Long Hole, is 30 feet over the rock where the body was found; on the other side of the Long Hole there are very high rocks; an isthmus, which joins the Broad Patch to the rest of the island is about 40 yards long, and it is 12 feet above high water. I saw the high water and the low watermarks at the Long Hole at both neap and spring tides; they are about 9 feet distant from each other. Between the rock on which the body was found and the sea there is rock 2 feet higher than the former rock; I took the tide for the 6th of September from the almanac; grass grows on the part of the rock where the clothes were found and that part which is next to the isthmus is such that you could step on it from the strand.

In response to Judge Crampton: A person could walk from the strand to where the clothes were without climbing during any portion of the way.

In response to Mr. Hayes: The way down the rock on which the clothes were found is easiest on the land side of the rock.

Mr. Butt: On your oath, sir, might not a person step from the strand to this part of the rock without climbing?

Witness: Yes; a person about to bathe might step down from the rock where the clothes were found to the strand.

Judge Crampton: I understand there was very little difference between the time of high water at the bar of Dublin and the Long Hole.

Witness: I cannot say whether there is any difference between the time of high water at Dublin bar and at Ireland's Eye; I took no measures to ascertain the fact.

Second Witness: Margaret Campbell
Examined by Mr. Pennefather

Witness: I have been married; my husband is dead; I keep a house in Howth; I was living there in September last; I had no one but my own family living in the house with me, in September last as well, and Mr. and Mrs. Kirwan; my own family consisted of two boys and a girl; the eldest boy was about 19 years old; it was in the middle of last June that I first saw the prisoner and his late wife; I knew nothing of them previously.

[The witness identified the prisoner after having approached the dock to look at him, being near-sighted]

Mrs. and Mrs. Kirwan came to me as lodgers; they occupied only one room; it was used as a sitting room and a bedroom; it was on the ground floor; it was opposite the kitchen; my bedroom was at the rear of their room; Mr. and Mrs. Kirwan had the room to themselves; Mrs. Kirwan always slept in my house from June until September; Mr. Kirwan used to sleep out about three times a week for the first month or six weeks after he came; he slept regularly at home [*i.e. in Campbell's house*], every night, for the last month or six weeks.

Mr. Kirwan used to be in town during the day, and would come home sometimes by the five o'clock train and sometimes by the last train; during the first month or six weeks they lodged with me, I observed quarrelling between them, more than once; I heard angry words from Mr. Kirwan to his wife; I heard him say he would make her stop there; I heard him miscall her; I heard him call her a strumpet; I heard him say, "I'll finish you." I do not think they had been with me a month at that time. It was before dusk in the evening; on the same evening I heard her say to him, "Let me alone, let me alone"; next morning I heard her say to him that she was black from the usage she had got the preceding night;

63

across her thighs, I think she said it was; the squabble had occurred before dusk in the evening, and Mrs. Kirwan did not go out afterwards; there was no person in the house but myself when it commenced, but before it ended, Anne Hannah came in and was with me. We were in the kitchen; Mrs. Kirwan's door was shut but the kitchen door was open; I heard no other dispute between Mr. Kirwan and his wife, unless a word, now and then; Mrs. Kirwan used to go out every day to bathe at Howth where ladies bathe; my house is distant from it, being situated at the upper end of the town; Mr. and Mrs. Kirwan slept at home [*i.e. in Campbell's house*] on the night of Sunday, 5th of September, and left immediately after breakfast the next morning; they were going to Ireland's Eye; it was the third time they had been there within a week.

They took a black travelling bag with them; it would not have held a bathing dress if there was anything else in it; they left my house together. Mrs. Kirwan had a bathing cap; I don't remember if she had a basket with her; I saw a bathing cap with Police Sergeant Joseph Sherwood after she was dead and I knew it to be hers. On the Thursday and Friday before they had been at Ireland's Eye; they spent the whole day out on these occasions, and returned about nine in the evening; they used to dine out; on the night of 6th of September, between ten and eleven o'clock, I think, I saw Mrs. Kirwan dead; she was brought on a car to my house by John Barrett; some police were with the car and Mr. Kirwan; I did not see the Nangles.

Mr. Kirwan was present when the body was brought in but I did not see him help to bring it in; there were three women in the house at the time: Mrs. Lacey, Mrs. Robinson and Catherine McGarr; the body was laid on the floor of her own room; it was wrapped in a sail and the face was covered; Mr. Kirwan went into the room with the body; I saw the sail taken off the body by the women; I think there was a bathing chemise on the corpse also; I did not examine her body; I could observe nothing particular about the appearance of the body; I could not, unless I were to examine it closely; I saw only her face.

The body was laid out that night by the women and Mr. Kirwan remained in the house until the next night [*and then he left*]; he came back early on Wednesday morning.

On the night of the 6th of September, when Mr. Kirwan came in, his feet were wet, and he put on dry stockings; I assisted him to change his stockings; I cannot say anything particular as to the general state of health enjoyed by Mrs. Kirwan; whilst living with me; I recollect her taking herbs; I did not suppose her to be in bad health; she was not ill while she was in my house.

Cross-examined by Mr. Burke

Witness: I understood that Mr. Kirwan had rooms in Merrion Street; I had lodgers before Mr. and Mrs. Kirwan came to me; it did not appear strange to me that a gentleman having rooms in town should sometimes remain away; I heard them quarrelling more than once; the first instance was shortly after they came; there was a second and I could not say there was a third; they had quarrelled at different times; I could not say when they had a fourth; it was in the first that he used the language to Mrs. Kirwan I have mentioned; it was almost a fortnight after they came to live with me; subsequently they had an odd word, now and again; he never used violence but the once.

I can't say I ever saw Major Brownrigg before [looking at him]; I think I saw him in Howth; I was not examined at the coroner's inquest; it was held in my house, and I was present when it was going on; I did not offer myself as a witness; I did not tell anything of what I have told today; the inquest was on the 7th of September; I know Mr. Furnace [*i.e. one of Brownrigg's team*]; I recollect being brought before him about the 15th of September; I see Mr. Dunne present; I had not seen him before the 14th of September; the sergeant of police brought me before Mr. Furnace; I was not sworn before him; I signed an information before him. [Acknowledged her signature to the information]

The document, which was a copy of the information of Margaret Campbell of Howth, sworn before P. Furnace Esq. on the 15th of September, 1852, was then read to the court by the Clerk of the Crown:

> Saith that the late Maria Kirwan who was drowned at Ireland's Eye, lodged in her home for nearly three months, with her husband, Mr. Kirwan; for the first fortnight they did not live happily together but during the remaining time, up to her death, informant considers, no couple could have lived more united; informant has heard Mrs. Kirwan's mother, Mrs. Maria Crowe, caution her daughter frequently not to be too venturesome in bathing.

Judge Crampton: The witness says she did not swear to that information.

Mr. Brereton: It is stated on the face of the information that it was subscribed on oath.

Cross-examination continued

Witness: The information was taken at Howth and my name and handwriting is to it; I did not consider I was sworn in making it; I was sworn but not before Captain Furnace; there was no book put into my hand. [Witness addressed the judges] There was no book put into my hand, none whatever. I was examined at Howth before Major Brownrigg, some questions were put to me by Mr. Dunne, and I was sworn afterwards.

The witness's statement to Major Brownrigg made on 8th of October, 1852, was then read.

> Mr. Burke: You say in that information that they only quarrelled once, yet you now say they quarrelled more than once?

> Witness: I meant that he only beat her once. I answered all the questions I was asked; I did not think of any more; when I was asked about it by Mr. Dunne, I was not sure whether he beat her or not, but afterwards I remembered that I had heard a rush in their room, and I thought he beat her; I was bound to tell everything; I don't recollect being asked by Mr. Dunne whether Mr. Kirwan had used any harsh language to the deceased or not; I am short-sighted; I saw no particular mark on Mrs. Kirwan's bathing cap; I used to see it hanging up in my room, and I know its colour; I will not swear to its identity now; I heard Mrs. Crowe, Mrs. Kirwan's mother, caution her about bathing.

Third Witness: Patrick Nangle
Examined by Mr. Smyly

> Witness: I am a fisherman and sailor, and live at Howth; I have lived there all my life; I know the tides there, and those at Dublin bar and Ireland's Eye; there is about a couple of minutes difference between high water at the bar and at Ireland's Eye; it is later at the Eye; I know every part of the Eye; I keep a boat to convey parties to the island from Howth. I recollect Mrs. Kirwan; she was about 28 or 29 years of age; she was a stout, handsome woman; I took Mr. and Mrs. Kirwan over to the island in my boat on three or four occasions; after I did so for the first time, I heard that they lived at Mrs. Campbell's; I took them over on the 6th of September; they both came to my place on the previous night and ordered the boat for ten o'clock the next morning; they came down

together to the boat at that hour; they had a bag with them and two bottles of water; the lady had a little reticule basket in her hand; Mr. Kirwan had a stick of the kind called a tuck stick.

Court: What was that?

Witness: I mean a stick like a sword cane. The island is a mile and a quarter from Howth, and it took ten or fifteen minutes to go across; it was a rowboat, we had a sail for occasional use; I landed them close to the tower; no one lives in the tower; I then came back to Howth; I took over Mr. Brew and a party to the island about twelve o'clock on the same day, and then returned to Howth; I went back for Mr. Brew's party at four o'clock, and when leaving with them, I saw Mrs. Kirwan; she hailed the boat, and Mr. Brew asked her did she want to come over, and she said "No"; she desired me to come back for her and her husband at eight o'clock; I saw Doyle's boat that day; after I went away with Mr. Brew's party, there was no one then on the island but Mr. and Mrs. Kirwan; at about twenty minutes to eight o'clock, I, together with Michael Nangle, Giles and Cavanagh, went over to the Eye for them; we reached there about eight o'clock; it was getting very dark then; before reaching the island, I could not see Mr. Kirwan, but we called and he answered; we landed close to the tower; he said "Nangle, come up for the bag"; I got out of the boat and left three men in it.

Mr. Kirwan was on the landing place and had a bag and a stick with him, and also a sketch book; he gave me the bag and the book to carry down; I took them, and on the way we met Mick Nangle; Mick said, "Mr. Kirwan, where is the mistress?" before I got to the boat; the prisoner said, "I have not seen her for the last hour and a half." Mick said, "Had you not better go and look for your wife?" Mick asked in what direction she had gone. Mr. Kirwan pointed out by the church and towards the Long Hole;

Mick and Mr. Kirwan then went away for about half an hour; I was overhauling the sketch book in the meantime; I was in the boat when Mick asked about Mrs. Kirwan; while they were away I did not hear anything; after looking over the book, I went up towards the tower stones, leaving the other two men in the boat and began to hail Mr. Kirwan and Michael Nangle; they did not answer; presently, they came up together, and when close to me my cousin said, "Paddy, did you get Mrs. Kirwan?" and I said, "No, didn't you get her?"; then Mr. Kirwan said, "Let us go back the same way and look for her."

Michael Nangle went away by the strand and I went towards the Long Hole with Mr. Kirwan, by the ruins of the church; I kept crying out, "Mrs. Kirwan," which he told me to do, and he himself went on exclaiming, "Oh, Maria, oh, Maria!"; you could hardly hear his voice; Mick met us on the Broad Patch side of the Long Hole and we went around the Broad Patch; Mr. Kirwan was at one time near the precipice and I pulled him back and I said, "Don't let us have your life to answer for"; we went towards the Long Hole; halfway down Mr. Kirwan slipped. Mick said, "Mr. Kirwan slipped and is killed"; Mr. Kirwan was with Mick, they were on the strand; I went two yards on, I saw something white and cried out, "Oh, Mick, I see something white here, there are no white rocks hereabouts," and on going over to it, I found it was the drowned lady.

She was lying on a rock, on her back and her bathing shift on her; it was high up on her breast, leaving the rest of her person exposed; there was a sheet under her; it was wet as also was her bathing dress; her head hanging back off the rock; her arms were stiff and her feet were in a very small pool of water; about half a gallon of water was in the pool; she had a pair of bathing boots on; her face was cut under the eyes, and over the forehead, as if it had been torn with a pin. Blood was coming from either the ears or down the head; there was a good deal of blood on her face; there was also blood coming from her side and private parts; there was a cut on her side; I covered her with the dress, and tied the sheet about her neck and across her legs before Mr. Kirwan and Michael came up; the head was in towards the rock, in a hole between two rocks, and the feet lying out; she was bleeding from the breast; the sea water was then six or eight feet away; the body was lukewarm, and quite pliant when I found it. I straightened the legs and arms.

After that they came up; Mr. Kirwan said, "Oh, Maria!"; he bid us go look for her clothes; that we would get them there on the rock [witness pointed]; I went up and searched where he pointed, but could not find them; Mr. Kirwan then got up, and went and found the clothes, and came and said, "One of you get up and go there for the clothes," pointing to the rock; I went and found them; I had searched the very same place before and did not find them.

Judge Crampton: How did he point out the place?

Witness: He went up the rock by himself, I remained with the corpse; after being three or four minutes away, he returned; it was too dark to see where he had gone; he pointed up where the clothes were, and sent me for them, and I went and found them; I said that it would break our hearts to carry her over to the tower; I proposed to go for the boat and pull round the island; Mr. Kirwan remained with the deceased; it took an hour to bring the boat round, and it was half past ten when we reached the Long Hole; the boat ran to within six feet of where the body was; it was in the same place as we had left it; we lifted it into the boat and covered it with a sail; the tide had turned and was then coming in.

Mr. Kirwan did not assist us to lift the body into the boat; he remained on the strand; the boatmen lifted in the body, and I put the sail over her; Mr. Kirwan then came on board and sat down by the head of the corpse, but I made him move, as he was in the way of our rowing, and said, "That is not the place for you; it was while she was alive, you ought to have minded her"; Mr. Kirwan got no wet; Giles went into the water, up to his knees; Mr. Kirwan got no wet with us.

We landed in Howth, and I went for a dray to convey the body away; Mr. Kirwan and Giles waited in the boat with the body; when we returned, the body was lifted out of the boat and taken on the dray to Mrs. Campbell's; next morning I went up to her house for the sail in which the body had been wrapped and found a great deal of blood on it, particularly about where the seat and private parts were, and the breast and a little from the face; I had to scrub the sail with a broom; I showed the rocks and the localities to Dr. Hatchell and also to Dr. Geoghegan; I also pointed them out to Mr. Jones; I know Ireland's Eye very well; it is in the county of Dublin.

Cross-examined by Mr. Brereton

Mr. Brereton: This case did not prove a good haul for you.

Witness: No, to my grief, I wish I had never seen it; it was a very bad haul; I went over to the island for Mr. and Mrs. Kirwan at half past six in the evening on the first day that I took them there; on the second occasion I went at seven in the evening, and on the third at eight; on the evening of Sunday the 5th, when they engaged the boat, they had no difference as to the time I should come for them the next day; Mrs. Kirwan said eight o'clock, and no sooner, and Mr. Kirwan did not say, "Seven o'clock" [*presumably in response to a suggestion that Kirwan said seven*].

I have seen maps like this before; I have seen maps in vessels, but I never saw one like that except once before in Kildare Street; I saw it with Mr. Jones; I don't know whether it was his house or not; I was brought there by a sergeant of police; I conned over the map, and was shown the places by Mr. Jones.

There were no boats near us when we hailed Mr. Kirwan; I shouted several times that evening; at the time when Mr. Kirwan and Michael Nangle came back after searching there were some fishing boats going by.

I heard no inquiry from Mr. Kirwan as to whether she was in the boat or not.

While Mr. Kirwan and I were searching, he went so near a steep place, that only I caught him, he would have fallen down the rocks; if a horse fell down he would have been killed; that was right over where the body was found; about a minute before I found the body, the prisoner fell.

I did not try to bend the arms of the corpse, but merely lay them alongside the body; I am sure it was not stiff; none of her limbs were; it was dark then; I saw her mouth, and blood enough upon it and froth; there were a good many scratches about her eyes.

Mr. Brereton: Upon your oath, did you see a single wound upon her body?

Witness: Yes, there were scratches like as if done by a pin.

Mr. Brereton: Did you see any deeper marks?

Witness: Yes, the private parts of her body were greatly cut; the blood would not have flowed if it were otherwise. The strand where we found her is covered with gravel; if the body had been in the water before the tide fell so low, and if a rock had not been between it and the mouth of the Long Hole, it would have been carried out to sea, that is, if the tide was running, and was high enough; the scratches on the face could not have been caused by crabs; there were no crabs where the body was; I have often seen crabs at the low watermark there, but not where the body was; I will swear that the marks on her forehead and eyes were not caused by crabs; however they were caused the crabs did not do it; I cannot say what caused them; I was at the inquest but I was not allowed to speak at it; before I came to my evidence about the sheet, I was put back, and the other man was brought forward; that was by Mr. Kirwan's direction; I had not mentioned about the blood, nor about the way I tied her up [*in the sheet*] when I was stopped.

Judge Crampton: No charge had been made at that time.

Witness: There was no shawl on or about the body when I found it; after we came for her with the boat, I saw a shawl; Mr. Kirwan was then lying across her breast, and the shawl was around her head; I don't think I mentioned at the inquest about Mr. Kirwan pointing up the rock to where the clothes were; I did not hear Mr. Kirwan say "Mrs. Kirwan must be in the boat," or that she went into the boat; no such word passed; he asked me if I had seen Mrs. Kirwan, he told us to search, and to shout out, "Maria Kirwan".

Only for us Mr. Kirwan would have lost his life; he was on the very brink of the rock when I caught him; if he took one step further, in the direction he was going, he would have gone over the rock; he would certainly be killed; a horse would be killed if it fell there; that was the very rock under which the body was afterwards found; about a minute before I found the body, Mr. Kirwan fell; I did not try to bend the arms of the body; it was not stiff; the knees were bent; I saw the face; there were several scratches; the mouth was frothing.

In my opinion, the tide was receding; the body presented the appearance of being checked by the smaller rock, but there was no swell to bruise the body.

There were wounds on the body; I could not say how deep; the seat and the side was wounded; the under part of the body was in a shocking state; the wound was severe; I think so by reason of there being so much blood; there were no crabs there, at least I did not see them; these injuries could not occur by scraping against the gravel, nor could they be caused by crabs; I was examined at the inquest; my evidence then went as far as where I stated having found the sheet under the body; I did not find any shawl under the body; I saw a shawl afterwards when I came back with the boat; then I found Mr. Kirwan just as I had left him, lying with his face on the breast of the body; it was then when I first saw the shawl; it was around the neck of the deceased; I do not recollect having said anything about Mr. Kirwan telling me the clothes were above on the rocks.

The statement made by the boatman to the inquest was then read to the court.

Cross-examination continued

Witness: I said nothing about Mr. Kirwan having found the clothes when giving my information, because I was ordered to draw back; when Mr. Kirwan went up the rock to look for the clothes he did not go up higher than I did; I will swear I searched the rock well; I do not care how dark it was, I searched the rocks and could find nothing; but afterwards Mr. Kirwan went up, and after being a few minutes away, came down and told me to go up again, and I would find them; I then went up and found them; I will swear that the clothes were not on the rock where I found them; they had not been there for me to find; I found them when Mr. Kirwan sent me up for them.Mr. Kirwan seemed to be in trouble when his wife was found; he threw himself on the body, and said, "Oh

Maria, oh Maria"; Michael Nangle and I went for the dray; I was not paid well enough for the assistance I gave; I got three shillings for the use of the boat; I demanded £2 for my trouble that night, and got it; Mr. Kirwan left £1, and the police sergeant passed his word for another; I caught the horse's head, and would not let the dray go until I was paid.

In response to a juror: No one could have been on the island after four o'clock, unknown to me; I could not say whether there was a sword in the stick Mr. Kirwan had or not, but it was like a sword cane; he had the same stick on the former days on which they went over to the island.

Another juror asked: Would a person bathing from the rock go to the place where Mr. Kirwan was near falling to get into the water?

Witness: Oh, no, sir.

In response to a juror: Mr. Kirwan could not have wet his feet in the pool at the deceased's feet, when he threw himself on the body; there was not above a quart of water in that pool; yes, about six o'clock there had been a shower; yes, there was fern on the island.

Fourth Witness: Michael Nangle
Examined by Mr. Hayes

Witness: I am a boatman and belong to the same boat as Patrick Nangle. [Identified the prisoner] I recollect taking him over to Ireland's Eye on Monday 6th of September; Mrs. Kirwan was with him; we landed them at the tower about 10 a.m..

It was 7.30 p.m. when we left Howth Harbour to go over for Mr. and Mrs. Kirwan; the wind had been from the north-east during the day, but was extremely light, we could carry a candle it was so calm; when we came to the Martello Tower we saw Mr. Kirwan; he ordered Patrick Nangle to come out of the boat and carry something down; I went up after Pat and met him coming down between the boat and Mr. Kirwan; before I spoke he had made two or three steps towards the bank to go down to the boat; I said, "Where is the mistress?"; he said, "I am after looking for her for half an hour"; I said to him "Sir, you should have had the mistress here, and not have to be looking for her at this hour of night, what way did she go?"

He said, "That way" [The witness pointed] "and I was sketching at the time. She left me after the last shower. She did not like to go to bathe where I told her to bathe because there was a bad smell"; Mr. Kirwan and I then went to look for her; we went by the John Winter Rocks to the strand; after that, we went up through the weeds; he kept calling Mrs. Kirwan; we turned then across the island towards the old church and he kept calling her, "Maria, why don't you answer? The boat is waiting": we next searched along the strand as far as a point called Caher Gran; I said, "She is not to be found here" and Mr. Kirwan said, "No, I see that"; we then went towards the Long Hole.

I had seen them coming from it the last evening I was on the Eye; we searched the Long Hole, as far as the state of tide at that time permitted; I heard Pat Nangle calling from another place; Mr. Kirwan and I then returned along the same strand we had traversed just before and we met Pat Nangle at the John Winter Rocks; I said, "This is a fine job to be here this time of the night. Where are we to find this woman? Let us leave the other two men at the boat and we will go round again and if Mrs. Kirwan comes in the meantime, they can go to the top of the bank and hail us."

Kirwan, Pat Nangle and I went over the same ground, back again, we searched all around the Broad Patch and

I said as it was now low water, we ought to go to the Long Hole again and, depend on it, we would find her; I never knew any ladies to bathe at the Long Hole; the usual place for them to bathe is on the strand; we proceeded to the Long Hole; Kirwan and I went down the channel on the left-hand side; whilst we were proceeding on the last search, Mr. Kirwan stumbled; I suppose he tripped against a stone.

Pat Nangle said "I see something here" and went over the rocks and found the body of the deceased lying on one of them; I was between 5 and 6 yards from him at the time; Mr. Kirwan went over to the body and leaned over it and began to cry; he bid me to see if I could go and find the clothes; I looked for them along the strand and Pat Nangle searched the rock; neither of us found them; Mr. Kirwan then went up the rock and I followed him; he said "Here they are"; I then saw Mr. Kirwan come down, bringing something white in his hand, like a sheet, also a shawl; he slipped coming down the rock; Patrick Nangle and Kirwan were putting things on her; Mr. Kirwan then told Patrick Nangle to go up the rock and bring down the clothes, which he did.

I asked Mr. Kirwan to go with us; he said no, he would stay with her; Pat Nangle and I then left Mr. Kirwan with the body and went to the other side of the island for the boat, which we rowed round and brought to the rock near where the body was; I, then, with the help of Patrick Nangle and Giles, lifted the body in over the oars and placed it in the bottom of the boat, wrapped in a sail.

No one got wet except Giles who wet his feet getting into the boat; we laid her head towards the head of the boat; I did not see Mr. Kirwan get wet; he could not get wet if he went the way I did.

The place where the clothes were found was a bad place to bathe, the rocks being sharp and dangerous; I did not see the body closely until the next day; I only saw the face; there were cuts and scratches on the face, the water in the Long Hole was as smooth as a well.

Cross-examined by Mr. Butt

Witness: A half an hour elapsed between our two visits to the Long Hole. I searched it at first, as far as the water would allow me; it was very dark then; when we went to search the second time, Pat Nangle went first into the hole; I kept 5 or 6 yards to his left, Mr. Kirwan was about 3 yards from Pat Nangle when the latter called out, "Here she is" and he immediately walked towards her; I was 10 yards from Mr. Kirwan when he found the clothes; he said "Here they are" and turned round with a shawl and something like a sheet; Mr. Kirwan slipped when coming down the rock; he was putting these on the body when we went away for the boat; there were only the sheet, and shawl and bathing dress on the body when it was put into the boat.

When we met him on arrival at the island he never made mention of his wife until he was spoken to about her; it was I who proposed to search the Long Hole and remarked that if anything had happened to the lady, we would be apt to find her in low water; Mr. Kirwan said he was afraid there was; he seemed uneasy while searching for Mrs. Kirwan.

Fifth Witness: Thomas Giles
Examined by Mr Pennefather

The fifth witness, the boatman Thomas Giles, had little of importance to add and apart from confirming that he had got wet when the body was being lifted into the boat and the curious fact that, when he had asked Kirwan if he had any grog, was told that he had already given his wife three glasses of porter. It was a remarkable fact, if true, and should have drawn some attention from the prosecution counsel.

Sixth Witness: Andrew Brew
Examined by Mr Smyly

The sixth witness, Arthur Brew, told Mr. Smyly that he saw the couple walking about the island, the artist sketching, and once Mrs. Kirwan alone, reading at that time. The last time he saw her was at the strand when he asked her if she desired passage back.

There was more vital evidence to follow.

Seventh Witness: Hugh Campbell
Examined by Mr. Hayes

> Witness: I am a fish driver and reside in Howth. On the evening of 6th of September I was leaning over the quay wall opposite to the lighthouse [*i.e. the old lighthouse at the end of the east pier*] and heard a cry which seemed to come from Ireland's Eye; the voice was weak when I heard it, it came from eastward of the lighthouse at Howth; I was right opposite the lighthouse.
>
> Mr. Hayes: What kind of voice was it?
>
> Witness: Like a person calling for some assistance.
>
> Judge Crampton: Were you able to distinguish any words?
>
> Witness: No, I could not distinguish any words.
>
> Mr. Hayes: Did you hear more than one cry?
>
> Witness: I heard three cries; in three minutes after I heard the first cry I heard another and shortly afterwards I heard a third.

In response to Judge Crampton: The cries were still weaker; they were nearly all the same and resembled the calling of a person for assistance, or for a boat to come.

Examination continued

Witness: In about half an hour after I heard the cries I saw the Nangles' boat go out of the harbour; the boat went out across to the island; I have often heard voices from the island before.

Cross-examined by Mr. Butt

Witness: It was between day and dark at the time; the sun was low; it was not sunset.

Mr. Butt: When did you first tell about those cries?

Witness: Not until the police came to ask me; I was sworn before Captain Furnace. I remarked to a person who stood near me on that evening, the voice was probably that of some person who had been left out on the island and was calling for a boat; I could not tell whether it was a male or female voice; it was weak as if of a person waking from a sleep.

Eighth Witness: Thomas Larkin
Examined by Mr. Pennefather

Witness: I am a fisherman and was out fishing on Monday the 6th of September; my boat is a hooker of 38 tons, and there was a crew of eight on board her with me; between day and dark I returned from the west of the island; we ran between Ireland's Eye and the mainland; we sailed within 10 perches of the Martello Tower on the west end of the island; I heard a loud scream when we had passed the tower about 20 perches; I was steering the vessel at the time; my back was to

Ireland's Eye; the other men were below when I heard the last two cries; I started up, stood to leeward of the helm and looked towards the island.

The wind was at the north-west; I went towards the left side of the boat which was turned towards the island; I cannot say whether the sound was from the direction of the Long Hole or not; in about seven minutes after, when halfway to Howth, I heard another scream, and afterwards, another lower cry, so low I could scarcely hear it; there were about two minutes between the second and the last; they seemed to come from the direction of the Long Hole; all the men were below when I heard the last two cries; we were about halfway between the Martello Tower and Howth Harbour then; afterwards I called the men to be ready to bring the vessel into the harbour; when they came up I told them about what I had heard; it is about two miles from the Martello Tower to the harbour.

Cross-examined by Mr. Butt

Witness: We were not sailing fast at the time; from the time I called the men until we got into to the harbour, was fifteen or twenty minutes, as near as I can guess; there could not have been eight minutes between the first and second cry; it was dark when we got into harbour; we could just see the daylight on the sky as we passed the island; I could have seen a man on the shore, if one had been there, but not to know him.

Chief Defence Counsel Mr. Butt then read the statement of information given by Thomas Larkin to the police. This was clearly a strategy to point up any differences, additions or contradictions, if they arose, between the original depositions and the evidence given in court. As well, if possible, to expose any coaching of witnesses by the constabulary, the purpose being to undermine the credibility of the prosecution witnesses.

There was nothing to in any way discredit the rock-solid and forthright account given by the fisherman who impressed all in the court as being a most credible and honest witness. There had been a three-week interval between the 6th of September and the date that Thomas Larkin gave his statement, which was not unusual, given the verdict found by the disastrous inquest. There was and could be no issue made of this. His account of the first cry was even more substantial and telling, as he recounted that it was so loud that it could be "heard all over the island".

Cross-examined by Mr. Curran

Witness: I suppose that there was about eight minutes from the time I heard the first bawl until I heard the other two; the night was a pleasant night but not a calm one; there was no sea, but a little breeze out; the night was neither rough, nor smooth; it was not eight o'clock when I heard the screams; it was between day and dark when we were passing the island; we could notice the daylight on the sky when we reached Howth Harbour.

The sergeant of the police came for me; I was telling of what I had heard at the churchyard; I did not know anything about Mrs. Kirwan.

I cannot swear as to minutes to the jury; I am positive that the cries came from Ireland's Eye; I could not rightly tell what they were; they were more like those of a person in distress than those of a person crying for a boat.

Ninth Witness: Alicia Abernethy
Examined by Mr. Smyly

Witness: I live at Howth; my place of residence is about seven yards from the ladies' bathing place and the Long Hole is just opposite to my window and is distant from it about a mile; on the evening of the 6th of September, I went to the next house to ask what o'clock it was; I found that it was five minutes past seven; I came back to my own place and leaned over my garden wall, with my eyes directed towards the Long Hole on the Eye, when I heard a dreadful screech, which was not so loud, and then another, and a weaker one; it was between the two lights [*i.e. the harbour lighthouse and the Baily lighthouse to the east of Howth*]; I could just see the island at the time; the cries were those of a woman; I never saw Mrs. Kirwan.

Cross-examined by Mr. Butt

Witness: I was not at the inquest; where I live is between the harbour of Howth and the Baily lighthouse; it is not found on the hill.

Mr. Butt: It is more round the hill than the harbour of Howth?

Witness: It is not round the hill; where I live is to the eastward of the pier; the reason I was looking towards the Eye was because a son of mine was out in a yawl, and I was expecting him home; I told no person except my own family I had heard the cries until the next morning, when I heard a woman was drowned; I told the police sergeant, Sherwood, about the cries I heard; I did so before the inquest, he was passing my door at the time, and I observed to him that the screeches I heard must have been those of the woman who had been drowned; about two minutes there were between the screams; I asked the hour before; I go every night.

In response to a juror: The last scream I took to be that of a person in agony and pain; the first was most dreadful; I never heard a female scream while struggling in the water; my child came in about 8 o'clock.

Tenth Witness: Catherine Flood
Examined by Mr. Hayes

Witness: I live at Howth; on the sixth of September last I was employed for the day in the house of a Mrs. Singleton in Howth; the house is situated on the quay of Howth and near the railway station; on the evening of that day, while at the hall-door of the house, I heard great screams from Ireland's Eye; I heard two and there was a lapse of a minute or two, between them; the first was the loudest; it was a very wild scream; the last was cut off, as if in the middle of it; this was at five or six minutes past seven o'clock; I was supplying the servant's place; I had come to the hall-door to wash the hall; I saw the late Mrs. Kirwan bathing at Howth during the season; the ladies' bathing place is a quarter of a mile from the pier; I live near Mrs. Abernethy; I saw Mrs. Kirwan swim in high waves; I have seen her bathing when many ladies would not go into the water.

Cross-examined by Mr. Burke

Witness: Mrs. Kirwan was very venturesome in bathing; I have seen ladies bathing at Howth for the last eleven years and she was the most venturesome bather I ever saw; after the scream I came home; it was when I opened the door at Mrs. Singleton's that I heard the scream; I opened the door to see if it was dark; after that I washed the hall; I left Mrs. Singleton's at eight o'clock.

Eleventh Witness: John Barrett
Examined by Mr. Pennefather

The eleventh witness John Barrett also gave evidence of hearing screams, at seven o'clock while standing at the door of his house at the east pier of Howth, which seemed to decline in loudness and seemed to come from Ireland's Eye. He moved to the pier itself and thought he heard more screams. Later that night he was called out of bed to bring the body of the deceased to Mrs. Campbell's house in a dray. He had not attended the inquest and never had a conversation with Catherine Flood about the case or anyone else. He told a sergeant of the police who was making inquiries about what had happened on the evening he brought the dray to move the body and later told him about the screams.

Twelfth Witness: Anne Lacey
Examined by Mr. Smyly

Witness: I live at Howth; I am forty years a nurse tender; I saw the body of the late Mrs. Kirwan at Mrs. Campbell's house on the night of 6th of September last about twelve o'clock; I was in the house before the body was brought, and saw it taken off the cart; it was wrapped in the sail of a boat; I saw blood on the sail where the seat was; when the sail was taken off the body, the men were sent out of the room; there was a bathing sheet around the body at the neck and knees; there was also a bathing dress on the body; there was a shawl around the head; only those three, the bathing dress, the shawl and the sheet were under the sail; I was employed with another woman to wash the body; I took off the sheet and bathing dress; I found her hair full of bits of seaweed and gravel.

The face was covered with blood; the blood still came from a cut above the eyes and on the cheek and forehead; the ears were also loaded with blood, which was running from the inside of them; I sponged and washed the ears but the blood continued flowing afterwards for nearly half an hour; I had to put a flannel petticoat to prevent it flowing down; the shawl was dark and wet; there was no mark on the neck; there was a cut on her right breast which bled freely after I saw it; I could not say the cut was very deep, but it bled freely; it was a clean cut; the right side was blackened from under

85

the arm to the knee; I washed only the right side; I did not wash her left side, Catherine McGarr washed it; the lips were swelled; I thought at first she had no teeth, nothing but swelled lips; the under lip was most so; there was a discharge from the private parts; it was not the natural discharge; the blood was clotted and much of it; the body was quite limber; I felt the belly, it was quite flat to the backbone; there was no water in it; one eye was open and the white of it was as red as blood; and the right eye closed; none of her bones were broken; her neck was slightly twisted; the body was healthy and beautifully clean; she was a beautiful creature; I saw Mr. Kirwan that evening, his boots and stockings and trousers were wet; when he was changing his boots and stockings, he turned up his trousers and I saw his drawers wet underneath; I stayed all night.

Cross-examined by Mr. Curran

Witness: I have for forty years been a nurse tender; I am certain from the appearance that the discharge I allude to was not natural; the natural discharge [*i.e. menstruation*] is clear and light; the other was dark and black; the scratches were not like crab scratches; Catherine McGarr washed the left side; I told her that the side was black.

Thirteenth Witness: Catherine McGarr
Examined by Mr. Hayes

Witness: I remember the 6th of September; I was at Mrs. Campbell's that evening and was engaged about the body of Mrs. Kirwan; I washed the left side of the body; I saw wounds about the eyes as if torn; her nose was crooked, and the lips were swollen and covered with slime; it was wiped off; it was a thick white slime [*i.e. froth*]; I could not see her teeth, her lips were so much swelled; blood was coming from her ears; the blood came from the inside of the left ear; when I washed her left breast, blood flowed from the nipple when I put the water to it; I saw a discharge of blood from her private parts, not like the ordinary discharge; the whole of the left eye was reddish; I did not examine the right eye; she was put in a coffin by candlelight; I saw Mr. Kirwan there and I remarked that the police would not allow a body to be touched until an inquest was held and Mr. Kirwan said, "I do not give a damn for the police or anybody else, the body must be washed"; when we commenced to wash the body, Mr. Kirwan left the room; I saw him sitting at the kitchen fire with his trousers turned up, drying his drawers; his stockings were changed; I do not know whether his trousers were wet or not; his top coat was not cloth but a polished thing; it was damp; I did not examine the right side of the body.

Cross-examined by Mr. Butt

Witness: I washed the left side; there was no cut on the left breast, but the blood flowed from the nipple; I saw a bruise and scratch on the right side.

Fourteenth Witness: Mary Robinson
Examined by Mr. Smyly

The fourteenth witness Mary Robinson, examined by Mr. Smyly, told the court that she held a candle for a woman who washed the body and she noted that one eye was open and bloodshot and the ears were bleeding. She saw Mr. Kirwan there at a chair in front of the fire in the kitchen and noticed some moisture on the floor, underneath the chair on which he was sitting.

—◇—

It now being five o'clock, the further hearing of the case was adjourned until the next morning. Judge Crampton said that the jury could not be permitted to separate; it was necessary that they should be accommodated for a night in a hotel. Every possible comfort should be afforded them. But he must forbid them the use of intoxicating liquor.

Special constables were sworn and the jury were conveyed to the Northumberland Hotel.

Throughout the first day's proceedings, from the opening address of the counsel for the prosecution and during the progress of the evidence, the prisoner remained cool and to some evidence he paid close attention and watched to see what effect, if any, it had on the jury. There was little he could tell as, for the most part, the twelve men were fully occupied following the evidence and remained impassive.

It was not, however, a good opening day for William Burke Kirwan and his very able defence team who were curiously lacking in energy when it came to cross-examination of what transpired to be very able and concentrated witnesses. No doubt the defence would up the ante as the trial progressed.

CHAPTER 5

THE TRIAL: SECOND DAY

Thursday, December 9th, 1852

The judges took their seats on the bench at ten o'clock. The jury having come into court and answered their names, the prisoner was again placed at the bar and the proceedings commenced.

Fifteenth Witness: Joseph Sherwood
Examined by Mr. Hayes

> Witness: I am a sergeant of the constabulary and am stationed at Howth; I remember the transaction of the death of Mrs. Kirwan on the 6th of September last; I was present at the inquest; I saw the face of the body before the inquest; I saw it on the night of the lady's death at the house of Mrs. Campbell where she had been lodging; the face was scratched, there was a cut on the right temple, above the eye, some swelling around the mouth and the eyes were slightly bloodshot; I saw the prisoner on the evening of 6th of September, first at the quay when the boat arrived and subsequently at Mrs. Campbell's house; he was sitting at the fire, and I

remarked that his clothes were wet from the knees down. This was about half an hour after the body was brought in; I saw the steam rise from his trousers and drops of water on the hearthstone which fell from them.

I went to the prisoner's house on the 7th of October, the morning after his arrest; I saw a woman on the second-stair lobby; she was a Mrs. or Miss Kenny, I do not know which; I saw two children in the house; one of them was a boy about ten years of age; I could not say whether it [*i.e. the other*] was a boy or a girl; I was in all the rooms of Mr. Kirwan's house; the children were in a room, the small one in bed, the boy standing beside it; I saw the woman Kenny afterwards at the Castle and at Howth before the magistrates; Mr. Kirwan was present.

Mr. Butt: Was Mr. Kirwan under arrest on these occasions?

Witness: He was.

Mr. Butt: Then I object to this evidence being received.

Mr. Justice Crampton: Were there any informations taken at the time?

Witness: There were.

Mr. Justice Crampton then said that, as informations were taken, oral evidence to their contents could be given.

Mr. Hayes: You say you were in all the rooms of the prisoner's house. Did you see a bed in it?

Witness: I saw but one bed in the house; namely, that in which the child was; this was about eleven o'clock; I saw some appearance of a breakfast; tea and bread and butter were on the table, and the teapot was beside the fire; I was on Ireland's Eye after the transaction; I was there when a bathing cap was found; it was found on the Saturday after the 6th of September, by a lady named Hamilton and I was just beside her when she picked it up; it was got at the high watermark at the Long Hole; it is now in the same state as it was when found on the island. [Produced bathing cap which was shown to Mrs. Campbell] The string appeared tied in a hard knot; the string of it is still tied; I have been thirteen months stationed at Howth; shouts from Ireland's Eye can be heard at Howth; I have heard them on the mainland.

Cross-examined by Mr. Butt

Witness: I saw Mrs. Kirwan's clothes in Mrs. Campbell's house the night the body was brought in.

In response to Mr. Hayes: I saw the bundle opened; I saw a flannel and a white petticoat, a gown, a shawl and stays. I am sure there were two petticoats; I did not see any chemise; I did not see any marks of blood or dirt on these clothes.

Sixteenth Witness: Anne Molloy
Examined by Mr. Smyly

The sixteenth witness called was Anne Molloy who lived as a servant with Mr. and Mrs. Kirwan both at 6 Lower and 11 Upper Merrion Street for a period of a year and was discharged by Mrs. Kirwan on the 15th of September, 1850. She said that the couple had always occupied the same bedroom during her employment. Mr. Justice Crampton interrupted the examination and told Mr. Smyly that he did not see what these things had to do with the question at issue. The prosecuting counsel explained that it was evidence of the prisoner's course of life but the judge replied that it was going too far back.

Mr. Smyly withdrew and the witness was allowed to leave the box.

Failure of Teresa Kenny to Appear

Teresa Kenny, the mother of Kirwan's children, was called but did not appear.

There was no explanation given or sought for the absence of the one and only witness who could give evidence in relation to the motive. Was she aware of Maria Kirwan's existence and vice versa? And if so, how recent had been the discovery? Could she shed light on Kirwan's mood and behaviour during the months from mid-June until September? There were a myriad of questions to be put to the "other" woman in the life of the artist. Counsel never got the chance and surprisingly did not pursue the matter by forcing Miss Kenny to appear.

On the other hand, it was more than likely a relief for Kirwan that she did not turn up and his defence team may have held the view that after all she had been called as a witness for the prosecution and thus could under examination have caused some damage to the defence.

In those circumstances Mr. Butt would have to accept the prosecution's theory on the motive for the alleged murder, without the prosecution providing any substantive evidence to back it up. Clearly, it did not upset Mr. Smyly in any way, but the spectators to the unfolding drama, the public and the media, must have been bitterly disappointed.

Seventeenth Witness: William Bridgeford
Examined by Mr. Pennefather

William Bridgeford told the court that he knew the prisoner; he and his father owned houses in Sandymount; Mr. Kirwan lived in one of four houses they owned in Spafield; he resided there for about four years; he became a tenant in 1848 and remained until the 5th of July 1852; he called at the house a few times and saw a woman there, who he supposed was Kirwan's wife; he had seen her since the 6th of September; he saw children in the house; he received notes from the woman and thought she signed her name as Teresa.

Eighteenth Witness: Catherine Byrne
Examined by Mr. Smyly

In the month of July last I lived at Sandymount Avenue as a servant; I lived as such with the prisoner at the bar; a lady was living with him who was called Mrs. Kirwan; she had seven children; Mr. Kirwan used to be in the house a good deal in the daytime; he slept there in the same bed with Mrs. Kirwan frequently at night; her name is Maria Teresa Frances Kenny; I did not see her since July.

Mr. Smyly: Do you recollect a strange lady ever calling there?

Witness: I do. She came to make some inquiries.

The witness was not asked the nature of those inquiries, nor was she cross-examined. It was obvious to any seasoned trial spectator or experienced court reporter that the identity of the woman caller could have been none other than the real Mrs. Kirwan. Perhaps with the non-appearance of Teresa Kenny both sides decided not to pursue the incident in the absence of the one person who could further corroborate the fact. Although it was of vital importance to the question of whether the women were aware of each other's existence, what occurred that day would remain a mystery. As would the precise date on which the strange lady called. It had to be after the 5th of July when the landlord Bridgeford said that Kirwan left the house in Spafield Terrace that he and Teresa Kenny had rented before moving to Sandymount Avenue. The landlady in Howth testified that she heard the row in which Kirwan threatened his wife's life and beat her about three weeks after the Kirwans came to lodge with her in the middle of June. The timing is such that it seems likely the row must have been caused by Maria Kirwan's visit to Sandymount Avenue, which would have entailed a day trip from Howth.

For the prosecution it should have been obligatory to tie the two occurrences to prove the motive. Mr Smyly asked Catherine Byrne but one question and there was no cross-examination. Given the importance of the evidence, one must speculate that some bargain had been struck between the prosecution and defence on the matter.

Nineteenth Witness: Anna Hanna
Examined by Mr. Pennefather

> Witness: I live at Howth; I knew the late Mrs. Kirwan and the prisoner; I washed for Mrs. Kirwan when she first came to Howth; I have been in Mrs. Campbell's house where she lived; I recollect being there on one occasion in the afternoon between five and six o'clock; Mr. and Mrs. Kirwan were in a room off the kitchen; I heard the voice of a man in the room; I supposed it to be that of the prisoner; there was a great deal of noise; I heard the voice of a man speak loudly about being robbed, and also something about a mother; I heard the words. "I'll end you"; I then heard the rattling of furniture about the room, as if they were knocked about; this was a day in July, 1852.

Cross-examined by Mr. Butt

> Witness: I never had a quarrel with the prisoner.

> Mr. Butt: Are you sure? Recollect yourself.

> Witness: He never threatened to prosecute me; I recollect his passing by the door one day, and we had a dog that barked after him; Mr. Kirwan threatened to summons me if the dog was not parted with; we sent the dog away; he never had occasion to threaten me.

Twentieth Witness: Alexander Hamilton
Examined by Mr. Pennefather

Witness: I am a medical student; I am studying for the profession and I have been attending lectures during the last six years; I have dissected during that time; I am familiar with the appearances presented by dead bodies; I was at Howth on the 6th of September last; I saw the body of the late Mrs. Kirwan on the following day, the 7th, between one and two o'clock at Mrs. Campbell's house; it was lying in a room next to that in which the inquest was going on; the body was ready to put into a coffin; it had a sheet around it; there was a cap on, and a sort of coarse shirt and a piece of calico around the lower part of the body.

I saw the face at first, and I removed the cap and made a superficial examination of the head in order to see if there was any fracture or depression of the skull; I did not detect anything of the sort; there was a kind of mark or scratch at the right temple, such as would be caused by the rubbing of a body against a rock; it was only an abrasion of the skin; there were scratches or abrasions of the skin around the eyes; the eyes were shut; the eyelids presented a livid appearance, as if in a state of decomposition; I did not open the eyes.

I remarked that the lower edge of one of the ears was cut, as if something were biting at it; the earring was held on by a slight strip of integument; I stripped the body down for the purpose of examining it; froth was all around the mouth, thin, light and stationary there; it covered the mouth from angle to angle; the face was rather pale; when I removed the clothes, I examined the abdomen, which was rather full and firm; I could not ascertain if there was any water in the body, but I thought at the time there might have been; there were no marks on the body that attracted my particular attention; I did not examine the body very closely; I did not examine the private parts; I did not see any blood where she was lying; I did not raise up the body in order to examine it; the neck and shoulders were stiff.

Cross-examined by Mr. Brereton

Witness: There might have been a cut on the breast, without me seeing it, but not a deep one; the skin around the eyes was rather more abraded; I do not think there could have been a deep cut on the breast without my observing it; on looking over the body, I did not see any mark that might be produced by violence; I never examined the body of a drowned person until Mrs. Kirwan's, but I would recognise the marks usually exhibited by such bodies; I would expect to find the abdomen swollen and paleness on the surface of the body. I saw no trace of blood mixed with the froth I saw about the mouth; I did not examine the froth to discover if there was any blood; there was a stain of blood about the size of a shilling piece on the cap above one of the ears; I did not examine the ears; the attaint on the cap appeared to have come from the ear; there is a cavity outside the tympanum from which blood would come; the appearance presented by the abdomen was such as I would expect in a case of drowning; I did not see any marks on the body that would lead me, as a medical man, to say that death was not caused by drowning.

In response to a juror: I was engaged by the coroner to make the examination.

Mr. Brereton: Do you think, as a medical man, that you discharged your duty by the superficial examination which you made in this instance?

Witness: I do not; but I knew nothing at the time to excite my suspicion.

Unless it was to expose the shortcomings of the inquest, there was no purpose in calling this witness, who was of no advantage to the prosecution and, as a medical student, merely confirmed and admitted his incompetence. As the medical evidence would be of vital importance in establishing the cause of death, it was essential that the prosecution, quite apart from the police surgeon who was next in the stand, make available to the jury the best possible expertise in the medico-legal field.

Unaccountably, the opinion of one highly qualified expert who had been part of the investigation and was entirely familiar with all the circumstances of the event, including the scene of the alleged crime, was not called to give evidence. However, his moment would eventually come.

Twenty-first Witness: Dr. George Hatchell
Examined by Mr. Smyly

Witness: I am a physician and surgeon; on the 6th of October last I was called to make a post-mortem examination of the body of Maria Kirwan; that was thirty-one days after death; I went to the cemetery at Glasnevin for that purpose; I saw the grave opened and the coffin raised; there was about two feet and a half of water in the grave; the water was attributable to the damp soil; the body was enclosed in a shell, placed within a larger coffin; the post-mortem examination was made in the yard, at a short distance from the grave.

Mr. Tighe, a surgeon, was with me; there were police present and some of the men belonging to the cemetery; the prisoner was not present; the grave clothes were taken off; they were wet and the body was wet; it had all the appearance of a body that had lain in the water for a considerable time; to a certain extent the body was macerated; the water had the effect of hastening the decomposition of the surface of the body; I made an exceedingly careful examination of the body; I examined the scalp carefully, but could not see any mark of violence there; over the right eye there was an abrasion, or marks of scratches and also on the prominent part of the right cheek, under the right eye; the right eye was rather protruded and the left one particularly so: that I presume was rather the result of decomposition. I partially opened the eyes and found that the white part of them was exceedingly vascular, or injected with blood; I examined the ears; there was an earring in the left ear, but the lobe of the right ear was wanting; there was nothing remarkable inside the ears; there were no injuries outside, inside or behind the ear, that I could observe, decomposition having set in too far; the upper lip was swollen and the tongue protruded between the teeth; the inside of the lips was very vascular; the tongue was marked by the teeth both above and below; there was a sort of a soapy matter about the face and mouth, such as usually presents itself on bodies in an advanced state of decomposition.

On opening the head, I found the membrane containing the brain in a very flaccid state; on making an opening in it, the brain, being in a semi-fluid state, flowed out freely; the brain was of a light pinkish colour, all over; the fluidity of the brain was owing to decomposition; the brain was a little more red than I expected; having been informed that blood flowed from the ears, and knowing that such symptom was often a result of a fracture to the base of the skull, I examined that part with great care, but I could not detect any fracture; I examined the trachea and the larynx and there was nothing remarkable about them; I examined the vertebrae of the neck but found nothing like dislocation there.

I examined the right breast, and found a superficial cut or scratch under the right nipple; I saw nothing to account for blood flowing from the nipple; there was an extensive lividity on the right side, but that is not remarkable in a dead body; the lividness depends on gravitation according to the position the body may be placed [*i.e. during the first 6 hours after death*]; the cuticle [*i.e. outermost thin skin*] of the hands and nails were coming off like a glove, but that was from decomposition.

About the lower part of the body, I observed some degree of swelling; the labia and anus were swollen, and the interior of the vagina was very vascular and injected with blood, much more than usual. These appearances I would say were produced by congestion of the veins arising from pressure, or by anything which would have impeded the general circulation of the blood through the body.

The body was that of an exceedingly well-formed woman; on making an opening of the chest, I found the lungs congested at the posterior, interior and at the lower portion of the anterior parts; the interior parts of the body were fresh and healthy, and completely untouched by decomposition; the congestion of the lungs was caused by the engorgement of the blood; their appearance was such as would result from a sudden stoppage of respiration; I examined the heart, and found it perfectly healthy: it was empty [*i.e. of blood*] on both the right and left sides; the large vessels from it were also empty.

I paid visits to Ireland's Eye on several occasions; I went to a place called the Long Hole; Nangle, the boatman, pointed to me the place where the body was found; the Long Hole is a deep creek running up to the island; the creek is divided by very large stones placed transversely; the stones are about midway between high and low watermark.

Mr. Smyly: From your knowledge of the place, the observations you have made at it, and from your observations of the body, are you able to form an opinion as to how this lady came to her death?

Mr. Butt: I object to this question as being illegal. The inference drawn by the witness from what he has seen at Ireland's Eye, and from what he has been told, ought not to be received in evidence. I do not object to the witness giving his opinion, founded upon his professional skill and knowledge.

Judge Crampton: I think there are two cases on record where such an opinion was held to be legal evidence. The question is, whether the admixture of the witness's personal examination of the body of the deceased, with his examination of the locality of the alleged crime, can disqualify him from giving an opinion founded on both matters conjoined. I am disposed to think the evidence admissible, but I would be glad to look into any authorities on the point.

Mr. Butt: There is a case cited in Roscoe, in which several of the judges doubted whether a medical witness could give his opinion on the very point the jury had to decide.

Baron Greene: I think the opinion of the witness on the matter of science is so mixed up with the matter of fact, that it cannot be legally put.

The court then ruled that the question should be put in some other form.

Mr. Smyly: From the appearances you observed, on the body, are you able as a medical man to form an opinion as to the cause of death, and what is that opinion?

Witness: I am of the opinion that death was caused by asphyxiation, or sudden stopping of respiration; from the congestion in the vagina, the engorgement of the lungs and other circumstances, I would say that in all probability the stoppage of respiration must have been combined with pressure of some kind, or constriction, which caused the sudden stoppage; I do not think simple drowning would produce, to the same extent, the appearances I saw.

In response to Judge Crampton: The congestion was caused by a combination of circumstances with drowning.

Mr. Smyly: Would simple drowning cause the appearances presented in this case?

Witness: Not to the same extent; there was a combination of circumstances with the drowning to cause the amount of congestion exhibited; I have seen the bodies of persons who have drowned and I don't think they presented appearances to the same extent as in this case; it does not follow that a person drowned must of necessity be full of water; it occurs often that there is no water in the body at all; bodies float sometimes immediately after drowning; I heard of a case of a gentleman, who was drowned in Kingstown Harbour, and whose body was stated to have floated immediately after drowning; he was stated to have tied his legs and arms.

Cross-examined by Mr. Butt

Mr. Butt: I understand you to have said, as a medical man, that the body of Mrs. Kirwan presented appearances that death by drowning would not cause.

Witness: Not to the same extent.

Mr. Butt: I ask you, as a matter of medical skill, were the appearances on the body such as could not be produced by drowning alone?

Witness: I don't think that I would have found the same amount of congestion in the vagina in a case of simple drowning.

Mr. Butt: Then your answer is, there were appearances not to be accounted for?

Witness: There were.

Mr. Butt: What were those appearances?

Witness: Extreme congestion of the vagina, and of the lungs, swelling of the upper lip, and extreme congestion of the inside of the mouth.

Mr. Butt: On your oath, when did you first form the opinion that death by drowning alone would not account for those appearances?

Witness: I formed it at the time I was making the post-mortem examination.

Mr. Butt: Do you swear that congestion of the vessels of the lungs could not have been produced by drowning?

Witness: I don't say that they were thoroughly incompatible with death by drowning.

Mr. Butt: Will you swear that the appearances presented by the lungs to the full extent could not have been produced by drowning alone?

Witness: I don't think they would to the same extent; I made the information in a day or two after the post-mortem examination.

Mr. Butt then read Dr. Hatchell's information given and sworn before Major Brownrigg on the 15th of October, 1852. The last line was less than unequivocal and would provide defence counsel with an opening: "The lungs and heart exhibited those appearances which are compatible with death produced by drowning or strangulation."

Butt went on the offensive. He was not known for the subtlety of his examination technique but he had to be careful that his aggression would not alienate the jury. It would be equally important for Dr. Hatchell not to equivocate about his findings while under the cosh of the examiner.

Mr. Butt: Will you say, on your solemn oath, that the appearances of the lungs were not consistent with drowning?

Witness: I have seen a great many –

Mr. Butt: I am not asking you, sir, what you saw. Answer yes or no to my question and remember the solemn oath which you have taken.

Witness: What is your question?

Mr. Butt: I ask you by virtue of your oath, were not the appearances presented by the lungs compatible with death by drowning alone?

Witness: I think the engorgement was more than I ever saw in cases of drowning before; this opinion is founded on what I have seen.

Mr. Butt [read the information]: Is it true that the lungs exhibited those appearances compatible with death produced by drowning?

Witness: You have not finished the sentence.

Mr. Butt [reading]: "The lungs and heart exhibited those appearances compatible with death produced by drowning or strangulation." Is that not true?

Witness: It is true.

Mr. Butt: Is it true that they are compatible with death by drowning?

Witness: To a certain extent they are.

Mr. Butt: Was the engorgement compatible with death by drowning alone?

Witness: I don't think it was.

Mr. Butt: You say it was not compatible?

Witness: It depends altogether on how the drowning occurred; if the drowning occurred very suddenly, the engorgement would not be so great as where the drowned person struggled to save himself or herself.

Mr. Butt: Was that what you meant to convey on your direct examination?

Witness: I did not mean to say whether she might have struggled by herself or with another; the appearance presented by the body would be occasioned by a person drowning, struggling with himself or herself; the appearance presented by the lungs must have been caused by struggling; I think it is very likely that the appearance of the vagina would have been occasioned by struggling in the water for life; a struggle and a compression amount to the same thing.

I went down to Ireland's Eye on several occasions, in company with Major Brownrigg and he is the Deputy Inspector General of the constabulary; he took a strong interest as a magistrate in the prosecution; I was asked by Major Brownrigg to go to Ireland's Eye; I thought it right for the sake of the prisoner, and for every other reason to make myself acquainted with all the facts.

Mr. Butt: Did you alter your opinion as to the cause of death after you visited Ireland's Eye?

Witness: I did not.

Mr. Butt: You had heard of violence used before you made the post-mortem examination?

Witness: I had; I heard of bleeding from the ears and other parts, and my examination was specially directed to what I had heard; there was no injury to the ears internally; I did not examine the tympanum, but I did not see any marks of violence about the ears, as far as I examined. Having been told that instruments had been run up the body, I examined to see if there were any traces of such things having been done, but I did not find any whatever; there was no appearance of violence in the vessels of the vagina, such as having a sharp instrument thrust up.

Mr. Butt: Suppose a person went into the water with a full stomach, would that be likely to cause congestion?

Witness: It would, but not to any great extent; going into cold water is likely to cause a fit, but it is not likely to cause bleeding from the ears; I think a fatal result might follow from a person going into cold water with a full stomach.

Mr. Butt: The congestion that would bring on a fatal fit would be congestion to a certain extent?

Witness: Of course.

Mr. Butt: Would congestion that might bring on a fit be more extensive than that which you saw on the body of Mrs. Kirwan?

Witness: No, I don't think it would.

Mr. Butt: Do I understand you to say those appearances presented were consistent with the fact of a person with a full stomach going into cold water?

Witness: I think it possible.

Mr. Butt: Is it not probable that such was the cause of death?

Witness: I am not prepared to say whether it was or not.

Mr. Butt: From your knowledge and judgements as a medical man, is such not probable?

Witness: Taking it per se, it is.

Mr. Butt: Have you ever heard of a fit of epilepsy being produced by a person going into cold water with a full stomach?

Witness: It is possible. If a person bathing got a fit, he or she might work against the rock or seized by a fit might fall on the face and be cut by a rock; if they rolled down, the sides might be bruised; I don't think the blackness I saw was occasioned by violence; it might have been occasioned by the gravitation of the blood to the particular part; it was not the blackness of bruise.

In response to Mr. Smyly: I have heard of persons falling in a fit of epilepsy, giving a very loud scream; I never heard of more than one scream.

Mr. Butt: Do you mean to say that a person in epilepsy will not give more than a single scream?

Witness: I will not say that they will not give more than one scream; but I never heard of more than one.

Mr. Butt: Will you undertake to say that a strong person falling in a fit of epilepsy, might not give more than one scream?

Witness: I think if such a person fell into the water, they would find it difficult to give more than one scream.

Mr. Butt: Did you ever read in the newspapers of the defendant in a case in Roscommon, in which I was engaged in the courthouse of Roscommon being seized with a fit of epilepsy and screaming so loudly and frequently that the court had to be adjourned?

Witness: I did not, but frequent screams are not impossible.

Twenty-second Witness: Mr. Henry Davis
Examined by Mr. Hayes

Witness: I recollect holding an inquest at Howth on the 7th of September last; the investigation was on the body of the late Mrs. Maria Kirwan; I first received notice of the death, along with the requisition for holding an inquest, at my home in Donnycarney upon the morning of the same day, from the police station at that place; the inquest was held at the house next to the police barrack; I saw Mr. Kirwan on that day; he was present during the investigation. I had never seen him on any previous occasion; he was examined on that enquiry and his evidence taken down. [A deposition was handed by the witness to the Clerk of the Court] That is the deposition of Mr. Kirwan and that his signature appended thereto.

Cross-examined by Mr. Brereton

Witness: I have held the office of coroner for upwards of ten years; during that time I have frequently seen the bodies of persons who have been drowned and am well acquainted with the appearances presented by them; I viewed the body of the deceased, Maria Kirwan, on that day and the [inquest] jury were with me at the time I did so; I then understood the body of the deceased lady to be in the same state in which it had been found and I held the inquest upon it under that belief; I afterwards, however, ascertained that it had been washed, prepared and laid out in readiness for my arrival.

There are frequently marks of small bites found on the bodies of persons who have been drowned; those minute bites are made by a fish called queen crabs; I am well acquainted with the appearances produced by them: there were marks of those bites upon the eyes as well as upon the breasts of the deceased, Mrs. Kirwan; bodies require to be in the water only a very short time before they are attacked by those crabs; very few hours are requisite for that purpose, and I have seen the case of one person whose body was not an hour in the water when it was attacked by them; the eyes are generally the first portion of the body attacked. The marks presented by the effects of crab bites are like small eating sores.

Mr. Hayes: They are totally unlike a cut or a scratch, I believe.

Witness: Totally unlike them.

I held the inquest, regularly, like the others; I read the deposition over carefully to each witness, immediately after he had concluded giving his testimony, and I requested him, if there were anything erroneous therein, to stop me and have it corrected; I then asked all the witnesses, separately, if they had anything further to say, and if they had I took it down; the jury wished Mr. Kirwan to be examined; and he was accordingly examined at their request; he was not a prisoner before me.

Re-examined by Mr. Hayes

Witness: I will undertake to swear that I read the depositions over to each witness according as he made it, and asked whether they had anything now to say; they each signed their depositions before the next witness was called; I remember calling upon the two Nangles as to whether they had anything further to say; I remember calling upon Michael Nangle to know whether he had any further evidence to give; to the best of my belief, he signed his deposition before the next witness was examined; I will not undertake to swear that he did so, but I believe such to be the fact; I am positive that he signed it with his name or his mark.

Mr. Butt: I think I ought to interpose, if only for the purpose of reminding my learned friend, that he is examining his own witness.

Mr. Hayes: I am endeavouring to elicit evidence from him, to suit me.

Mr. Butt: I think it unfair that the Crown should endeavour to throw discredit upon the testimony of its own witness.

Judge Crampton: I think Mr. Hayes ought to treat him more gently than Mr. Butt and Mr. Brereton have done.

Re-examination continued

Witness: Mr. Kirwan took an active part in the investigation; I remember his interrupting one of the witnesses who was giving his testimony; I do not remember what he said to him; I believe the witness in question was one of the Nangles; one of the Nangles also interfered with the other.

Mr. Brereton: Did you ask Mr. Kirwan if he wanted to put any questions to witnesses who were examined at that investigation?

Witness: I did; my reason for doing so was because there was more or less suspicion attached to him at the time.

The Clerk of the Crown then read out the deposition of Kirwan, sworn before the inquest on the 7th of September at Howth.

The Case for the Crown then closed.

◄○►

Mr. Butt's Address to the Jury on Behalf of the Prisoner

Gentlemen of the jury, I am sure you will agree with me that it would be impossible to exaggerate the solemnity of the duty you have to discharge. I need not tell you, that on your verdict in this case, the life of the prisoner at the bar depends; and more than life, even, for your verdict may not only consign him to an ignominious death, but will also subject him to the most fearful imputation that could rest upon any man, or that ever rested on any man in the annals of crime. And if your duty be a solemn one, I need not say that mine is too. It is no part of my duty, even to protect the man who has entrusted to my advocacy the defence of his character, his honour and his life, to attempt to lead you astray, or pervert a single fact of the case.

I would rather look at myself altogether in the light of a person having to assist you in the discharge of your arduous duty, as one bound unquestionably to suggest everything in the case favourable to the prisoner, but certainly not bound, even in protecting him, to misstate a single fact, or to wilfully mislead your judgement. Certain rumours have been spoken of; Dr. Hatchell has told you that there were such; but I implore of you to dismiss from your minds every one of the rumours which, I regret to say, have been industriously circulated to the prejudice of the unfortunate prisoner, and to poison the public mind against him. I would ask you to dismiss all those slanders from your minds, or only to recollect them in order to feel how cruel has been the injustice to him.

Gentlemen of the jury, I will now proceed to examine the evidence on which you are asked to come to the conclusion that the wife of the prisoner met her death by violence at his hands. Three pieces of evidence have been offered to your notice, for the purpose of leading you to that conclusion. The first was founded on the appearance

110

of the body; second, suspicion against the prisoner, and the cries from the island; and third, what is impossible to put out of consideration, that which is founded on the grievous stain that rests on the matrimonial character of the prisoner. I will deal with the three.

In the first place, with regard to the cries and the suspicion raised on this point against the prisoner, I would observe from the whole case for the prosecution it is impossible, from its nature, for it to be encountered by any evidence except his own, which cannot now be given, but which was given at the coroner's inquiry. It cannot be denied that this is a case for investigation; but I hope that you, after this investigation, will declare, by your verdict, that the prisoner leaves this court acquitted of the crime with which he now stands charged. It is impossible for him to bring forward any evidence on that point.

He and his wife were alone on the island when she met her death, no human eye witnessed her dying struggles, and it is impossible for him to offer evidence to contradict the case of suspicion made against him on this part of the case. But suspicion is not sufficient to warrant a verdict of guilty. You should look at all the facts, and ask yourselves, if they established his guilt, or left a reasonable doubt upon your minds, though it might be better for him to be carried back to a felon's cell than to be acquitted on that ground. Allow me to remind you that the law and Christianity presume every man innocent till he is proved to be guilty. If that be the rule in a case where some person had done the fatal deed, it applies infinitely more strongly to a case where the question is raised: was there a crime committed at all?

The evidence, as to the cries, if they came from the deceased lady at all, is consistent with the belief that she met her death in a fit, and that the cries heard were hers; it is still but a conjecture. You recollect the evidence of

111

Larkin upon this part of the case. He was unable to say whether they were the cries of a man or a woman, and he stated he supposed about eight minutes elapsed from the time he heard the first cry until he heard the second, and that the daylight was vanishing from the sky when he came into harbour.

Is it not possible that the cries he heard may have been the cries of the prisoner and the Nangles on the island when they were looking and calling for the deceased? For it appears to me that the time mentioned by Larkin became identical with the time of their so crying out; besides, Michael Nangle deposes, that when he went to the Long Hole, he distinctly heard his companions calling him from where the boat was. But, assuming them to be the cries of the deceased, in the interval between the time of Larkin hearing the cries and the landing of the boatmen on the island, it would be impossible for the prisoner to arrange the body on the rock where it was found, and return to await the landing of the boat.

It would therefore be much better for the prisoner if you could come to the conclusion that the cries which Larkin heard were the dying shrieks of Mrs. Kirwan; for the time must have been very short from the hearing of cries until the Nangles landed: and if they were her dying screams, it is clear, beyond all doubt, that she had not come to her death by the hands of her husband. Larkin's is the only evidence on this point on which you can safely rely. You will not, I think, be much disposed to attach credit to the testimony of the lady whom I cross-examined yesterday. She was a mile further from the island, and appeared to have prepared everything to hear the screams. She crossed over to the pier, and placed her hands behind her ears to enable her to hear more distinctly. Can you give faith to testimony such as that? No evidence has been offered to you of any other person on shore having heard them. Neither the police, the railway, not coastguard, who would have been the most likely persons to have heard them, were produced; and upon such vague testimony you are asked to consign a fellow-creature to an ignominious death; but I feel sure you will give it no more weight than it merits.

Larkin's evidence as to hearing a cry might be fairly given, but the guilt of the prisoner cannot be deduced from it. The deceased was a strong woman, and would not be accidentally drowned without uttering a cry. The evidence of Larkin is accounted for that by Nangle; if you attach any weight to it, you will recollect that Mr. Kirwan had been looking for his wife for half an hour before the boatmen arrived, and the cries might be his while doing so. It is impossible to take them on reliable evidence as dying cries; but even if they were dying cries, there was nothing to fix the prisoner with guilt. You should have some distinct notion in your own minds of the manner in which he did it. How? Dr. Hatchell talked of compression, which was a convenient phrase; but I ask you, as rational men, to fix in your minds any one way, in which, consistently with the evidence, he could have murdered her.

Did he strangle her? Did he go into the water and drown her? It would not do to say they were alone on the island, and that he must have killed her in some way, for you must have distinct grounds for arriving at such a conclusion. Dr. Hatchell's ingenuity would not be sufficient, for I defy even a doctor's ingenuity to show, consistent with the evidence, in what mode the deceased met her death at the hands of the prisoner. If her death was the result of violence, and that Larkin heard her death cries, how was it that eight minutes elapsed between the first and the second? What would a strong woman be doing in the meantime? Is it consistent with any conceivable way in which he could kill her, that she cried once and then in eight minutes again?

113

One natural supposition, and which is consistent with the innocence of the prisoner, is that she had been attacked with epilepsy, produced by her going into the water after her dinner, which Dr. Hatchell admitted was compatible with the appearance of the body, and with the suggestion that she shrieked first, revived afterwards, and shrieked again. On no other supposition could it be accounted for.

Gentlemen of the jury, there is another part of the case that I approach with pain. It is undeniable and the prisoner has his punishment in having his humiliation proclaimed in a public court. It is undeniable that he had formed an unfortunate connexion; but surely, that is a long way from coming to the conclusion that he, therefore, murdered his wife. Evidence was given on this point to supply motive for the crime. Did it supply a motive? The connexion alluded to was not a new one; his wife knew of it, and forgave it, and she and her husband were reconciled. Did the evidence then, on this point, supply a motive for the commission of the crime?

Let not your indignation and reprobation of his moral conduct prejudice you against the prisoner at this solemn hour. Let him who is without sin cast the first stone. Remember the frailties of human nature, and that men have at all times yielded to seduction from the path of virtue, who were incapable of the cowardly crime imputed to the prisoner. I am not palliating or excusing the offence of the prisoner, arising from the unfortunate connexion alluded to, as I believe he has humbled himself here for the offence, which no man could justify, and I hope that, in the solitude of his prison, he has humbled himself before that Judge, in whose presence we shall all one day appear, and who will judge more mercifully of man's frailty than the ill-nature of the world. I ask you solemnly, and with reverence, in the language of inspiration, "Judge not, that ye not be judged"; and when you come to scan the offence of a brother man, remember that you could know but half the case. You know nothing of the temptation which preceded the fall, not the agony of remorse that followed it.

While you might condemn him for that offence, against his wife, let it not lead you to the conclusion that he was capable of imbruing his hands in her blood. Such a supposition would be monstrous. I do not shrink from this part of the case, but I leave the frailties of man to your charity, and demand, if you believe him innocent of the crime with which he has been charged, an acquittal from your justice.

Gentlemen of the jury, I now come to the evidence relative to the examination of the body, and the appearances presented by it; and I may here observe, so powerful was the effect of this melancholy death upon the prisoner that he was confined to bed for a considerable time.

Let me impress upon you, in the first instance, the important fact deposed by Dr. Hatchell, namely, that the blackness which some of the witnesses said they observed upon different parts of the body of the deceased woman, was not such a blackness as would be occasioned by a bruise, but that which might have resulted from the gravitation of the blood to the particular parts upon which the body was lying. That blackness, I assert, upon the authority of the medical testimony, was caused in the parts where it existed, by the body resting or lying upon those parts for a considerable time. You have it also established that there were no marks of violence, of such violence as would occasion the blackness presented. Any medical men will tell you, gentlemen, that there are clear and distinct marks or appearances, by which they can discover the difference between a blackness resulting from violence and from gravitation, and which would prevent them from falling into any error on the subject.

Bearing this in mind and coupling it with the fact that the marks of violence are negative by the medical evidence, even by Dr. Hatchell, we have it manifest that the blackness said to have been seen on parts of the body of the late Mrs. Kirwan, and respecting which so much was said, and which impressed the females who examined it so much, has nothing at all of any consequence in it.

But then there is the congestion of the lungs and the other parts of the body; and there is also the bleeding from the ears, and those other parts. In relation to those matters, let me call your attention to the fact that whilst my learned friends, prosecuting for the Crown, were willing to ask and did ask Dr. Hatchell a great many questions about the congestion exhibited in the lungs and elsewhere, they were at the same time most unwilling to put to him this question: whether from the medical appearances alone, he was able, as a medical man, to form an opinion as to the cause of this lady's death? They would not put to him that question; but they were most anxious to obtain from him an opinion, combined with the officious zeal and suggestions of constabulary officers, and agents of the Crown solicitors, who brought him down to Ireland's Eye to tutor and instruct him. They did not require his opinion as a medical man, founded on the appearances presented by the body at post-mortem examination; but an opinion, partaking of all the stories he had heard, and into which he had been tutored by the chief of his force.

It was proved that there was bleeding from the ears, and oozing of blood from the right nipple, and from other parts, but that there was no mark whatever of violence, nor was there any conceivable injury or external impression discernible on the entire body, that would cause the bleeding from the ears and other parts. But it was proved that, if this lady, while bathing had been seized with a fit of epilepsy, that she fell and was drowned, struggling in the water, this would be calculated to produce bleeding from different parts of the body at the same time.

This is a reasonable supposition, and I assert boldly that there is no other way, in reason, or sense, to account for this otherwise unaccountable bleeding. Dr. Hatchell, in making his information, thought proper to introduce the word strangulation, when he was giving his opinion as to what form or manner of death the appearances were compatible with. He proved, however, on that table [*presumably table where medical specimens were exhibited in court*], that he carefully examined the vertebrae and the trachea, and there was not the least sign of strangulation, or violence of any kind, but he said compression must have been combined with drowning.

What, in the name of common sense, did he mean by compression? Did he mean or intend to convey that the prisoner seized the deceased around the waist and crushed her to death, as a bear would his victim? But that would not cause bleeding from the ears; and nothing was more likely than the circumstance of being seized with a fit while bathing, to cause the congestion in the lungs and elsewhere, which congestion is nothing more than sudden stoppage of the blood and the gathering of it into a particular place. If, as seems likely from the evidence given, she ate her dinner on the island, and went afterwards to bathe, and that she was seized with a fit in consequence of going into the water with a full stomach, then the exudation of blood from various parts would probably take place.

In that way, the appearances described as to the causes of which so much has been said, could readily be accounted for. This, I submit to you, is the most probable explanation of the appearances, and I defy a man to say, or show, there could have been a forcible compression, sufficient to force the blood from the ears and other parts, without that compression injuring a vital organ. I ask any one of you to suggest any other mode than I have stated to you, by which the blood could be caused to exude from various parts, as it did, in this case, without leaving visible marks behind. I tell you this exudation could be caused, and probably was caused, by the very congestion that terminated this unhappy woman's existence.

The froth would result from a fit of epilepsy or drowning. Well then, if it was caused by drowning, who drowned her, or how was she drowned? If you come to the conclusion that she died from the effects of a fit, there is an end to the case. I rely upon the existence of the froth, and the swelling of the lips, as being perfectly consistent with the occurrence of a fit; and I affirm that every particle of the medical evidence given in this case is fully and perfectly consistent with the idea of the deceased having been seized by a fit, while in the water. I cannot discover one particle of evidence that would show her death to have resulted from violence at the hands of another.

Then we come to the statements respecting the left ear, the cut on the breast, and the scratches on the face. I may remark that the observation I am about to express is not meant as a slight towards my learned friend, Mr. Smyly. He smiles at my comments; but I know he would regret that an inconsiderate smile from him would weigh a feather against the prisoner in the scale of which his life depends. Now, with reference to these scratches. If you have ever been present where the body of a friend or one with whom you were acquainted, and who met his death by drowning, if you saw, I repeat, the body taken out of the water, you will remember the horror you must have experienced at seeing it covered with those crabs that fasten so voraciously upon the poor body, almost the very moment it is immersed in the water.

Mr. Davis, the coroner, whose capacity to speak on the subject is beyond question, from his long and great experience as a coroner, and from his constantly being obliged to hold inquests on persons who had been drowned, tells you that these small green crabs do fasten upon the drowned body, and disfigure it, nay more, he mentioned to you an instance in which he held an inquest on a body that had been only one hour in the water, and which on being taken out, was found to have been assailed by a number of these very green crabs. No man who resides near the seacoast can require to be satisfied of the fact that these crabs almost immediately attack the body of a drowned person, and disfigure it.

In corroboration of this, you have Dr. Hamilton, the medical gentleman who examined the body of Mrs. Kirwan on the morning of the inquest, stating that some of the marks he observed seemed to have been caused by something biting at the parts. But independently of that, it is clear that the deceased must have fallen among the rocks; and is there anything more likely than that she was scratched and marked by them? Is that a more reasonable way of accounting for those marks than to ascribe them to violence by a human hand? It is, highly, or by the agency of these green crabs. Is it not probable that a person seized with a fit, falling amongst the rocks and struggling amongst them, would be scratched and marked thereby?

I will ask you, gentlemen, however, to bear in mind that if I cannot account for those scratches and marks, I am not bound or required to account for them, in order to make out the innocence of my client. Remember, gentlemen, that it is not a case in which we know and can prove what passed on that island, and at the place where this lady met her death. It is not a case in which there is evidence to show that the prisoner was at the scene of death, and that it becomes necessary for him to show why he was there, and to explain what occurred.

There is no such case before you; it is one in which, if the prisoner is innocent, he knows as little and can tell as little of what occurred, or in explanation of the appearances and circumstances that seem doubtful, as anyone in this court. But I think I can account for the scratches, either on the very probable supposition that the deceased was seized with a fit, and fell and worked and struggled among the rocks. You recollect that one of the witnesses said that the hair of the deceased was filled with sand and seaweed. That would look like a struggle amongst the rocks, after falling down in the water. I submit that it will be perfectly consistent and reconcilable with all the appearances, whether you come to the conclusion, and I do not think it by any means an unreasonable conclusion, that these small green crabs, of which I have spoken, assailed the poor, perishing remnant of this unfortunate lady, or that she received those scratches while struggling about in the water.

Are these scratches at all reconcilable with the supposition that the prisoner is guilty of the murder of his unhappy wife? If a man goes to murder a woman, surely he will not begin by scratching and tearing her forehead, her face or her eyelids?

If there was a scratch upon his face, or a mark of a blow or struggle, which there is not, then I would understand the learned counsel for the Crown, in alleging that these were caused by the deceased in her struggles with the prisoner to save herself, and that therefore they were evidence against him. But it is perfectly absurd to say, or imply that, in order that the prisoner should murder the deceased, it was necessary for him to scratch her eyelids, or cut her breast skin deep. I am confident that all these little circumstances, which have been relied upon as proofs of the prisoner's guilt, will, on being calmly, carefully, and fairly investigated turn out to be the strongest proofs of his innocence.

If he be guilty of the foul crime charged against him, my prayer is that you will this day declare him so; but, if he is innocent, I pray that Providence will clear him, and will interpose to elucidate and make manifest evidence of his innocence, even the most trifling circumstances brought against him, in the assessment of evidence laid before you, in the most extraordinary manner. I trust that the most minute and most insignificant fact, that now seems inexplicable, will soon be explained and cleared up in the most satisfactory way, and that it will all the more conclusively demonstrate his innocence.

No man will venture to tell you, or ask you to believe, that the prisoner murdered the deceased by any other means than drowning; and that he could have undressed her, put on her bathing clothes and then placed her where she was found, for the purpose of having it thought that she had drowned by accident. If such an allegation like that was made, let me ask, how could he have killed her? There was no mark of violence or strangulation. If you do believe the prisoner to be the murderer, I see no other possible way for him to have done the deed, except by following her into the water, when she went to bathe, and holding her under until she was drowned.

To make out and sustain that extraordinary supposition, evidence is brought before you to show that his boots and trousers were wet. Why, if the prisoner did commit the dreadful deed in that way, it would not be his boots and trousers, but his coat and arms that would be wet. I may here observe, if you come to the conclusion, as you must inevitably do, that the deceased of her own free will went into bathe in the Long Hole, you get rid of all that has been said about the improbability of her going to bathe in such a place. It is established, beyond all question, that she was fond of bathing, and that she was an expert swimmer, which would materially tend to remove the impression that she would be afraid to bathe in such a place.

But good swimming, gentlemen, is no protection against drowning, if a person be seized with a fit. It is an incontestable fact that good swimmers very frequently meet their deaths by drowning. I do not believe that it has been stated or alleged, that where the body of the deceased was found is a place of danger; on the contrary, it appears to be, for a person who did not wish to be disturbed, or intruded upon, a most likely place for bathing.

I contend that you have not one particle of evidence to cause you to think that the lady received a single blow from her husband. Dr. Hatchell, it is admitted, had the body taken up for the express purpose of looking for marks of violence, but he could find no trace of violence, whatever. He told you he had heard of sharp instruments having been inserted into the body, and into the ears, and of her having been strangled; he examined carefully for marks that would and should exist if these things had been done, but he found no such marks, nor any traces of them. He said he heard of her breast being cut, and behold the cut turns out to be only skin deep. You recollect Nangle's examination; you remember him, because he had heard the infamous suggestion as to the use of sharp instruments, throw out that the stick, which he said Mr. Kirwan brought to the island, was a sword cane. This too, was disproved, as being now admitted that it was only a stick.

Gentlemen, people don't usually die from violence inflicted on them, without leaving some mark or marks by which the medical men can discover the nature and amount of violence used. If a person is strangled, surely there will be marks of strangulation, by which medical men can discover the fact. And if a sword is inserted into any part of the body, will there not be a wound inflicted upon them which medical men cannot overlook or mistake?

I may call your attention to the fact that a medical man who assisted Dr. Hatchell in making the post-mortem examination, who is not under the control and influence of the constabulary authorities, as Dr. Hatchell is, and who was not brought to the Long Hole to be tutored, that gentleman, Surgeon Tighe, has not been produced. Why, let me ask, was he not produced? Why did the Crown only produce Dr. Hatchell, who after swearing that the appearances presented at the examination were quite consistent with simple drowning, was then brought down to the Long Hole, there to be induced to alter his opinion upon being shown the position of some rocks?

After the exhibition Dr. Hatchell made upon the table, a more disgraceful exhibition I never witnessed, it was surely due to the case, it was due to the prisoner and to the administration of justice, to produce some person who had assisted at the post-mortem examination, and upon whom a jury could place reliance. Why did they not produce Dr. Tighe, who is, perhaps, at this moment, within reach of my voice? I say the Crown has not brought forward evidence which ought to have been produced; and I must rely on the high characters of the Crown counsel when I state my belief that they did not withhold such evidence. Dr. Hatchell's examination was, however, perfectly satisfactory.

It is quite true that a month had elapsed from the time of Mrs. Kirwan's death until the examination. Dr. Hatchell said he found the brain in a fluid state, but that, he added, was the result of decomposition; the pinkish colour of the brain was produced by the determination of blood, and that would produce a fit in the water. In point of fact the length of time that the body was buried did not at all conceal any marks of violence or injury that might have existed, or could have resulted from an injury calculated to cause death. As to the supposition that death had been produced by strangulation, I may remind you that neither the medical men nor the women who washed the deceased saw any marks of strangulation.

If there were marks, particularly from strangulation, you could have evidence enough submitted to you to show that the decomposition, so far from destroying those marks, would on the contrary have deepened those marks. You have it reluctantly admitted that death did not result from any internal injury. I will say that if a little of the zeal exhibited on the 6th of October had been shown early in September, it would have been much better for all parties. On the 16th of September the attention of those who took up the case and the prosecuting of it was called to the matter. The prisoner knew nothing of the case that was being drawn up against him; he rested quietly in the consciousness of his own innocence, and was not alarmed or apprehensive.

Gentlemen, let me now ask you to remember what the conduct of the prisoner was on the evening of this lamentable occurrence. He proceeds to sketch, as was his practice, near the ruin [*i.e. the Martello tower*], while Mrs. Kirwan goes to bathe a second time. Coming on eight o'clock, the prisoner, becoming anxious for the return of his wife, commences to search for her, but is unable to find her. Michael Nangle, one of the witnesses who deposed as to what took place at the island that evening, has given his evidence very fairly. Do you remember him stating that while he and Mr. Kirwan were looking for the deceased, he said to Mr. Kirwan she might have gone to the Long Hole, and that it would be well to search for her there? I put that statement against all that has been said, as to it not being likely that she would go to bathe in the Long Hole. Well, the body is at length discovered, and the afflicted husband, in his agony of mind, heightened, perhaps by the reflection that he had wronged her, flings himself on it and then exclaims, "Oh, Maria!" When the boatmen returned, after bringing the boat around the island, and being absent for upwards of an hour, they find the prisoner in the same position. You have it sworn, when the men proposed to go for the boat, this alleged murderer volunteered to remain amid the darkness and silence of this fearful scene, to guard the lifeless remains; and it is proved that he did so for more than an hour.

I ask you, can you believe that he was the murderer of the unfortunate woman, beside whose body he proposed to remain, and did remain for such a length of time, without a human being near him in that desolate and solitary spot? If he had been the murderer, would he, on the contrary, gladly have embraced the offer of the boatmen to accompany them, and thus escape the sight of his victim, shocked and horrified at its ghastly appearance before him on the bleak strand? I dwell, gentlemen, on these little incidents and circumstances, because they strongly refute the slanders that have been circulated on every side against the prisoner.

If she was the wife he wronged and he did wrong her, I can well conceive the gush of sorrow and affection that took place. If he loved and deplored [*i.e. lamented*] her, it was natural that he should be willing to remain by the body, guarding it alone, amid the darkness that hung around. I cannot, for the life of me, conceive how, if he was the murderer, he could be able, no matter how great the amount of his nerves, to remain alone for such a period, and in such a place, lying across the body of his supposed victim.

Gentlemen, I now come to the question of the sheet, on which my learned friends appear to place a great reliance. I may remind you, in the first place, that you have no evidence on that subject but the statement of Patrick Nangle. Supposing him to be correct in his statement, it is conceivable that if the deceased was

125

seized with a fit, while in the water, she may have struggled or worked over to the sheet where it lay, and grasped at it. But are you satisfied that the sheet was near her at all? You have it sworn by Michael Nangle that the prisoner brought down a shawl, and something white to the body and that these things were afterwards, wrapped around the body. Let me ask, what necessity would there be for the prisoner bringing down the sheet at all?

Does not the place and position in which the body was found afford the strongest proof that the prisoner did not place it there; for if he wished, he could have gone a step further, and by raising it over the reef of rocks, it would have gone with the ocean's water, perhaps, forever.

Gentlemen, you will also recollect Michael Nangle's evidence, wherein that witness swore, that from the position of the body, lying across the rock, with the head jammed in between two fragments of or parts of that rock, it seemed if the body had been there stopped and prevented from being carried out with the tide. I believe such was the case; that it had been those rocks, or this divided rock, which prevented the body being brought out to sea by the receding tide; and this fact, taken together with other clear and undenied portions of the evidence, shows that at the time when the sad event had been discovered, and for a long time afterwards, neither the witness, Patrick Nangle, nor any of the other men who were examined, had entertained the remotest suspicion that there was anything in this sad case but the result of the merest accident.

The witness, Michael Nangle, in giving his evidence, had testified to seeing Mr. Kirwan bring down a portion of the deceased lady's clothes and a shawl and a sheet. The other witness Patrick Nangle had sworn that he saw no shawl or sheet in Mr. Kirwan's hands, on his coming down from the rock. Both men happened to be quite near Mr. Kirwan at the time. Now, it is obvious, that if you believe the testimony of the former of those witnesses, you will be compelled to refuse credence to the other. Patrick Nangle had sworn that Mr. Kirwan had nothing in his hands when he came down from the rock; on the other hand, Michael Nangle positively swore and asserted, that when Mr. Kirwan came down from the rock he carried in his hand a shawl and something else which was white and looked like a sheet, and added that Mr. Kirwan sent Pat Nangle up the rock for the remainder of the clothes.

It is utterly ridiculous, in the face of this clear and positive evidence of Michael Nangle's, to suppose that the clothes had not been on the rock when Patrick Nangle first went to look for them. It is clear that the clothes must have been lodged higher up on the rock, where Patrick Nangle had not searched, and yet in the face of the clever and conclusive testimony of Michael Nangle as to those clothes, you find Patrick Nangle obstinately asserting that the clothes had not been there, and Mr. Kirwan brought down no portion of them with him.

I would ask you, therefore, to attach no weight to Patrick Nangle's testimony, but, on the contrary, to accord due credit to the evidence of Michael Nangle, to this effect, that when Mr. Kirwan discovered the clothes, he brought down with him such portions of them as sufficed to cover the body at the time, and that he then desired Pat Nangle to go up and fetch the remainder of the garments.

Mr. Kirwan is stated to have dried his boots and to have changed his stockings after returning to the house. The boatmen were called on to swear that he could not have got wet whilst with the body on the island. Now, you will remember that the body was found lying with the feet resting in a small pool of water.

It has been also sworn, by all the witnesses who were present when the body was found, that Mr. Kirwan threw himself across the body and bewailed bitterly her loss. Surely, when you remember that he remained still prostrate across the body, alone with the dead during the time the boatmen were away, if he loved his deceased wife as evidently he did, are you prepared to say, that whilst extended beside, or lying across the body, he might not have got his feet wet from the very pool of water which lay at the feet of the deceased? In fact, every one of those incidents seem to present proof, when maturely considered, more and more conclusive of the prisoner's innocence, and his perfect unconsciousness of any necessity to conceal a single act of his.

Larkin told the sergeant of police the nature of the cries which he had heard and a very old woman in the vicinity had heard or fancied she had heard a cry or a shout, and began to suit her imagination to the point. In fact if it were not for this story of Larkin's, not a word would ever have been heard of the cries and screams which were alleged to have been heard at such distance by others. Even if you believe that those cries had been the death shrieks of the deceased, those shrieks, or their occurrence rather, is perfectly compatible with the case submitted on the part of the prisoner; but if, as Larkin himself admitted, these cries were the shouts of some person calling for a boat, no greater importance should be attached to them in connexion with this case, than they deserve.

You should also remember that the Long Hole is situated in a kind of a gulley, hemmed in at either side by high cliffs, constituting, in fact, that picturesque division of the little island of Ireland's Eye so often remarked by all who pass the bay of Dublin. This creek or gulley, thus hemmed at the sides, might re-echo with cries which would scarcely be heard at other parts of the

128

island, by reason of the high rocks or banks at either side. But the cliffs open towards Howth, so that the cries which could not be heard by a person on another part of the island, might be easily heard across the water at Howth.

I would then ask you, gentlemen, when you patiently go over and review the facts of this case, to cast aside all extraneous suspicions. You are bound to come to your conclusion on the evidence before you. Gentlemen, I have spoken as I feel regarding this foul accusation brought against the prisoner. As regards the one stain on the prisoner's previous character, which, in fact, caused this prosecution, it is doubtless a crime, a serious crime, to have been unfaithful to his wife, and to have formed a connexion with another; but you should not, because of that lapse, be disposed to give credence to a charge as heinous as that brought now against the prisoner: and surely, the torture of mind, the humiliation and the ignominy to which he is exposed on this trial, constitutes an amount of suffering which is, in itself, sufficient punishment.

Do not, because yielding to the impulses of human frailty the prisoner had been unfaithful to his wife, do not on that account believe him to have been instrumental in the perpetration of a shocking murder. I call on you to repudiate and dismiss from your minds all considerations in connexion with previous events. If you do so, I hope the prisoner will leave this court a wiser and better man, at least not branded with the stigma and infamy of having committed the fearful crime of which he stands accused before you.

◀◦▶

Evidence Called for the Defence

First Witness: Dr. Rynd
Examined by Mr. Butt

Witness: I am a surgeon; I have been present during the trial and have heard the evidence, given this day by Dr. Hatchell, as to the post-mortem examination, and likewise as to the appearances presented by the body.

Mr. Butt: Judging from all these appearances, which you state you have heard described, what cause would you assign for the death of the party upon whom they were found?

Mr. Smyly: My Lord, I must really object to that question. Here is a medical gentleman produced who was not present at the post-mortem examination, and who, for all we know to the contrary, may never have seen the deceased, and yet is examined for the purpose of proving the cause of her death.

Mr. Butt: It is a perfectly legal question.

Judge Crampton: I think, in strictness, this question cannot be asked. But where the question is merely one of science, or where certain facts are admitted, or not disputed, and the question thus becomes substantially one of science only, it may be convenient to follow it to be put in its general form, in order that the testimony given by one medical witness may be assisted by the experience of a man of science in the medical art; that is to say the question might be put in this form: "Supposing such and such facts occurred, what would be your opinion relative to them?" but to ask "You have heard the whole of the trial, and all the evidence that has been given, what is your opinion of the cause of death?" is evidence too close to home to the jury box, for it is exactly what the jury have to try, and is, in fact, substituting a witness for the jury.

Mr. Butt: Now, Dr. Rynd, there were appearances such as you have heard described, upon the body of the late Mrs. Kirwan, what is your opinion as to how they originated?

Mr. Smyly: That is precisely the question that I object to, my Lord.

Judge Crampton: I am afraid that you have mistaken my meaning, Mr. Butt; but I will endeavour to render myself intelligible to you. Assuming certain appearances to exist, a medical witness may be examined with safety as to his idea of how those appearances arose; but the question cannot be asked in the manner you have put it.

Mr. Butt: Supposing certain appearances to exist in a person after death, such as those described by Dr. Hatchell, such as congestion of the lungs and other parts of the body, to what cause would you consider the death of the person to be assigned?

Dr. Rynd: Judging from those appearances you mention, I would attribute them to congestion of the brain.

Mr. Butt: That is not my question.

Dr. Rynd: That is the answer to the question I was asked.

Mr. Butt: I beg your pardon, the question I asked was what kind of death would arise from those appearances?

Judge Crampton [to witness]: What I understood you to be asked was, supposing certain appearances to be discovered in a body after death, to what kind of death would those appearances, in your opinion, be attributed?

Dr. Rynd: I have already said: death from congestion of the brain.

Mr. Butt: And supposing there was a considerable degree of congestion of the lungs and likewise of the vessels in the other parts of the body; supposing those circumstances to be combined, what kind of death would they point to, in your opinion?

Mr. Smyly: This form of question resembles too closely the evidence given by Dr. Hatchell.

Mr. Butt: I have endeavoured to ask the witness, from such and such appearances, what kind of death he thought they would indicate, which I believe, is the manner of the query suggested by His Lordship.

Judge Crampton: That is certainly what I suggested, but your manner of putting the question is certainly putting the matter too much to the jury box.

Mr. Butt: I will put the question again. Supposing all the appearances which I have before described, congestion of the lungs et cetera to exist in a body, what kind of death, would they, in your opinion be attributable to?

Dr. Rynd: All those appearances you have described would produce asphyxia, and the person should die; in other words, it would cause stoppage of the breath, and of the circulation of the blood, which would end in death.

Mr. Butt: In your judgement, as a medical man, do you think those appearances could be caused by extreme violence, supposing there to be no external marks of violence on the body?

Dr. Rynd: There should be manifest marks of external violence to produce them.

Mr. Butt: Would you consider a cut, skin deep or a scratch on the forehead and eyes sufficient to produce them?

Dr. Rynd: Certainly not.

Mr. Butt: In your judgement, as a medical man, would those appearances be produced by a fit of epilepsy?

Dr. Rynd: They would.

Judge Crampton: Without any concurring cause?

Dr. Rynd: Without any concurring cause.

Mr. Butt: Are you able to say, from your experience as a medical man, whether epileptic patients scream?

Dr. Rynd: They do.

Mr. Butt: Is it probable that a person in that situation would give more than one scream?

Dr. Rynd: They might give several.

Mr. Butt: In your opinion, as a medical man, would bathing with a full stomach produce epilepsy?

Dr. Rynd: It would be very likely to do so, because the repletion of the stomach would cause a flow of blood to the head in that case.

Mr. Butt: And would an epileptic fit, so produced, leave all those appearances which I have described?

Dr. Rynd: It would.

Mr. Butt: Would it be more likely to be produced in a person of full habit [*i.e. a condition of the body characterised by congestion of the visible blood vessels and a tendency to stoutness*]?

Dr. Rynd: Of full habit, in which case it would, I think, bring apoplexy with it, but epilepsy would surely produce those appearances without the person being of full habit.

Mr. Butt: Would there be any pink colour of the brain, more than would normally be the case, a month after death, supposing the woman's death to have been the result of apoplexy?

Dr. Rynd: If the brain were more than naturally pink, a month after death, it would be proof that there was a greater quantity of blood present in minute vessels of the head, than perhaps was natural, which would tend to cause apoplexy.

Mr. Butt: Supposing there was blood flowing from the external cavity of the ears, without any injury being done to the internal parts thereof, would you be able to account where the blood came from?

Dr. Rynd: Yes, I think I would be able to do so, upon a very strict examination of the organs of the ear, for the blood might have oozed from the tympanum, or if congestion were very great, it might have been the result of external oozing.

Mr. Butt: But with nothing more to guide us than the fact immediately after death there was a flow of blood from the ear, could that, in your opinion, be produced from congestion of the brain?

Dr. Rynd: Yes, I think so, for I have seen bleeding from the eyes of a person in an epileptic fit.

Mr. Butt: Then, could all those appearances, and the flow of blood from other parts, in your opinion, be satisfactorily accounted for by a person having gone into the water, shortly after a meal and being seized with epilepsy?

Dr. Rynd: I think it very probable that such might be the case; general congestion would produce a flow of blood from the vagina, and that general congestion would, very probably, be produced by sudden immersion in the water with a full stomach.

Mr. Butt: Supposing a strong person, going into the water, and bathing after dinner, was seized with epilepsy and general congestion followed, is it your opinion, as a medical man, that it would provide bleeding from the several parts of the person I have enumerated?

Dr. Rynd: I think it would do so, if apoplexy were combined with it.

Mr. Butt: Do you know, or, as a medical man, can you assign any external violence which may be offered to the human person that would produce the general congestion and the bleeding from the ears, breasts and other parts without injuring any other organ or leaving marks of violence?

[The witness appeared to hesitate for some time]

Mr. Butt: Have you heard or do you understand my question.

Dr. Rynd: Yes, but it requires some consideration. [Witness spent a few minutes in deliberation] Apoplexy might be produced by a blow to the head that would not leave a mark, and yet the congestion would be so great that an exudation might take place; the blow might leave a very slight mark upon the scalp, but that abrasion might be so slight, that it might not be perceived.

Mr. Butt: Supposing there were marks of strangulation upon the neck, would decomposition remove them?

Dr. Rynd: If there were marks of strangulation upon the neck, the place where the compression was made would be decomposed sooner than the other parts around it, and consequently be in a greater state of decomposition when the body came to be examined.

Cross-examined by Mr. Smyly

Mr. Smyly: On the post mortem on the body of a person who had been drowned, would you expect to find congestion of the lungs and congestion of the brain?

Dr. Rynd: On making an examination on a body which had been taken out of the water, the person having died in the manner you describe, I would expect to find congestion of the lungs and of the brain and I would not be surprised to find congestion of the vagina.

Mr. Smyly: Would you expect to find bleeding from the ears?

Dr. Rynd: Such a thing might be, but I never knew of any instance of it, where a person was simply drowned.

Mr. Butt: The blood, I believe, continues fluid in the bodies of persons who have died from drowning for some time after death; can you tell me how long it remains in that state?

Dr. Rynd: I am aware that it continues to flow for some time after death, but I cannot say for how long.

Mr. Butt: Would the blood continue to flow the next day?

Dr. Rynd: It would.

Mr. Smyly: You mentioned that froth came from the lips of those who had died from epilepsy; can you tell me the difference between the froth so produced and that that comes from the mouths of those who are simply drowned?

Dr. Rynd: Froth remains stationary on the lips of those persons who die from epilepsy for some hours after death, whereas in the case of those simply drowned, it continues to flow, for some time.

Mr. Smyly: How long would the froth continue to come forth in the case of a person who had simply drowned?

Dr. Rynd: That depends entirely on the quantity of froth formed in the mouth; as long as there is any therein, it will continue to come forth.

Mr. Smyly: Could you form any idea as to the amount of froth that would be formed?

Dr. Rynd: Of that I have no idea.

Mr. Smyly: Could you describe the difference between epileptic and other froth?

Dr. Rynd: I could not positively say; an epileptic generally bites his tongue, which tinges the froth with red.

Mr. Smyly: Is there any other difference?

Dr. Rynd: No describable difference.

Mr. Smyly: Would the lips of a simply drowned person be swollen?

Dr. Rynd: I have seen the lips of a simply drowned person grow large and swell.

Mr. Smyly: Would you expect to see a considerable degree of congestion in those persons who had been simply drowned?

Dr. Rynd: That depends on the efforts made by the persons to save themselves.

Mr. Smyly: I now ask you, whether, without any extreme marks of violence, but simply by the stoppage of respiration, a high degree of congestion of the lungs et cetera, might not take place?

Dr. Rynd: Would you be kind enough to repeat the question.

Mr. Smyly: You have heard of the celebrated Burke case, where although there were no external marks of violence visible, suffocation was produced. My question is, whether the application of a wet sheet or any other wet matter, placed over the mouth, would produce a high degree of congestion and the appearances described, although there were no marks of external violence?

Dr. Rynd: It would, undoubtedly, produce a high degree of congestion, which would be followed by bleeding from the several parts of the body described, although there might be no marks of violence.

Judge Crampton: You say that epileptic patients scream; is that scream given at the moment of seizure; or when the patient is about to fall?

Dr. Rynd: It is generally given at the moment of falling or of becoming insensible.

Judge Crampton: Can they scream after falling, or have you ever known them to do so?

Dr. Rynd: Certainly there can be screams for two or three minutes after.

Mr. Smyly: Have you ever seen the deceased lady, Mrs. Kirwan?

Dr. Rynd: I saw her about six years ago when I attended her in a fever.

Mr. Smyly: Had you then any opportunity of knowing she had, at any time, been subject to epileptic fits?

Dr. Rynd: I had not. She seemed to be, when in health, a fine, strong young woman.

Mr. Smyly: Have you ever seen her since?

Dr. Rynd: I have not; I was told that her father died of a fit of that nature.

Mr. Smyly: May I ask if it was a person who has taken an anxious part in this trial who gave you that information?

Dr. Rynd: It was indeed; it was a person deeply interested therein.

Mr. Smyly: What length of time would the struggles of a person in an epileptic fit continue?

Dr. Rynd: That would depend on the severity of the seizure; the struggles might last fifteen minutes if the seizure was not a severe one.

Mr. Smyly: In the case that there are more cries than one, which would be the loudest?

Dr. Rynd: The first scream is always of a terrific nature and the cries might be continued for ten minutes.

―◇―

This was a deeply interesting, important and compelling passage of evidence in which both the prosecution and defence theories of the cause of Mrs. Kirwan's death were fully emerging. It was also notable for the exposition of the contrasting style of examination by the opposing leading counsel. Butt was typically bombastic in his approach which got him off to a bad start with his star medical witness, Dr. Rynd, a prominent and accomplished Dublin physician. Having to rephrase his opening question proved to be a lengthy and somewhat humiliating process for Butt. However, he soon recovered and developed a strong rhythm of questioning of the witness who had also settled down.

The counsel's purpose was twofold: first, to establish the fact with the help of the medical opinion of his witness that a certain form of drowning could produce the same degrees of congestion and appearances as evidenced by Dr. Hatchell on the victim; and secondly to provide an explanation for both the cries and the superficial injuries by suggesting that the victim had a fit of an epileptic nature after having gone into cold water with a full stomach.

On the other hand, Smyly employed a quiet and incremental style of examination, designed to elicit the information in a manner that would not produce any confusion in the minds of the jury members. Interestingly he did not confront a central issue of fact in relation to the defence proposition of the victim entering the water with a full stomach. At post mortem Dr. Hatchell found that the stomach was *empty and contracted*. There was no sign of food or even particles in any of the air passages.

What was mystifying from the defence point of view was that to take this line on the fit being brought on by immersion with a full stomach, surely it should have been established at what time Kirwan and his wife had eaten the food that they had brought over for the day trip? A simple consultation between the prisoner and the solicitor would have confirmed the fact. But therein lay another mystery in this case of mysteries.

It appears that Mr. Smyly was more intent on testing the prosecution contention that death was as a result of suffocation effected with no marks of external violence on the body. And in a very subtle fashion he established that Mrs. Kirwan, who had been examined by Dr. Rynd, six years previously, was a healthy, strong woman with no medical history of epilepsy. Counsel also got the agreement of the witness, quoting the famous case of Burke, that suffocation with a material such a wet sheet, with no marks of external violence, would produce the medical appearances of Mrs. Kirwan's body, noted by both witnesses and Dr. Hatchell's post mortem.

The defence knew that the medical evidence would play a large part in the minds of the jury when they were forging their decision, and called in a second witness. It is a course that the prosecution should also have followed but did not, which might prove to be a risk. While Dr. Hatchell was a highly regarded and competent physician, he displayed some lack of forthright expression of his conviction about the cause of death, especially towards the conclusion of his testimony.

When asked by Mr. Butt if the appearances presented by the body could be consistent with those of a person with a full stomach going into the water, the doctor agreed it was possible, and when pressed if it could be probable, he said per se it was. What Dr. Hatchell forgot to say was that it was in no way applicable to the case, as the post mortem proved that this theory could not withstand the fact that there was no food in the stomach when Mrs. Kirwan went into the water. It was an incredible oversight and it remained to be seen how unfortunate for the prosecution case.

For whatever reason, some scientific and medical experts are uneasy in the adversarial cauldron of the court. Dr. Hatchell did not impress in the witness box. This created in some observers' minds the impression that the medical evidence itself was weak. It was anything but that; the question was, what impression would the rebuttal of his evidence leave in the minds of the jurors?

◄○►

Second Witness: Dr. Robert Adams
Examined by Mr. Brereton

Witness: I am a member of the Royal College of Surgeons.

Mr. Brereton: You have heard of the appearances described by Dr. Hatchell, as presented shortly after death; what, in your opinion were they originated by?

Mr. Smyly: I object to that question being answered; His Lordship has already decided that the question cannot be put in that form.

Judge Crampton: The better course would be to put the question in the manner in which Mr. Butt has already done.

Mr. Brereton: Supposing such appearances were presented in two or three weeks after death, what, in your opinion, would be the manner of death by which they originated?

141

Dr. Adams: Congestion of the lungs.

Mr. Brereton: From what would congestion of the lungs arise?

Dr. Adams: The lungs are perhaps the last organs which would undergo much change; congestion of the lungs might arise from a variety of causes, from drowning, suffocation or from an epileptic fit.

Mr. Brereton: From what cause would exudation of the blood arise?

Dr. Adams: Any cause that produces congestion of the whole muscular system, will cause an exudation of the blood, which is nothing more than the overflowing of the surplus quantity of blood in the veins.

Mr. Brereton: Do you think that general congestion would cause the flow of blood from the nipples of the breast?

Dr. Adams: It might be possible, but I have never heard of it.

Mr. Brereton: Do you think that it is likely that epilepsy would be caused by a person going into the water after a meal.

Dr. Adams: I think it probable that epilepsy might be occasioned in the manner you describe.

Mr. Brereton: Does the blood of a person who drowns remain liquid after death?

Dr. Adams: The blood of a person drowned generally continues in a liquid state for some time, in the same manner as that of a person who dies from the effects of lightning.

Mr. Brereton: Could you specify the length of time it remains in that state?

Dr. Adams: I could not do exactly; but I fancy it would remain so for a day or two, or more.

Mr. Brereton: Would abrasions or skin wounds cause exudation of blood while it remained in that state?

Dr. Adams: It would not cause the exudation, but the consequence would be that the surplus blood would exude more freely through those abrasions, than through the portion of the skin that had received no injury.

Mr. Brereton: Does a person usually scream before or after being seized with epilepsy?

Dr. Adams: The scream is generally a precursor to the fit, that is to say that the seizure is generally announced by a loud scream.

Mr. Brereton: Does a person seized with epilepsy usually scream more than once?

Dr. Adams: A person seized with epilepsy may scream more than once, but it is not usual; the first scream is the rule; where there are more screams than one the first is the most violent.

Cross-examined by Mr. Hayes

Mr. Hayes: Suppose a person were to put a wet cloth over the mouth and nose of another as we have heard of being done in a celebrated case, would that cause congestion?

Dr. Adams: It would be very much the same as drowning or hanging.

Mr. Hayes: Would it produce the appearances described by Mr. Brereton?

Dr. Adams: It would produce all the effects of hanging or drowning; whatever effects hanging would cause, would be produced in this manner.

Mr. Hayes: Would it produce bleeding from the vagina?

Dr. Adams: It would produce congestion which might produce the bleeding you speak of.

Mr. Hayes: Would it produce bleeding from the ears?

Dr. Adams: The bleeding from the ears might be produced in the same manner.

Mr. Hayes: Could the congestion be also produced by any external violence, such as extreme pressure on the chest, suppose by one person kneeling on another's breast?

Dr. Adams: I doubt very much if pressure on the chest would produce congestion; pressure on the windpipe, would, however, do so.

Mr. Hayes: Suppose I put you into the water and put my foot on your breast, would that produce congestion?

Dr. Adams: If my mouth were under the water, it would.

Mr. Hayes: And would not the effects be increased by my putting you under water?

Dr. Adams: It all depends on the mouth and nose being underwater; that would produce all the difference, which, in my opinion would not be much.

Mr. Hayes: Is it your medical opinion that it would not add much to the effects?

Dr. Adams: I have already stated that it all depends on the mouth and nose being under the water.

Mr. Hayes: Very well, Dr. Adams, now suppose we add this ingredient, that while the individual was in the water, there was an extreme struggle. What effect would that have on the bodily symptoms?

Dr. Adams: I suppose it would cause a great deal of air and water to get into the windpipe and produce congestion.

Mr. Hayes: Would a protracted struggle increase those effects, think you, Dr. Adams?

Dr. Adams: The longer the struggle, the greater the congestion would be.

Mr. Hayes: You said it would produce froth. That froth, I think I gathered from Mr. Rynd, is the air coming out and mixing with the saliva?

Dr. Adams: It is the air getting into the windpipe, and mixing with the water and mucus, which produces the froth.

Mr. Hayes: Now, Dr. Adams, [*can you say*] whether it is more likely that air would remain in the body in the case of a person who died from accidental drowning, or in that of a person who was drowned by being thrust down suddenly and kept under water?

Dr. Adams: It would be very hard to say; but the difference would be so trivial as not to be worth calculating.

Mr. Hayes: In which case would there be most froth?

Dr. Adams: There would be most froth in the case of a person who had struggled violently and it would continue to come for longer than in a case where death had occurred from mere accidental drowning.

Mr. Hayes: Have you ever known a case of accidental drowning where bleeding from the vagina or ears was produced?

Dr. Adams: I cannot bring any such to my memory.

Mr. Hayes: Have you ever heard, or during your experience, have you ever known of a case where death from epilepsy was accompanied by either of these things?

Dr. Adams: I have never known such a case to occur, during my experience, nor have I read of such.

Re-examined by Mr. Brereton

Mr. Brereton: Would such pressure, applied to the chest, as would leave no external mark of the application, be sufficient to produce the appearances I have stated?

Dr. Adams: That is a doubtful question; in the case of any such pressure being applied, out of the water, it would leave some external mark of violence.

Mr. Brereton: In the case a wet sheet was put over the mouth and nose of a person, would it produce loud and terrible screams?

Dr. Adams: That is not a medical question.

Judge Crampton: Supposing death to have taken place by forcible submersion or from accidental drowning, would you be able, from the appearances described, to state to which species of death they were attributable?

Dr. Adams: My Lord, in my opinion, no living man could do so.

Mr. Brereton: That is all I will trouble you for.

The information of Mrs. Campbell was then read to the court, and the case for the defence closed.

—◇—

Dr. Adams was a highly respected surgeon and fellow of the Royal College of Surgeons and as admired for his professional integrity as his skill as a medical man, not as biased or implacable as the previous witness Dr. Rynd, a brilliant physician also but with a matching ego, with a penchant for fine clothes and the ladies and an immovable belief in his own views.

Dr. Adams was in the tradition of the best medico-legal witness who would at all times give an objective assessment of the medical matters he was asked to address in court. While he was chosen by the defence team for his unquestionable qualifications it was clear from his evidence that he was not, in any manner, adverse to answering prosecution questions with the same professionalism as those posed by the defence. Whether it was with prior knowledge of this fact or not, Mr. Hayes, providing an object lesson in skilful cross-examination, effectively turned the evidence of a defence witness into a distinct advantage to the prosecution.

In doing so, Mr. Hayes, in a most subtle fashion, revealed the prosecution theory that Mrs. Kirwan had been killed by the application of a wet sheet over the mouth and nose combined with forcible immersion in the water and accompanied by compression of the chest and a great struggle for life and managed to have the appearances noted on the body and the effects confirmed as being so by the defence medical witness.

There was a telling point for the prosecution in Dr. Adams' opinion that out of the water there might be some marks of violence from compression, which by inference would not be the case if the pressure was applied under the water.

But most tellingly the prosecution counsel elicited the fact that Dr. Adams had never come across a case in which accidental drowning had produced bleeding from the ears or vagina and had never come across or heard of a case where death from epilepsy had produced those post-mortem appearances.

—<o>—

Mr. Hayes' Address on Behalf of the Crown

It now becomes my duty, the evidence on both sides having closed, to address you in coming to a just and sound conclusion. To the prisoner at the bar, the case is all important, his life is at stake, and as Mr. Butt has told you, something dearer than life: his honour and his fair fame among his fellow men.

Gentlemen, you are not to decide upon the rumours which have been circulated, or on the reports that have been spread abroad, but solely and exclusively upon the evidence which has been given in the case. I heartily subscribe to the statement made by Mr. Butt that these rumours should be discarded from your judgement; that they should not be thought of one moment except to be thrown aside. You should not take them into consideration either for or against the prisoner.

Because rumours prejudicial to him have been circulated; you should not be induced to find him guilty; nor because other rumours have been circulated, which I say are totally unfounded, are you to believe him innocent, if the evidence leads you to the conclusion that he is guilty. My learned friend has thought it right to go a little out of his way in speaking of the manner in which this case has been got up; and he seemed to indulge in something like unnecessary strictures upon those engaged for the Crown in the conducting of this case, and in its investigation.

While I am willing to bear my share of all the responsibility that can attach to us, I have yet to discover in any part of the case, and Mr. Butt did not condescend to put his finger upon any fact or circumstance, that there is anything circulated or tending in the slightest degree to cast discredit upon those concerned for the prosecution. In my humble judgement we have done our duty, nothing more or less. We thought the case was one, and Mr. Butt admits it, deserving of a careful and fair investigation before a jury and we brought it before a jury accordingly.

Mr. Butt talked of witnesses being tutored; I say Mr. Butt has no foundation for that assertion; and when he spoke of a witness whose character and reputation are unstained, being tutored and instructed for the occasion by official authorities, he stated that for which he had not the slightest foundation. Dr. Hatchell's testimony, I will admit, did not come up to what the Crown had been led to believe and expect, but I see no ground for the assertion that he did not state the truth. His evidence, which had been given fairly, candidly and impartially, amounted to this: that the symptoms and appearances presented by the body of the deceased were consistent with death produced otherwise than violence.

This testimony, in its general aspect, was favourable to the prisoner; and yet the gentleman who gave it has fallen under the lash of Mr. Butt's indignant eloquence.

Let us now, gentlemen, having disposed of these matters, proceed to consider the facts of the case, and let us state them in a regular order of time. Let us, in the first instance, apply ourselves to the evidence which is rather introductory, and which goes to supply a motive for the perpetration of the alleged murder. It is a painful fact, clearly proved, that for ten or twelve years before this unfortunate transaction, the prisoner had been living in illicit intercourse with a female, who has been named more than once today.

By her he had a family, for her he supported an establishment at Sandymount, kept a house servant; and as, one of the witnesses told you, it was his custom to sleep with this woman, at the house in Sandymount, abandoning the place that should have been his marriage domain retreat. This woman went by the name of Mrs. Kirwan. She is received there and known as such; the landlord, Mr. Bridgeford, knows her only as such. While the prisoner is carrying on this horrible intercourse, and is, I will say, shamelessly introducing this woman in public as his wife, he has at the same time a wife.

Mr. Butt: I wish to correct my learned friend. There is no evidence that the prisoner had introduced this woman to the public as his wife.

Mr. Hayes: Mr. Bridgeford, I repeat, who was the landlord of the house in which they resided, knew her only as Mrs. Kirwan. And here I beg of my learned friend to correct me, if I mistake any of the evidence, but if it is only word-catching, I beg he will not.

Mr. Butt: I submit I am entitled to interrupt the learned counsel when he is misstating the facts.

Mr. Hayes: I insist that she passed as Mrs. Kirwan; the servant called her so; and all the time Mrs. Kirwan was living in Dublin, he had no family by her, and, in that respect, the marriage may not have fulfilled the prisoner's expectations. Things so continued until the month of June last, when this gentleman took lodgings in the house of a Mrs. Campbell at Howth. Mrs. Campbell has detailed to you the circumstances of a dispute which took place shortly after their removal to her house. She told you that there were loud and angry words, and the dreadful expression of the prisoner, when alone in the room with his wife, not imagining of course he was overheard by others, "I'll end you, I'll end you, I will finish you," and then described the rumbling around of furniture, as if a beating was going on.

Mrs. Campbell tells you of the deceased's complaint the next morning that she had been beaten. Are these facts consistent with the kind and genuine affection that ought to exist between the husband and the wife? Are they not the very antipodes of affection? Is it reasonable to suppose that a man who had been living with a concubine for ten years and during all that time gave her his name, while he was beating his legitimate wife at Howth, could be supposed to entertain affection for the woman he treated so grossly and who ought to have been the partner of his dearest affections?

I will not insult your understandings by venturing to suppose that affection could exist in the breast of such a man. You are told there is no evidence of any further cruelty having been used towards the deceased and that Mrs. Campbell stated they lived together afterwards as happily as any couple do. I will admit that he did not beat her after the occasion in question; and what is more I will admit that he endeavoured to inspire confidence in her. I will admit, if it serves Mr. Butt's purpose, that he did everything to give her amusement and enjoyment, and then I will see whether these admissions will not bear strongly on the case for the prosecution.

For some days before this transaction, they had been in the habit of going to Ireland's Eye. They went three times. Nangle states that on the first occasion they went in his boat and returned from the island at half past six o'clock; on the second occasion they returned at seven o'clock and the third time they went it was fixed that they should return at eight o'clock; that was all arranged by Mr. Kirwan and if you like with the concurrence of Mrs. Kirwan.

Let us now come to the day in question. Preparations having been made to go to the island at ten in the morning and return at eight in the evening of this the 6th of September, the parties were ferried across. At four o'clock, Mr. Brew and his party left the island; after that the island was utterly desolated and uninhabited, save for the prisoner and his wife until eight o'clock. They were sole occupants of it. What takes place in that interval?

At seven o'clock, shrieks were heard, which are deposed to by five witnesses; therefore, as to the fact there cannot be a possibility of doubt, and as to the ingenious attempt of my learned friend to attribute them to epilepsy, as being the shrieks of epilepsy, there is no evidence to support that assertion. If there was any evidence that this lady had been previously affected with epilepsy, or anything of the kind, there might have been a shadow of a ground upon which to found that assertion. As the prisoner has forborne to produce such testimony, it is not too much to infer that there was none to produce; and we must take it that the deceased was a perfectly healthy woman.

The five witnesses deposing to the fact of the shrieks are incapable of concert. One of the witnesses did not mention it until several days after. Hugh Campbell swears that about a half an hour after he heard the shrieks, he saw Nangle's boat leave the quay to go to the island. How accurately does that tally with the statement of Nangle himself who says he left the quay about half past seven o'clock, and with the other witnesses who state they heard the shrieks about seven o'clock. We have it indubitably established then that the cries were heard before Nangle left Howth; and that puts to flight the airy phantom Mr. Butt has conjured up, that the cries might have been the cries of Nangle and those who were with him.

He says, however, he would rather have the cries accounted for the other way. Let us take that proposition then and proceed to discuss it. But we must first, get rid of the rest of Mr. Butt's poetry in this case; for even poetry must not be allowed to weigh in a case of this kind. When the five witnesses, at Howth, could hear the cries from the island, may I ask did the prisoner who was on the island hear them? Pressed by this fearful question, Mr. Butt had to recourse to the science of acoustics and he spoke of the probability of persons on the mainland hearing noises that a person on the island, who was only at a distance of 280 yards could not hear.

Mr. Curran: Oh, no, 890 yards.

Mr. Hayes: That was the distance from the Long Hole to the landing place; but I am taking him where he was sketching at the old ruin.

Justice Crampton: We have no evidence to show where the prisoner was when the cries were heard.

Mr. Hayes: I don't care where they put him; I will suppose him at the farthest extremity of the island. I will imagine any of you gentlemen on the island, at any part of it; and then I ask, will you come to the conclusion that these shrieks heard on the mainland were not heard by the prisoner, no matter what part he was at? They were heard at seven o'clock and Mr. Kirwan's own evidence is: "She left me at a later period of the day, about six o'clock to bathe again." That was the prisoner's own evidence, given at a time when he was not charged with any crime. He never saw her alive after six o'clock; she is an hour away; and yet this affectionate husband, whose ears should have been alert to catch even the rustling of the fern, that would bear him tidings of his absent wife, is deaf to those dreadful shrieks.

Suppose that he knew her to be subject to fits of epilepsy, would it not be the duty of any man, in such a case, not pretending to love, but even to one particle of humanity, would he not run on the wings of wind to give her assistance lest she be suffocated in the water? When the boatmen come to the island, is he found searching for his wife? He is standing on the western side of the island, the boat hails him, he answers, and you will be astonished to learn that instead of this man giving way to the natural ebullition of an affectionate mind, grieved for the loss of his partner at such a time, his words to Nangle, as he came up to him were: "Nangle, take up my bag"; and the witness swore, that when he came up to take the bag, the prisoner proceeded two or three yard towards the boat; while Pat Nangle is carrying the bag before him, Michael Nangle comes up and stops him in his course and says, "Where is the lady, Mr. Kirwan?" and that is the first mention of the lady.

It came not, as you will observe, from the distracted, agonised husband, but from the boatman, who seems to have known what his duty was, on such an occasion. What is the reply? "She went away from me, in that direction, after the shower, and I have not seen her since." I believe he added, "I have been looking for her and I cannot find her." Accordingly, about eight o'clock, two hours after this lady set out to bathe, the search for her is begun by the prisoner and Michael Nangle, a time when Nangle said he should not allow his wife to be waiting for him, and when the night was very dark. The first search is fruitless.

You have it that Patrick Nangle, standing at the Ordnance stone near the boat, began to cry out, "Maria Kirwan"; and you have it sworn by Michael Nangle that he heard the cries at the Long Hole; and it was not too much to suppose, that if the prisoner was standing where Patrick Nangle was he would have heard the screams coming from the Long Hole. I have no desire, in this case, gentlemen, but for the cause of truth. If I am earnest in the prosecution of this case, I am so, first, because I feel it is my duty to be earnest in the discharge of my duty; and secondly because I know the prisoner has been ably defended.

Well, on their return from their ineffectual search, they were joined by Patrick Nangle who suggested that before entering the Long Hole the piece of high tableland called the Broad Patch should be carefully searched; and accordingly it was searched. In the course of the search, the prisoner walked close to the edge of the cliff; it is not for me to say whether it was by accident, or otherwise; but it appeared from the evidence that the very spot from which Nangle pulled back the prisoner was immediately over the place where the body was afterwards, found. I do not suppose that any one of you would attribute to the prisoner the intention of laying violent hands upon himself; but, be that as it may, we have it that shortly after they left the Broad Patch and went down to the Long Hole, into which the prisoner followed them.

There is, if I recollect rightly, a rock of considerable height in this hole, which divides the hole into two channels and has at the further extremity a rugged surface. Down one side of this hole, Kirwan and Michael Nangle went and the other was searched by Patrick Nangle. Patrick Nangle said that he found the body on the back, with a sheet under it, and that the bathing dress was drawn up under the arms, so as to leave the person of the deceased exposed.

We are now, coming, gentlemen, to a deeply important part of the case. The question, you have to consider, gentlemen, is whether this was accidental, a suicidal or a homicidal death. It is not suggested that this lady laid violent hands upon herself. I will dismiss that idea, therefore, from my consideration altogether; and now the question arises, whether upon all the facts and circumstances of the case, death was caused by accident, or by Mr. Kirwan. If the death was by criminal means, that criminality must involve him, and must amount, if it is not denied, to the crime of wilful murder; for it has not been suggested on behalf of the prisoner that there is any other person concerned; or that if he be guilty, he is fairly chargeable with anything less than the crime of murder.

As to the alleged crime, we can give no direct evidence; no mortal eye beheld the occurrence; and it is only from circumstantial evidence that you can arrive at a conclusion. Every minute fact, therefore, is of the last importance. Now, the first question is what brought the sheet under the body where it was found? That sheet ought to have been left high and dry for her use on coming out of the water. On either of the suppositions, that she died of drowning or epilepsy, this circumstance is inexplicable. My learned friend, in the course of his able address, challenged you or me to imagine a state of things criminatory of the prisoner and consistent with the evidence.

I accept the challenge; it is for you to judge of the probable inferences; and you are to judge of these probabilities as men acquainted with life and conversant with human affairs. Let us suppose, and for the present, it is only a supposition, that this man induced or allowed the deceased lady to bathe, meditating her death. At seven o'clock, while this lady was in the water, the tide was going out. And at that time, the water in the hole was 2 feet 9 inches deep, being one foot 9 inches over the rock, which was one foot high.

You will judge whether in water of the depth of 2 feet 9 inches, it was possible this young woman could have fallen victim to accidental drowning, and she an expert swimmer. Let us suppose her in this water, 2 feet 9 inches deep; let us suppose the prisoner coming into the hole with the sheet in his hand, after taking it from the place in which it was left, ready to put it over her head; let us suppose that she saw his dreadful purpose, can you not conceive and account then for the dreadful shrieks that were heard, when the horrid reality burst upon her mind, that on a desolate and lonely island, without a living soul but themselves upon it, he was coming into that Long Hole to perpetrate his dreadful offence? Would not the consequence have been the fearful shrieks heard and sworn to? If he succeeded in putting her under the water, notwithstanding her vain efforts to rise, struggling with all her energy against his greater strength, can you not imagine the fearful, agonising and fainter shrieks that women and men depose to having heard? That is not a mere imagination; it is a rational deduction from the evidence. It is for you to say, upon all the facts of the case, that that might have occurred; or whether the prisoner lost his wife without any fault of his own.

The matter must have occurred at seven o'clock at the end of the barrier formed by the rocks, beyond which she could not get without being lifted upon them.

I will now come to after nine o'clock. Pat Nangle swore that, as they were coming along, the time drawing late, the prisoner kept saying in an undertone, "Oh, Maria, oh Maria," and that on coming to where the body was, he immediately threw himself upon it and continued these exclamations. I can imagine grief making a man eloquent; but I cannot imagine intense grief venting itself only in such monotonous repetitions, as "Oh, Maria."

An attempt has been made to cast discredit on the evidence of Pat Nangle, who was acquainted with many of the facts connected with the occurrence, and to substitute that of Michael Nangle, who, by his own admission saw very little of the body until he assisted to carry it into the boat. This attempt, I will show you hereafter to be ineffectual.

I need scarcely call to your recollection the strange fact, respecting the finding of the clothes by Nangle on the rock, after he had searched in the same place and had come back and told the prisoner he could not find them, and after the prisoner went up to the place. How the clothes came there, it is for you, men of the world, to judge and decide. It was to say the least of it, passing strange, that if the deceased left the prisoner, as he stated after six o'clock, and that he did not see her after, he could notwithstanding be able to find the clothes in a few minutes, in the spot he pointed to, and where Nangle, who knew the island so well, could not, on his first search, find them.

There is an alleged discrepancy between the Nangles, with respect of the sheet; but it is reconciled with this fact: that Kirwan brought down the chemise with the shawl in his hand from the rock. It is a remarkable fact that the chemise is not forthcoming; at least it was not found in the bundle of the clothes brought down; and whether that article might not answer to the "something white" said to have been in the prisoner's hand is for you to say.

The next fact to which I will call your attention is, that when the body was brought to Mrs. Campbell's house, the prisoner ordered it to be washed and laid out; and when Catherine McGarr spoke to him about police interfering to prevent the body from being washed, he, a gentleman of station and education, is sworn to have said "I don't care a damn for the police, the body must be washed." He insisted on this being done, although it was his duty to have afforded every facility to the investigation he knew was about to take place; and therefore, that every minute circumstance as to how the body was found, and every circumstance connected with it was most important for the ends of justice.

He could not shelter himself behind the plea of ignorance, as to this, for the woman had reminded him of the coming investigation. The women who washed the body have told of the lividity on one side, and of the scratches on the face and right cheek. They were not, as Mr. Davis said, likely to be caused by the crabs that have been so eloquently spoken of; for they were scratches. You will ask yourselves, gentlemen, whether, or not, these scratches have any reference to the time when this horrible sheet was about to be put on the face of the deceased; whether, at that awful time she might have put up her hands to try to remove the sheet and in endeavouring to do so, tore herself in the manner described.

Another proof or argument against the supposition that death was occasioned by epilepsy or accidental drowning, is the fact that the bathing cap of the deceased was not on her head, but found in five or six days after her death at high watermark, with the strings tied. Might not that cap have been torn off her head in the struggle that took place before the sheet was put on her face?

I may remind you a gentleman, second to none in this city, in skill, experience and talent, has sworn that in the whole course of his experience he never knew of a case from accidental drowning or from epilepsy in the water, in which there was bleeding from the ears and other parts.

And yet in the face of all these facts, and of this evidence, you are called to come to the conclusion that Mrs. Kirwan's death was accidental or resulted from epilepsy? Bring the whole conduct and demeanour of the prisoner before you, together with all the facts and circumstances of the case and ask yourselves what conclusion would you have come to without the aid of medical testimony. After you have done this, then call into consideration the evidence of Mr. Adams, who said he never knew the bleeding described as having occurred in a case of accidental drowning and I am sure you will come to a fair and just conclusion.

I have now, gentlemen, gone through all the parts of the case with more zeal, Mr. Butt thinks, than is consistent with my position as a Crown prosecutor. If so, I ask you not to let the prisoner be prejudiced by my zeal. Consider all the facts; combine and compare them; bring your knowledge of human nature and human affairs to them, and try, if you can, in Heaven's name to come to the conclusion that the prisoner is not guilty of the crime laid to his charge. In the name of justice, come if you can, to that conclusion. I call upon you moreover, if you have reasonable doubt of the prisoner's guilt, give him the benefit of it, although my learned friend Mr. Butt would spurn such an acquittal, and in God's name, open his prison doors and let him go free.

But, on the other hand, after bringing your calm and sober judgement to bear on this all-important case, if, after carefully considering every circumstance and fact, you are forced to the conviction, without a rational doubt, for there are doubts which may be suggested by a cowardly mind to a wicked heart and which ought to have no place in your jury box. If, without a rational doubt, you are conscientiously convinced that this woman came by her death by the hands of him who ought to have been her protector, come well or ill, come weal or woe, it is your duty, painful though it be, to bring in the dreadful verdict of guilty and leave the rest to God.

—◦—

The adversarial court game was now over. There were two more phases for the criminal trial to go through: the judge's charge to the jury and the jury's verdict. Before that the addresses by the opposing counsel would have been ringing in the ears of the jury. The prisoner had maintained his composure throughout the proceedings, there was little in his general demeanour to tell the observers what had been going through his mind. If he had been beset by nerves or suffered from the intense pressure for being tried for a capital crime, there was no obvious sign.

The opposing counsel, Mr. Butt and Mr. Hayes, had of course by the exigencies of making their respective addresses to the jury, shown their cards to the court. Their styles of examination and cross-examination had been followed through in the speeches. It was no easy task for either to address and take command of the volume of evidence and express it in their obviously different interpretations. The objective was to convince the jury that the evidence elicited would lead to the conclusion that the prisoner at the bar was either guilty or innocent of the charge.

By the fact that there was no witness to the event, that evidence would rely on the circumstances of the tragedy, for whatever the outcome no other word would describe it. A strong, beautiful and young woman had lost her life and all of the life expectation and her husband, if convicted, would suffer the same fate.

Both counsel had urged the jury to put the moral character of the prisoner out of the equation when making their decision, as they rightly should. On the other hand, this was easier said than done, as this element was a major role in the motive for the alleged crime, if, as Mr. Butt remarked, there had been a crime at all. While adultery had no place in the criminal code, not for the first time the eternal triangle was capable of providing an incentive for the commission of crime. Otherwise, there was no rational reason for the accused, if he did so, to get rid of his wife.

Mr. Butt, wisely avoided confronting the issue of the evidence of Mrs. Campbell about the row in her lodging house in which the accused had threatened his wife's life and apparently subjected her to violence. What could be the possible explanation for this behaviour? The answer to this must have been connected to the prosecution's contention in regard to the motive. Mr. Hayes placed special attention on this incident, compensating for the curious lack of evidence on the timing of the alleged knowledge on behalf of the wife about the existence of the mistress and her children. A matter of months, Mr. Smyly claimed in his opening speech, but where was the evidence for that?

But if that knowledge had been long established then what could have prompted the relatively recent nasty confrontation? The absence of evidence from Teresa Kenny, who simply did not turn up, and the nature of a visit to her abode by a certain lady must have impressed the jury in some fashion that might not have been of such advantage to the defence as was imagined. Why the substance of that undoubted confrontation was ignored or suppressed, denying the jury a crucial piece of evidence, would remain a mystery.

There were some patent absurdities in Mr. Butt's address to the members of the true and good twelve men. Such as the suggestion that the cries heard by the witnesses on the mainland and Larkin on the fishing vessel were those of either Kirwan in his search and/or he and the boatmen in their efforts to find the wife. The timing was completely at odds with the evidence given. The defence counsel went further on this subject when he described the geography of the island and maintained that as a result of its nature that cries could have been heard at Howth but not at the point where his client said he was at the time, less than half a mile from the Long Hole.

There was another strange contradiction. Mr. Butt found Dr. Hatchell's medical evidence perfectly satisfactory while Mr. Hayes admitted that it was wanting and not what the prosecution expected. Mr. Butt, for his own reason and bias admittedly, was in fact, although he might not have wished it, closer to the mark. The truth was that a man of undoubted professional skill simply did not perform up to expectation in the witness box. But Mr. Butt somewhat diluted his point by attacking the integrity of the witness by claiming that the fact Dr. Hatchell visited the scene of the crime was evidence that he had been tutored by his master Major Brownrigg, head of the investigation.

Mr. Hayes refuted this attack, justifiably, but unaware of course that within three decades such practice would be promoted by the great French Professor Alexandre Lacassagne and his colleague Dr. Edmund Locard in Lyons and set for all time the basic standards of crime-scene investigation. Nonetheless, the fact was, as the jury would be well aware, the medical aspects of the case would be paramount in the result.

What the jury did not know was that the prosecution did not employ the services of a medical witness who was available and who could have assessed the appearances of the body of the deceased beyond any reasonable doubt. Why the evidence of this brilliant physician and medico-legal expert was not employed was another mystery of this extraordinary case. But more on that subject later.

While it would be almost impossible to assess the impact of the opposing counsel's speeches on the jury, it could be posited, on the basis of the respective content and in particular the delivery, which one attained an edge. Mr. Butt relied somewhat more on rhetoric, while Mr. Hayes on a sober assessment of the facts and circumstances presented. Both were extremely eloquent in delivery. But could it be that eloquence would win out over the sober presentation of fact?

If there was an edge to be had, it was not founded on delivery but more so on the medical facts of the appearances on the body. The scratches on the face and breast and the lividity on the right side could be subject to any biased conjecture to suit opposing opinion in relation to the circumstance that led to the death. However, Mr. Butt's reliance on the crabs to explain the scratches on the basis of the evidence of the incompetent coroner Davis and the medical student Hamilton, who admitted the shortcomings of his examination in evidence at trial, was weak to say the least of it. And, in actual fact, the lividity provided no evidence at all as to the position the body had been in at the point of death, as it is a result of the natural pooling of blood from gravitation and can shift its location on the body during the first six hours after death if the body is moved. In this case, it was moved before medical examination, being transported wrapped in a sail in a boat and later carried in a dray.

The most important evidence in the medical appearances was the bleeding from the ears and the vagina. In that regard, Mr. Hayes scored his most effective point when eliciting from the defence witness Dr. Adams that he in his long experience had not seen such signs from accidental drowning, from whatever preceding cause. Or from a fit of epilepsy.

All those facts and circumstances had been presented to the jury. All the members had to wait for before arriving at their decision was the charge by Judge Crampton which would concentrate on the legal aspects of the evidence presented to the court.

Mr. Justice Crampton's Charge to the Jury

Gentlemen of the jury, the prisoner at the bar, William Burke Kirwan, stands indicted before you of the wilful murder of Maria Louisa Kirwan, his wife. I can well re-echo the sentiment uttered by the learned and able counsel, who addressed you with so much eloquence and zeal for their respective clients, that it is impossible to exaggerate the importance of the case now before you, and the solemn duty which devolves upon you. You are now called on, upon the evidence which you have heard, to decide upon the guilt or innocence of the prisoner at the bar.

I will, therefore, take it for granted that you will do what both the counsel called on you to do, namely, to discharge from your minds, as far as possible, all remembrance of anything that you may have heard out of court upon the subject of this case, to put away all prejudice, and to give your verdict solely upon the evidence that has been lain before you on the part of the Crown and the defence.

Gentlemen, the charge is one, undoubtedly, of great enormity. The offence, at all times, is classed with those most heinous in the catalogue of our legal crimes; but in the case of a man, having violently and feloniously deprived of life the partner of his affections, the enormity is greatly increased.

When I mention this circumstance, I do it for the purpose of calling on you to give your most earnest, you most anxious, your most cautious consideration to the evidence that has been laid before you, and to the deductions and inferences which you are called upon to make from that evidence. It is the duty of every jury sworn to find truly between the Crown and the subject, upon every occasion, even the most petty; but it is emphatically the duty of a jury empanelled to try a case of such magnitude and importance as the present case.

A young Maria Kirwan sketched by her husband with the cool eye of an artist
(Courtesy NLI)

Teresa Kenny and child waving goodbye to Kirwan as he returned to his wife?
(Courtesy NLI)

Untitled. Apparently a grieving Teresa Kenny and child, captured beautifully and emotively *(Courtesy NLI)*

Kirwan's fine representation of the Martello tower and landing place on Ireland's Eye
(Courtesy NLI)

Isaac Butt in 1849, Chief Counsel for the
Prisoner, founder of the Home
Rule Movement

Dr Robert Adams, medical witness for the
defence, fellow of the Royal College
of Surgeons

Highly romanticised sketch of the Long Hole (Sir Cusack Patrick Roney, 1874),
with the "elevated rock" behind the ladies

Howth Harbour and Ireland's Eye (Richard Lovett, 1888), Lambay Island in the background

Howth Harbour and Ireland's Eye, present day

Kirwan's island prison: Spike Island today with its 6-bastioned fort

Spike Island: Fort Westmoreland (now Fort Mitchell) from which patriot John Mitchell was transported in 1848, first to Bermuda and then to Van Diemen's Land

Prison block, Spike Island

Distant view from Spike Island: Cobh (formerly Queenstown), 1870, last port of call for the Atlantic crossing (including that of the *Titanic*); Kirwan sailed to America in 1879

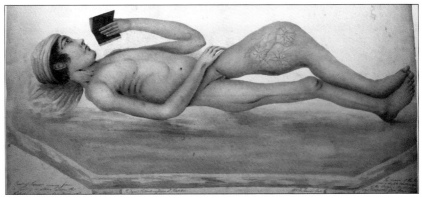

P. Fagan, Jervis St Hospital, under the care of Surgeon Wallace: large swelling on left leg
and a heart condition; two quarts of coloured water removed from the interior of his body

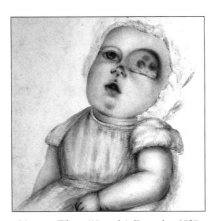

Margaret Tibery (10 weeks); December 1838

Margaret Tibery (4 months, 2 weeks);
February 1839

Kitty Stapleton (12): lesion of the mouth

Margaret Kells (8): Meath Hospital;
skin disease; 1845

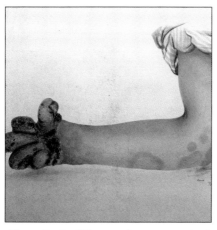

Thomas Keating (12): apparently a gangrenous hand

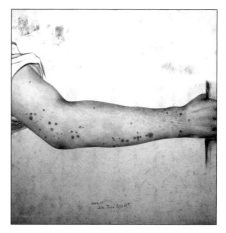

John Price (67): skin disease.

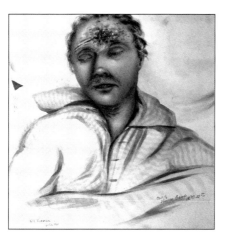

Thomas Eames (55): skin disease

Dissection of a joint with faded clinical notes

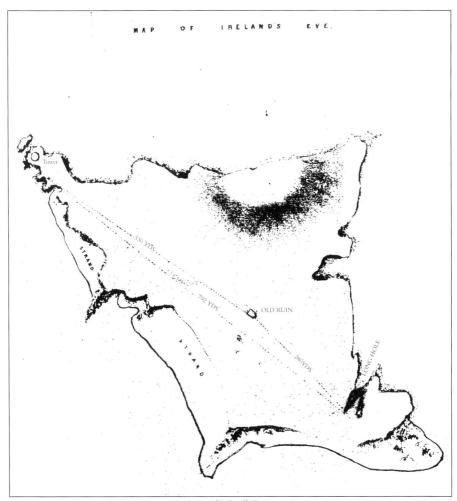

Map of Ireland's Eye

Gentlemen of the jury, you have been apprised that in this case there is no direct positive testimony against the prisoner. There is no person who has seen, who has witnessed the mode in which the unfortunate deceased met with her death. The mantle of mystery is spread over that subject; and, gentlemen, you are called upon to exercise your judgement on what is called circumstantial evidence, that is facts and circumstances, bearing directly on the question that you have to try, namely, the guilt or innocence of the prisoner, from which you are called upon, naturally and I may say necessarily to infer, on the one hand, guilt, and on the other hand, innocence.

If, gentlemen, in such a case of circumstantial evidence, you cannot in your consciences reconcile the innocence of the prisoner with the facts that are laid before you, and the circumstances relied upon in the evidence against him, it will be your bounden duty, upon that circumstantial evidence, to find the prisoner guilty.

If, on the other hand, gentlemen, you can reconcile the facts and circumstances that are relied upon, as affording a chain of evidence against the accused with his innocence, you are bound to find him not guilty. And I only re-echo the sentiment of the learned counsel on both sides, when I tell you this: that if you are not able, honestly and fairly, to arrive at a conclusion in your own minds, on the evidence, as to the prisoner being guilty; if your minds are in a state of honest doubt on the subject, gentlemen, it will be your duty also to find a verdict of acquittal.

Gentlemen, the material date to which you have to fix your attention, on this occasion, is the 6th of September, 1852. Circumstances there are, preceding that date, which are relied upon by the Crown, and circumstances there are immediately following it which have been made the subject of your consideration. The circumstances preceding and following the body of the deceased, and the declarations of the prisoner at that period, are of the greatest importance for you to dwell upon.

The evidence before the 6th of September had not a necessary connexion with either the guilt or innocence of the accused. You have heard a good deal with respect to the character and immoral habits in which it appeared the prisoner indulged previous to the 6th of September. There is no necessary connexion between the character and conduct of the prisoner previous to that date, with perhaps one exception, and his liability to the charge which is the subject of this indictment. They may furnish you with a motive, unquestionably; but you will recollect how difficult it is to connect a single motive with the subsequent act. I do not wish to dwell on the earlier part of the case, and I bring you at once to the 6th of September.

On the 6th of September, I will say about the hour of nine o'clock in the evening, the deceased, Mrs. Kirwan, was found lying dead upon a little rock, in the place called the Long Hole at Ireland's Eye, her head hanging down at one side of the rock and her feet in a pool of water at the foot of it. She had a bathing shift and bathing boots on her, but there is some conflict in the evidence as to whether she was lying on a sheet or not. One witness positively deposes that it was partly under her; another witness differs from him as to this circumstance; and these are two witnesses of very great importance: the two boatmen of the same name.

Gentlemen of the jury, your great inquiry will be: what was the cause of death? There are some indisputable facts in the case to which, before I enter more on the evidence, I would wish to call your attention, as a guide through those parts of the evidence which are more perplexed. It appears that Mr. and Mrs. Kirwan came, in the month of June, to lodge in the house of Mrs. Campbell. The period of their engagement as lodgers there was to expire, I think, on the 7th of September, that day after the occurrence.

Mr. Butt: That is only statement, my lord; there is no evidence of it.

Judge Crampton: Very well. It appears that the prisoner and his wife lodged at the house of Mrs. Campbell; there was a passage between their room and the kitchen; and Mrs. Campbell lived at the rear of their room. It appears from her evidence that language of a very threatening character was used by the prisoner to his wife, one evening at the end of June or the beginning of July, which would lead to the conclusion that they were not living on very happy terms as man and wife. The language was not only that of unkindness, but was of a threatening nature. It might be only the language of passion, but it was evidence of treatment unbecoming any man, but especially a husband.

Mrs. Campbell states that during the first month there was disagreement between them, but she was not aware of any other subsequently; that there were some words, but not enough to lead to a disagreement, and after the first month they lived as happily as any man and wife. All this will be for your consideration. That the prisoner did not entertain a single and entire devotion of heart and affection to his wife is beyond all doubt. How far that circumstance is material for your consideration, is for you to say.

It appears that Mr. Kirwan was an artist and was fond of sketching and Mrs. Kirwan, who was an extremely healthy and strong young woman, about twenty-eight or twenty-nine years of age, was extremely fond of bathing, and was in the habit of bathing at the ladies' bathing place at Howth; and it appears on three occasions before the 6th of September, she accompanied her husband to Ireland's Eye. He occupied himself sketching, and she in bathing and walking. On the 5th of September both Mr. and Mrs. Kirwan engaged with a boatman to bring them over to the island, the following day.

They went over, accordingly, on the morning of the 6th; and Mrs. Kirwan was last seen alive when the boat was leaving the island that evening with Mr. Brew and his party. It is uncontroverted that after four o'clock no persons remained on the island, up to the return of the boat at eight o'clock, except Mrs. Kirwan and Mr. Kirwan; and it further appears from the deposition of Mr. Kirwan, made at the coroner's inquest, she went to bathe at six o'clock. She was a good swimmer and had bathed before in the morning; and according to Mr. Kirwan's statement, she determined to bathe again at six o'clock. The sun [began to set] set on the 6th of September at 36 minutes past six o'clock, so that it was not long before sunset when she went to bathe, according to that evidence.

I have now recapitulated nearly all the uncontroverted facts in the case. Another fact has been relied upon by both sides, namely, that she took a bathing cap with her; and a bathing cap, which no doubt you will conclude was hers, was found on the island a week afterwards at high watermark.

The next evidence to which I will call your attention, is the appearances on the body of the deceased lady. There were external injuries, undoubtedly, on her frame; but none of them appears to have been, on the full medical testimony that you have had, of a serious character. None of them could have been the cause of her death. She was found with those appearances on her, and after the lapse of an hour, was brought over to Howth in a boat; she was conveyed to the house of Mrs. Campbell where she was washed and laid out; and on the next day the inquest was held, at which Mr. Kirwan as well as other witnesses were examined.

I may as well, perhaps, at this moment, refer to the evidence of the medical gentlemen who have been examined. Some of them have been treated, perhaps, with a little harshness by learned counsel; but zeal on the part of a counsel in the discharge of his duty is only natural, and it is on the whole laudable. Harshness has been especially used towards Dr. Hatchell, a respectable physician, whose evidence, I must say, was in the main essentially the same as that of those eminent men, Dr. Rynd and Dr. Adams. The evidence of all the medical men is substantially this: that the cause of death could not have been from any external injuries.

I put the case of suicide on the part of the lady, as has been done by a learned counsel, out of the way. The question you have to try simply is was this accidental death, or was it designed by a felonious hand, I think I may say by the hand of the prisoner at the bar, because there was no other person on the island by whom it could have been effected. The evidence of all the medical gentlemen concurs in this, that there was no external cause of violence that could have accomplished it. When I say "violence", I do not mean of course to include under that term the process of destruction which the very learned and able counsel for the Crown has suggested in reply, namely, applying a wet cloth or sheet forcibly to the mouth or nose, a mode of destruction, which would, according to all the doctors, leave, undoubtedly, no external marks different from those that would be produced by either suffocation or drowning.

They were of the opinion that no violence by imperfect external pressure was the cause of death; and with the exception of Mr. Hamilton, the medical student who made but a very superficial examination of the body, not suspecting anything at the time, all the medical gentlemen, Doctors Hatchell, Rynd and Adams are agreed that the symptoms and appearances of external and internal injuries would all be consistent with a person being drowned either by simple drowning, or by what we might call forcible immersion, being kept under the water. Dr. Hatchell went a little further than the other two in stating that his conception was that the appearances of congestion would be to a greater extent developed where the drowning was forcible, than they would be where it was merely simple drowning.

Dr. Adams was decidedly of the opinion that from the appearances that were suggested to him, no conclusion could be arrived at as to whether death had been by forcible means or by simple drowning.

Therefore, on the subject of the cause of death, you are left even by the doctors in a great state of uncertainty and mystery. The learned counsel for the prisoner has challenged the learned counsel for the Crown to suggest a mode of death, administered by an unfriendly hand, which could account for all those appearances; and the learned counsel for the Crown has in reply suggested that possibly the prisoner might have used a wet sheet, and while the lady was in the water, might have forcibly pressed it upon her mouth and nostrils; and that all the circumstances and appearances of the body, externally and internally, might be accounted for in that way.

According to the evidence of the doctors, there is hardly anything to be accounted for, if the drowning were taken into consideration, except some of the external appearances: those upon the eyelids, temples, cheeks and breast. The prisoner's counsel accounted for these by supposing they were the bites of crabs; and on the other hand it was suggested that there might have been a violent struggle, in which some of those scratches and injuries might have been received. There may have been precipitation from a height. All these circumstances are for your consideration.

You cannot find any man guilty of the most trivial crime upon suspicion or conjecture; your verdict should be found, on a firm, stable basis; and that should be either direct testimony which you believe and cannot reconcile with the innocence of the prisoner.

I now revert to the evidence relative to the conduct of the prisoner, on the 6th of September, and which was relied on as proof of hatred and hostility on his part towards the late Mrs. Kirwan and of his pre-determination to kill her. You have the evidence relative to his conduct in company with the Nangles on the island on the night; and you will have to consider and determine whether the exclamations, sworn to have been made by the prisoner, were occasioned by genuine sorrow or they were merely effected for the sake of appearances.

There is a discrepancy in the evidence of Pat and Michael Nangle in relation to the finding of Mrs. Kirwan's clothes. Michael Nangle swore that after Mr. Kirwan came down from the rock on which the clothes were found, he had in his hand a shawl and something white. Whether it might have been a chemise or a sheet was not mentioned. It was remarked by counsel that no chemise was found in the bundle of the deceased's clothes brought to Mrs. Campbell's. I may state here that there was no stain of blood or dirt on the clothes that were brought down. Pat Nangle said he did not see the shawl until the boat was rowed to the Long Hole for the body, and that he saw it there for the first time, wrapped round the deceased. Michael Nangle stated that Mr. Kirwan brought something white with the shawl from the rock where the clothes were, and that they wrapped them around the body. It will be for you to consider and decide among yourselves as to which of the witnesses was in error. I do not think that there was any desire on their part to state anything unfairly. It was very dark at the time, and it was possible that the shawl might not have attracted Pat Nangle's attention. It is clearly proved, with respect to the clothes, that they were on the rock, and that the prisoner desired Pat Nangle to go and look for them. He did so, but could not find them. The prisoner then went up himself and came back in a few minutes, when he told Nangle to go again and he would find them. Nangle did so, and said he found them in a place that he had previously searched.

It has been suggested by the learned counsel for the prisoner that the cries deposed to by Larkin may have been the cries of the Nangles, when on the island, looking for the deceased. You will take that matter into your consideration, and see if it is borne out by the evidence upon the subject. It is an important circumstance to have regard to, that the cries of the boatmen might have been more numerous than the screams.

It was also remarked by the counsel for the prisoner that no allusion was made at the inquest to the appearance of blood on the face or about the sheet by Patrick Nangle. But the evidence given, in such a court as this, is generally more detailed and protracted than that given at a coroner's inquest.

Mr. Davis, the coroner, swore that he read over the depositions to the witnesses, and asked them if they had anything to add; but it is of importance to recollect that Nangle said he was stopped by Mr. Kirwan when he was going to speak about the sheet; this, in some degree, was corroborated by the coroner, who said that Mr. Kirwan did interfere with one of the Nangles. The strength and force of the evidence in a case like the present does not, however, depend on a single point or link, but upon a general connexion of the entire; it derives its force from its continuity.

I now come to the most important portion of the case. I allude to the cries that were sworn to have been heard coming from the island. It was admitted, on all sides, the cries of some voice were heard coming from

Ireland's Eye, a little after seven o'clock, on the evening of the 6th of September. Larkin who was in the boat, to the westward of the island, swore that he heard a very loud scream. If the screams were heard by him, and that they came from the Long Hole, they must have come across the entire island and consequently must have been heard by Mr. Kirwan.

Larkin said the first scream was very loud; he heard a second scream, which was lower, and a third, still fainter; they were, he said more like cries of distress than calls for a boat. The credit of the witnesses, who said they heard the cries on the mainland, was unimpeached, and they all fixed the time they were heard about seven o'clock. It will be for you to say if the screams came from the Long Hole, and, if they did, they undoubtedly came from the deceased lady. Were they the cries of a drowning person requiring help, or of a person suffering from violence? What caused them? Undoubtedly, pressing and imminent danger of some kind.

Were they the screams of someone seized with epilepsy; or were they caused by pain or fear, occasioned by another person? These are questions which you will do well to consider carefully, and see how they are to be answered or explained by the evidence. The general effect of the medical testimony is that the appearances presented internally, might have resulted from simple drowning, combined with epilepsy, or from forced immersion; you will consider whether the cries deposed to were consistent with an attack of epilepsy to a person bathing. You will also consider if this lady, an experienced bather and expert swimmer, while in the water, or perhaps I may say out of it, was seized with a fit of epilepsy so suddenly that she fell on the rock called the Body Rock, and there remained.

It was after six o'clock in the evening at that time when there was only one foot 9 inches of water over the rock; and was she swimming in that depth, and if so was she, while in that position, seized with epilepsy, and did she then give the screams described? As to the bathing sheet, it is not to be supposed she placed it on the rock where she was found with it, as the rock was then covered in water. How came she on the rock? You will consider whether it was possible or probable that the tide water threw her on it. Again had she ever had a fit of epilepsy in her life? If she had fallen over the rock where Mr. Kirwan was near falling, when Nangle pulled him back, and that she fell on the spot where she was found, there would have been bruises on her body.

Let me implore you not to confound suspicion with evidence. If you cannot account for these facts and circumstances which I have called to your attention, if you cannot reconcile them with the prisoner's innocence, you cannot go beside them. If you cannot satisfy yourselves that Mrs. Kirwan's death was the result of violence by any other person, you must give the prisoner the benefit of any rational, well-founded doubt you may entertain, and acquit him.

I have exhausted, I believe, all the material facts of the case. I now conclude, by imploring you again to recollect the solemn duty you are called on to discharge. Life and death, and the honour and reputation of a man in a respectable walk of life, are hanging on your verdict. You are under a solemn obligation, the obligation of an oath taken before this court, and in the sight of God, to find a true verdict according to the evidence. Give then, the utmost, the most anxious, the most painful consideration, to all the facts and circumstances of this extraordinary case. And, gentlemen, find such a verdict that will be satisfactory to your own consciences, consistent with the solemn oath you have taken, and with the demands of justice.

◄○►

That Mr. Justice Crampton gave a fair and just assessment of the evidence in the case must have been evident to all the observers and professionals involved. In fact, it leaned more in the favour of the prisoner than anyone present could have expected. He impressed again and again that if there was any rational doubt in the jury's minds the accused should be acquitted. In relation to the medical evidence, which was of vital import to the outcome, his charge was hugely to the benefit of the defence.

He relied on Dr. Adams' final statement that no conclusion could be arrived at as to whether death had been of forcible means or by simple drowning. Therefore the judge stated that, on the subject of the cause of death, the jury were left even by the doctors, in a great state of uncertainty and mystery. This was not strictly true as during Mr. Hayes' cross-examination of Dr. Adams he had put to him two vital questions which contradicted the medical man's conclusion.

The passage was as follows:

Mr. Hayes: Have you ever known a case of accidental drowning where bleeding of the vagina and ears were produced?

Dr. Adams: I cannot bring any such to memory.

Mr. Hayes: Have you ever known of a case where a death from epilepsy was accompanied by either of these things?

Dr. Adams: I have never known such case to occur, during my experience, nor have I read of such.

Therefore there was no such mystery as alluded by the judge in his charge as to the import of the medical evidence. Dr. Adams' evidence corroborated Dr. Hatchell's post-mortem findings by the answers to the prosecuting counsel's examination. For what possible reason the judge missed this point there could be no explanation offered other than the pressure of his charge at the time or the inadequacy of his note-taking. The pressure, if that is what it was, would manifest itself in a more detrimental effect to the case in a short time.

◄○►

It had been a long and exhausting day of proceedings, the court having sat nine hours earlier.

The jury at seven o'clock retired to their room, and the judges left the bench. At twenty minutes before eight o'clock the judges resumed their seats and Mr. Justice Crampton directed the sheriff to summon the jury. Mr. Justice Crampton, addressing the foreman, asked him if they were likely to agree. It had been an incredibly short time passed in deliberation, for the judges to be already seeking any reaction from the jury.

Foreman: I don't think we are likely to agree.

Juror: There is not the most remote chance of our agreeing.

Another juror: There is not the slightest chance of an agreement.

Mr. Justice Crampton: It will be necessary for you, in that case, gentlemen, to remain in your room during the night.

The foreman enquired what would be the latest hour at which His Lordship would receive a verdict, in the event of an agreement. Mr. Justice Crampton, after a brief conversation with some of the jury, said that he would return to court at eleven o'clock for the purpose of ascertaining if they had come to an agreement.

The jury then retired and the court adjourned.

The clock in Green Street Court made its progress, slowly and incrementally, towards that hour. The prisoner at the bar had been removed to his cell, the judges had left the courthouse in search of dinner, the spectators to the nearest hostelries and the reporters stayed sharpening their pens and consulting their notes. The special constables stood guard outside the jury room as the twelve men deliberated on the evidence presented to them. All would ruminate and speculate about the outcome but none would know for sure what verdict awaited.

—◁○▷—

In a lonely grave in Glasnevin Cemetery the reinterred and dissected remains of Maria Louisa Kirwan lay, unconscious to the drama that was being enacted. But, nonetheless, in the midst of that darkness, desiring of the justice which should be done for her. For despite all that had occurred, her demise, her voice, now dulled and inanimate, cried for a proper answer. The victim, if that was what she was, deserved no less. In spite of everything, the dead scream from the grave.

During the process of a criminal trial, particularly of a capital nature, the victim is a mere concept, referred to as "the deceased", "the unfortunate lady", who had managed by some strange circumstance to lose her life. She is described in evidence like some sort of dead meat, a lifeless entity, the cause of whose death is subjected to endless interpretation by people who never knew her in any shape or form – other than the pathologist, who in doing his duty became acquainted with her outer and inner organs in a manner, of necessity dealing with the same dead meat.

Her character, by virtue of this objective proceeding, was not given any importance, while that of the prisoner was acceded every weight. Was she a good woman of true and unstained behaviour and constant in the conduct of her life? Nothing but nothing of this is the concern of the court. In fact, the opposite. The defence assign to her a medical condition of which there is absolutely no proof offered in her history: of epilepsy none, of fits none, of an experienced swimmer entering the water with a full stomach, even less.

A further stain is cast on her character by the defence by suggesting that she knew all along of the long-standing liaison between her husband and his mistress and not only forgave him but was reconciled to that totally ludicrous situation.

But the life of her perfidious husband, now charged with her murder, assumed an all-important position in the order of human and legal affairs. The demands of justice for him, as the judge in his charge emphasised, was paramount.

But the charge and plea of Mr. Justice Crampton was now out of the equation. Unless he unfairly intervened, the jury would be the arbiter of the fate of the accused.

—◦—

Mr. Justice Crampton returned to court at eleven o'clock, to ascertain whether the jury had agreed. His Lordship having taken his seat, the jury were called out, and the prisoner was placed at the bar.

The foreman, in reply to an inquiry from the judge, as to whether they had agreed, stated that they had not.

Mr. Justice Crampton: Are you likely to agree?

Foreman: Upon my word, My Lord, I don't think we are.

Mr. Justice Crampton: Is there any use in my remaining, in expectation of you agreeing?

Foreman: I don't know, My Lord; I cannot say; but I will take an opinion of the jury again.

Another juror then said he did not think there was any likelihood of their agreeing.

Mr. Justice Crampton: If I thought you would agree to a verdict within any reasonable time, I would think it my duty to remain; but if you are not likely to agree, all I can do is let you remain together for the night, and adjourn the court until tomorrow. Consult together for some time and let me know if you can agree.

The jury having conferred for a few minutes, the foreman stated that there was not any likelihood of their agreeing, and that they had not made any progress towards an agreement.

A juror asked if His Lordship could take the verdict at nine o'clock in the morning.

Mr. Justice Crampton: If you are agreed to a verdict at that hour, I will come down to court; but if you have no question to ask now upon the evidence, you had better retire, as I can be of no assistance to you. I hope you have your great coats.

A juror said they wanted chairs; they had only two forms in their room, and some of them had to walk about while others sat. The judge directed the sheriff to provide every accommodation for the jury, except refreshment, which the law did not allow.

Foreman: There are several of the jury who would wish to hear the testimony of Surgeon Adams again, if possible.

Mr. Justice Crampton: I wish I had known this earlier, for unluckily I have left my book of written evidence behind me; and the gentleman in question is, I suppose, now fast asleep. If, however, there is any particular part of the evidence, which any gentleman would like to hear, I will direct my attention towards it. I think I will be able to satisfy him, for my recollection upon the subject of his testimony is quite clear; and I believe counsel on both sides are present, who will correct me if I err in my rendering thereof.

Foreman: The jury, My Lord, wish to know what Dr. Adams' opinion was as to what the appearances on the body were attributable to.

Mr. Justice Crampton: With respect to that, and I think I put it distinctly to you, it was to this effect: the congestion in the lungs, and in the other parts, that were the subject of evidence, might have arisen from simple drowning, of from drowning caused by forcible immersion, or from force in other ways. Those symptoms might have been caused by simple drowning, and they might have been the result of forcible drowning.

A juror: Then those appearances might have been the result of simple drowning?

Mr. Justice Crampton: They might.

Foreman: The jury wish to know Your Lordship's opinion as to how far they may attach importance to that evidence.

Mr. Justice Crampton: The testimony of Surgeon Adams is exactly the same as Dr. Rynd's and substantially the same as that of Dr. Hatchell, and was to the effect that the appearances of the body might result from simple drowning, under peculiar circumstances, or might be the result of strangulation or of suffocation. Neither of these gentlemen [*i.e. Adams and Rynd*], however, saw the body. May I wait now, gentlemen?

Juror: If your lordship would be kind enough to wait for five minutes more.

At the expiration of that period, the foreman came forward and said that there was a likelihood of their agreeing, and requested a few minutes more on the part of the jury, to consider the matter.

Mr. Justice Crampton: Very well, gentlemen, you had better retire to your room.

The jury returned after about fifteen minutes into the court, the foreman bearing in his hand the issue.

The names of the jury having been called over, the Clerk of the Crown asked:

Gentlemen, have you agreed to your verdict?

Foreman: Yes.

Clerk of the Crown: How say you, gentlemen? Is the prisoner, William Kirwan, guilty or not?

Foreman: Guilty.

Clerk of the Crown: You say he is guilty.

The court then adjourned until the morning.

◄○►

The fate of William Burke Kirwan had been decided after a two-day trial and upwards of four hours of deliberation by the jury. It was interesting, to say the least, and in a way predictable that their one request was to hear again the evidence provided by the defence medical witness Dr. Adams, for it was he, ironically, who confirmed the fact, played down by Mr. Justice Crampton that neither accidental drowning nor epilepsy could have produced the bleeding from the ears noted on the victim's body.

It also appeared that the jury's decision, in concert with the circumstances of the event, had at the end of the day relied on the medical appearances on the body. Dr. Hatchell's post-mortem examination had been vindicated despite the weakness of his performance in the witness box. It was, however, somewhat unfortunate that, for whatever reason Mr. Justice Crampton had left his notes of evidence at home at the most important juncture of the trial.

It also seemed somewhat strange that he had enquired of an agreement from the jury after such a small period of recess. It had been a long and tension-filled day, but the jury had been forewarned by the judge in his charge of the solemnity of their duty, so there was no justification to rush their judgement. Mr. Justice Crampton had also reminded them that if they were to deliberate all night, they would, by law, not be allowed any refreshment, a daunting prospect in a room that by one juror's account contained only two benches.

It obviously was not an environment conducive to the comfort of a jury who were faced with bringing in a verdict that might lead to the destruction, by hanging, of the accused. That is not to say the jury were unduly influenced by the paucity of their resources, although it left open to the supporters of the prisoner the claim that this might be so.

The jury had been given the benefit of the best prosecution and defence counsel of the day and a highly experienced and fair judge to assist their assessment of the evidence presented. Also top-class medical witnesses, bar one. Any omission on the part of any of those parties could not be laid fairly at the door of the jury, no member of which would harbour any bias in reaching a decision regarding the guilt or innocence of the accused.

Their decision had been made and William Burke Kirwan, in his cell, awaited the inevitable sentence for the murder of his wife.

CHAPTER 6

THE TRIAL: THIRD DAY

Friday, December 10th, 1852

At half past ten o'clock the judges took their seats on the bench, when the Clerk of the Crown directed the county gaoler to put forward William Burke Kirwan. After a lapse of a few seconds, Kirwan made his appearance and at once advanced to the front of the dock. He seemed to have retained the firmness and composure that had marked his demeanour throughout the progress of the trial.

> Mr. Butt: My Lords, I believe that this is the proper time for me to make an application on behalf of the prisoner with reference to points which are now of considerable importance. After the conviction of a prisoner is the proper period to raise the reserved questions for appeal, and there are two questions which I wish to bring under the notice of Your Lordships, one of which has reference to what occurred yesterday, and the other to the establishment at Sandymount and of another person passing there as the prisoner's wife. I consider the admission of that evidence as illegal and, if the court feel any doubt about it, Your Lordships will reserve the point.

The evidence I refer to is that, from 1848 to 1852, the prisoner lived with another woman, at Sandymount, who called herself Mrs. Kirwan. We think such testimony is inadmissible, and not very fair, as calculated to give rise to a motive.

Mr. Justice Crampton: That is a matter for future consideration, but is no reason for postponing the sentence.

Mr. Butt: I am aware that it is not a reason for postponing the judgement of the court, but it is a matter, nonetheless, worthy of consideration. The second point to be reserved is whether the verdict of the jury was founded on the testimony of Adams, who was examined on behalf of the prisoner.

Mr. Justice Crampton: It may have been.

Mr. Butt: There can be no doubt about it. Mr. Brereton proposed to ask him, had he heard the testimony of Dr. Hatchell; and if he had, to state his opinion as to the cause of death, and whether he agreed with that gentleman or not? Now I submit that this was a legal question and the court, having refused to allow the witness to answer to it, might have caused prejudice in the minds of the jury; and on that ground your lordships will feel justified in reserving the point, under the statute giving the court jurisdiction to reserve questions of law arising in a criminal case, and respite judgement, if they think proper in the meantime.

Mr. Justice Crampton: My learned brother Greene and I have both carefully considered these matters when they were under discussion, and are clearly of the opinion against the prisoner, whether right or wrong.

Mr. Curran: There is another matter I would wish to bring under notice of the court. There are several authorities as to whether the examination of a prisoner can be used against him, and it has been decided that depositions on oath cannot be admitted; yet in this case, they were admitted as part of the Crown case.

Mr. Justice Crampton: That is only applicable to a prisoner; but Mr. Kirwan was not a prisoner at the time.

Mr. Curran: We think there may be something in these points. There are a vast number of authorities on the reception of depositions.

Mr. Justice Crampton: I will take every authority you refer to me with pleasure.

Mr. Hayes then inquired if it would be necessary for him to make some observation. Mr. Justice Crampton said that he did not require to hear him. They would be overturning first principles to admit that point.

‑◦‑

The only recourse for appeal (established in 1848) at the time of the trial was the Court for Crown Cases Reserved, an appellate court to hear references from the trial judge. It did not allow a retrial, only judgement on a point of law. Neither did it create a right of appeal. It could, however, reverse judgements. It heard only a few selected cases every year. The Court of Appeal wasn't established in England until 1875 and in Ireland until 1877, and allowed for one division hearing criminal appeals and another for civil appeals. This was superseded by the Court of Criminal Appeal in 1907.

There is no evidence that any such appeal was in fact made in this case.

‑◦‑

It only remained for the prisoner to address the court before the sentence was passed.

The Clerk of the Crown formally invited Kirwàn to speak:

> William Burke Kirwan, you have been indicted for the wilful murder of your wife, Maria Kirwan, at Ireland's Eye on the 6th of September last. You have thrown yourself on God and your country, and your country has found you guilty. What have you now to say why sentence of death and execution should not be passed against you?

All eyes turned to the dock. During trial proceedings attention is deflected from the prisoner to the participants who happen to dominate the stage of the court as it would in a theatrical presentation when the spotlight focuses on the character actor speaking the lines and others in exchange of dialogue. Now the character of the accused had been transformed to that of a convicted murderer. An imagined backdrop would portray in relief the gallows and the spectre of the hangman, the last human participant in the drama of legal retribution.

Already the prisoner had become a talking ghost, all that was missing was the improvised sound of the wind and wisps of ethereal smoke on the battlement of the dock. Nothing could fix the attention of the spectator so completely as the sight of a condemned man, his last act on this earth, and every moment of his past life predicated to oblivion on a rope from a gallows mechanism so ill-designed as to produce strangulation as opposed to instant death. An irony under the circumstances that could certainly not have escaped the educated observer, not to mind the prisoner if he was wont to consider such a thought.

But it was hardly likely that William Burke Kirwan harboured such a thought, certainly not if one was to attempt to speculate thus from the form and content of his address. Most murderers, especially ones who premeditate their crime are gamblers and a gambler will play their card to the very last until the reality of their loss can no longer bear the intervention of fantasy. That normally occurs in the loneliness of the prison cell when all hope has been exhausted or before the first step on the short journey to the gallows, arms pinioned and the cap placed over the head and eyes. But the black cap donned by the judge is but a prelude: anything might happen in between.

Kirwan's Address to the Court

My lords, might I claim the indulgence of the court for a few moments for the purpose of stating some matters connected with this unfortunate affair, that have not been brought out on trial.

On the morning of the day in question, before we left Howth for Ireland's Eye, we brought a bag containing some provisions for the purpose of dining on the island, as usual. Your Lordship may recollect that when you were speaking of the matter to the jury, you made an observation with regard to Mrs. Kirwan's bathing dress being in the bag with the provisions. You said it was unlikely they would be in the same bag. Now, on that morning, Mrs. Campbell was desired to give the bag with the bathing dress and the sheet to Nangle's daughter. There was also a basket containing some provisions. Nangle's daughter received those things from Mrs. Campbell, and brought them down to her father Michael Nangle who put them in the boat. We got into the boat but we did not proceed directly to the island, as we sailed about to accommodate other men, for taking passengers. We at length arrived at the island.

There are two large strands and one smaller. Mrs. Kirwan went to bathe near the Martello Tower, and while she was bathing, I was walking about. After a short time she came to me, partly dressed, and said she saw a boat advancing with another party. These men had told her they were to come with another party. She remained behind at the boat speaking to Pat Nangle, while I was walking about with Michael Nangle. As I have stated, I was walking about when Mrs. Kirwan told me she saw a boat advancing; the wind was direct for the island and the boat came very rapidly over.

We then walked about for some little time. After a little we proceeded to the old church where we remained a considerable time. I made a couple of sketches, Mrs. Kirwan occasionally reading and walking about. We afterwards left there previous to the company leaving at four o'clock, after which there was a shower. Previous to that we went to another part of the island, where under the shelter of some rocks we partook of the dinner we had brought with us. After that I went to make a study, or sketch towards Howth.

From that place, Mrs. Kirwan left me, stating she would go to bathe, taking her bathing dress with her and that she should walk around the island and meet me at the landing place. This was usual with us, we having been there on former occasions, in other boats besides the Nangles'. I continued at the sketch for more than a couple of hours, till it was getting duskish, which was a common thing with me. I then washed my brush and colours and put them into my bag. I came to the landing place and deposited it there. I saw that Mrs. Kirwan had not come to the appointment.

I walked towards the high ground to see if she was coming along the hill. I called out her name, saying the boat was coming. I saw the boat advancing. I turned back and called out from the edge of the bank to the men. Nangle states he did not hear me, but one of his companions did. The boat advanced; I knew none of the men by name except the Nangles.

I called out and asked them what delayed them; to hurry and make haste. One of the men, Pat Nangle, came up and took the things off the bank; but not from me, for I had not got them in my hands as he stated. I still continued calling [him] Nangle, for I did not know this man's name. The other man, Michael Nangle, whom I recognised as the proprietor of the boat, came up. I advanced a couple of steps towards him, but as he came up he said: "Where is the mistress, sir?" I immediately told him she went to bathe after the shower, that I was looking and calling for her and that we would go and look for her.

I told the other man who remained behind in the boat, that if Mrs. Kirwan came, she was to go to the boat, and that he was to call for us. We went along the bank, and struck inwards towards the old church. There is a great quantity of thick, rank grass there, and weeds and wild fern; and passing through those things I got very wet; for Your Lordship may be aware that thick, close grass after a shower of rain may retain water for a long time. I had on light trousers and boots passing through this.

Previous to going to the left, to the high ground, I expressed to Nangle my opinion that Mrs. Kirwan, in going over the rocks on the high ground, might have slipped and hurt herself and that if we called out, she might hear us. Nangle put his hand up to his mouth in this manner and gave a loud halloo; we waited a second or two to hear if there was any response. I called out loudly for Mrs. Kirwan by her Christian name, not lowly but loudly, and he called too. When we got on a line with the larger strand, I told him to call out a second time.

He did so; there was no answer. I still occasionally called "Maria Kirwan". We went to the old church, over where the land is flat, to where there is a hill that shuts you out entirely from Howth; you cannot see Howth at all. We shouted again, there was no response. We went again to the Long Hole, as it is called, as far as the water would permit us; we looked narrowly and closely and could see nothing. I then suggested to this man we would go round back and see if Mrs. Kirwan might have hurt herself and was delayed by it.

At that time we heard the cries of Pat Nangle from the bank. Pat Nangle states he did not hear Michael Nangle but Michael Nangle did answer his cries. I told Michael Nangle to answer and expressed my gratification that Mrs. Kirwan, I was sure, had come to the boat.

At this point Mr. Justice Crampton interrupted him.

I am sorry to interrupt you at this painful moment, but you must be well aware that your counsel entered into all these subjects. It is impossible for me to now go into the evidence.

Kirwan: I beg your pardon, My Lord, for the interruption. I consider myself to be a doomed person, from the trial that has taken place, and the sentence about to be passed; and I state these matters as well out of regard for my own memory, as for the sake of those friends who have been with me, who know my character from childhood, who know my innocence, and who feel it yet as I do. If Your Lordship be willing, I will proceed, if not I will stop.

Mr. Justice Crampton: If you wish to add anything, you may do so.

Kirwan: I have only to state with regard to the provisions being found, there was no evidence on the subject. Sergeant Sherwood was one who had charge of the bag, and he was not asked about it. The coroner also knew of it, but he was not asked about it, and therefore he did not state what he knew. My sketch book was examined by the jury; it was produced for them.

—◦►—

190

Kirwan had spoken in a firm and perfectly calm voice but it cannot but strike a reader that, however calm he appeared, the narrative which concerned his version of what went on during the fateful day on the island was rambling and did not seem to have any coherent point or theme that might provide any alternative version to what happened. He used up his chance to make a strong plea for innocence on trivia, when it would have served him better to explain, for instance, why he ordered the body to be washed against the advice of the attendant.

It is, however, worth considering at close quarters – as I will do later – as it contains one detail, unwittingly revealed, which was capable of undermining the whole defence theory and which by-passed even the most astute observers of the proceedings. Suffice it to say the prisoner's address did little in the way of providing any sense of his innocence. For example, not once did he mention that he loved his wife or express any emotion in regard to her death.

◄◦►

The Sentence

Mr. Justice Crampton then passed sentence on the prisoner. He seemed deeply affected by the task he had to undertake and spoke in a low and solemn tone:

> William Burke Kirwan, it now becomes my very painful duty to pronounce on you the sentence, necessarily consequent on the crime of which you have been convicted. That crime is murder, a crime denounced by both human and divine law as the most heinous crime that man can commit against his fellow man. Your case has been most patiently and deliberately investigated. You have been tried before a very intelligent and, I believe, a very impartial jury, and you have had the aid of some of the ablest and eloquent counsel at our bar; and the result has been that, after a very mature,

191

protracted and deliberate investigation, that jury has found you guilty of the murder charged in the indictment under which you were tried.

Upon that verdict, it is not my province to pronounce any opinion; but after what has been said, I cannot help adding this observation, that I can see no reason, or grounds to be dissatisfied with it; and in saying this, I speak the sentiments of my learned brother who sits beside me, as well as my own.

Now, William Burke Kirwan, according to the evidence and the finding of the jury, yours is not an ordinary murder, great as the guilt of murder must always be. You raised not your hand in daring vengeance against a man for whom you had received or thought you had received injury, provocation or insult; but you raised your hand against a female, a helpless, unprotected female, one whom by the laws of God and man was entitled to your protection, even at the hazard of your life, and to your affectionate guardianship.

That victim was the wife of your own bosom. In the solitude of that rocky island to which you brought her, on that fatal 6th of September, under the veil of approaching night, where there was no hand to stay, and no human eye to see your guilt, you perpetrated this terrible, this unnatural crime. And what was your motive? It appears that for years you had been leading an immoral profligate life. You were living with a female who was not your wife, by whom you had a large family; and thus circumstanced, it would appear you married the unhappy lady whose death you no doubt deeply regret. You gave her the title and character of your wife, whilst you continued to give to the partner of this illicit connexion, which I have alluded to, the affections, the rights, the duties which you owed your lawful wife.

I have been looking for a motive for the unnatural act which you, by the verdict of the jury, have been found to have perpetrated. Embarrassed you may have been by the painful predicament in which you had placed yourself, under this double engagement, and you seem to have resolved to extricate yourself by a desperate crime. Instead of dismissing the mistress, and providing for her as well as you could, you appear to have meditated the destruction of your wife. You took lodging at Howth and, according to the evidence, during the first month of your sojourn there you treated you wife with rudeness, cruelty, and on one occasion made use of threatening language, threatening her life. In a moment of passion or excitement you did threaten her life. It does appear, from the evidence, that after the first month of the sojourn you treated your wife more kindly and lived with her on better terms than you had done before.

You were by profession an artist. It appears that your wife was passionately fond of bathing and she had opportunities at Howth for indulging it. Frequently you visited, with her, a little island, Ireland's Eye, a mile from the mainland. On three [*two*] occasions before the 6th of September, you and she seem to have gone together, returning late at night, having spent the day, you in sketching and she amusing herself; and on this fatal 6th of September, you and she paid your last visit to that island; and on that day it was, and under circumstances wrapped up no doubt in great mystery, that the unfortunate lady was deprived of life.

She was in the prime of her years; she was in sound health; and suddenly her life was cut short. No human eye could see how the act was done, none but your own conscience and the all-seeing eye of Providence could develop this mysterious transaction; but the verdict of the jury has established that by some means or other, by violence after a struggle, your unfortunate, unhappy wife, became the victim of your cruelty and vengeance. Now I shall not enter into any further detail on this matter, nor did I state what I have stated with any view to inflict pain upon you. I feel for the painful predicament in which a gentleman of your condition, or your education, and of your habits now stands.

It is to me deeply painful to refer to these matters, but I feel that it is my duty to do so for two purposes. First, the purpose of public edification. Let the young take warning from the subject to which I have been referring, the cause which has led to your now degraded and painful position. Let them be aware of forming immoral engagements and of entering into profligate courses. The steps of crime are very gradual, there is not much descent from one step to another, and the first leads naturally to the second and so on until the last fatal step, which has placed you where you are now.

I also allude to those circumstances in the hope, it may be vain that I should do so but I sincerely trust it may not be a vain expectation, that during the brief interval which must remain for your painful sojourn on this earth, you may withdraw your mind and affections from secular affairs, from worldly objects and fix them upon that which is the proper subject for every man's most serious consideration: the awful subject of the judgement to come.

I cannot hold out to you one ray of hope of pardon on this side of the grave. The die is cast and I fear it is against you, and cannot be reversed. Consolations, you can have none now. Henceforth, you can have but the consolations of religion. Hope, you can have none now, but the hope of pardon and salvation through the sacrifice and merits of an all-loving Saviour. No human being can be saved but through that Saviour, and through faith in his atonement and his merits, not even to the most virtuous man that lives; and thanks be to God, we know upon authority that cannot err, that the door of the Saviour's mercy is not shut against the greatest sinner that lived. The blood of Christ can cleanse all. I entreat you to turn your thoughts to those solemn and sacred subjects.

Do not, I implore of you, consider what I am saying now as words of course, or matters of mere official duty. I speak as one feels what he says, as one who is convinced that your eternal happiness or misery will depend on what passes in your soul during the short period that is now left to you on this earth. Do then, cast yourself on that Saviour.

Having said much, it now remains for me to pronounce upon you the last awful and solemn words of the sentence fixed by the law.

Here the judge assumed the black cap which sent a shudder down every spine in the court.

The sentence is, that you, William Burke Kirwan be taken from the place you now stand to the place from where you came, the gaol, and that from thence you be taken to the place of execution, the gallows, and that you be there hanged by the neck until you be dead, and that your body be buried within the precincts of the prison in which you are now confined. And may the Lord have mercy on your soul.

The prisoner, a few minutes later, spoke in a clear and firm tone.

Convinced as I am that my hopes in this world are at an end, I do most solemnly declare in the presence of this court, and that of God, before who I expect soon to stand, that I had neither act, part or knowledge of my late wife's death; and I will state further that I never treated her unkindly, as her own mother can testify.

The prisoner was then removed from the dock and shortly afterwards conveyed to Kilmainham jail in a covered car, escorted by a party of mounted police.

—◇—

The electric tension that accompanies the verdict and the sentencing in a capital murder trial, often virtually unbearable at the end, now evaporated as did the audience: the reporters to burn the midnight oil, which would continue to be burned for many months and years to come; the legal men to their clubs first and then to other briefs; the spectators to a lifetime of recounting their presence at this mouth-watering event; the medical men to their hugely demanding schedules in the hospitals, the dissecting rooms and the lecture halls of the Royal College; and the constabulary to more crimes and misdemeanours.

None would be let, for other reasons, forget this momentous trial and most likely would not have anyway. William Burke Kirwan had been sentenced to death. But this extreme sentence was commuted by the Lord Lieutenant to transportation for life after the usual consultation with the judges, in this case Crampton and Greene. It was abundantly clear from the former's emotional address to the prisoner before sentence that he was not of the hanging judge variety, quite apart from the obvious and deserved merits of clemency arising from certain shortcomings of the trial process.

If the coroner's inquest should have provided a full stop as opposed to a comma it seemed that the trial marked the end of the story. But there would be at least one or two more twists to the mysterious saga of Ireland's Eye.

CHAPTER 7

THE DEFENCE

Just as the tide of public opinion had flowed against William Burke Kirwan in advance of the trial, in an extraordinary twist it flowed in his favour following his conviction for the murder of his wife. It would be entirely normal to mount a campaign for the commuting of the death sentence to one of life which partly explains an effort on behalf of a convicted gentleman but the campaign, orchestrated by Dublin solicitor John Knight Boswell, went far beyond that. Claiming that Kirwan was entirely innocent of the crime, he presented a meticulously researched and highly convincing case on behalf of the prisoner which was completed on February 28th, 1853:

> Junius tells us that prudence and self-preservation will oblige the most moderate dispositions to have common sense even with a man whose conduct they censure, if they see him persecuted in a way in which the real spirit of the laws will not justify. This generous sentiment, from one of England's ablest advocates of constitutional freedom, is well adapted to the subject of the accompanying statement, who has been persecuted and slandered to death. With Kirwan's moral conduct we have nought to do. To convict him of the sixth, he

197

has been charged with the seventh commandment; but without being his apologists, it strikes us that it is a redeeming feature in his character that he did not desert the woman he betrayed; and in language the rule of all: "Let the man that is without sin cast the first stone."

This is the case presented by Boswell, which he organised under headlines into various subjects. It was subscribed to by an impressive number of top medical professionals in Dublin and most notably by the greatest medico-legal practitioner of his generation in England, Dr. Alfred Swaine Taylor.

Reports of Murder of Bowyer and Crowe

When Mr. Boswell was asked to investigate the circumstances in connection with this mysterious case in which the public mind had been prejudiced and false reports circulated that Kirwan had murdered his brother-in-law Crowe and Mr. Bowyer, the latter charge investigated by the Commissioners of Metropolitan Police, Mr. Boswell succeeded in reputing the charges and establishing the innocence of Kirwan.

Source of Reports: Mrs. Byrne

Looking at informations from the Crown, on 21st September, 1852, Maria Byrne provided an affidavit which stated that, Mr. and Mrs. Kirwan having left the residence at 11 Upper Merrion Street about three weeks, she suspected that Kirwan had taken his wife some place to destroy her. She had no doubt that Mrs. Kirwan was wilfully drowned by her husband and she had strong reasons to believe that he had made away with other members of his family under suspicious circumstances. She spread the rumours that Kirwan had murdered Crowe [*his brother-in-law*] and Bowyer.

Mrs. Crowe, the mother of the deceased, referred to the statements: "If there could be a quieter husband to her daughter it was Mr. Kirwan who had a full supply for every need and desire and the information of Maria Byrne was wholly false and unfounded." Maria Byrne had on one occasion said that "bloody Billy Kirwan and Hodges and Smith had murdered her husband" and Mrs. Crowe on hearing that he was in hospital called at the house in Lower Merrion Street where Mrs. Byrne introduced her into a room in which was laid out tobacco and said to her: "Here is a wake but no dead man."

Mrs. Bentley, a lady of the highest respectability, has sworn that the said Mrs. Byrne used to instigate the late Mrs. Kirwan to quarrel with her husband, she and they being next-door neighbours; that Mrs. Kirwan had no peace of mind until she forbade Mrs. Byrne the house; and that Mrs. Kirwan had always represented her husband as a gentle and good-mannered man.

Ellen Malone, who had been in the service of Mr. and Mrs. Kirwan, says that Mrs. Byrne was in the habit of telling stories to Mrs. Kirwan to aggravate her husband and Mrs. Byrne had been turned out of the house. She also said that he treated his wife with the greatest kindness and generosity.

The next person who charged Mr. Kirwan with murder and robbery was a Mrs. Bowyer. This person has claimed from the Commissioners of the Dublin Metropolitan Police a large variety of pictures, which are now in Kirwan's house and which she alleged were stolen from her husband, many of which were of great value. On investigation and examination, it appears that almost all of the paintings so claimed are paintings which were sent by third parties to be cleaned and an immense number were copies made within a few years by Kirwan himself.

She also claimed a modern bookcase full of books, which she told the police constable was just as it was with all the books in it when stolen from her husband in 1837. The books, on examination, were found to be nearly all of a modern date, with many being published between 1845 and 1852.

Yet upon the testimony of such witnesses was the charge of murder got up against the wretched and absent convict and in the language of the coroner: "His character was his ruin."

Mrs. Bowyer was some years since in a lunatic asylum.

Bigamy

The next charge Mr. Boswell successfully exposed was an attempt to get a case of bigamy against Kirwan. The authorities, being contacted, dropped the investigation.

Conspiracy

Kirwan immediately after his arrest wrote a letter to Major Brownrigg, Deputy Inspector of the Constabulary, stating that the charge of murder was the result of a conspiracy and named the party [*possibly Mrs. Byrne?*]. Among the many reports circulated against Kirwan, it was said that the deceased did not know of his intimacy with Miss Kenny until a short time before the death, thus filling the public mind with a motive for the murder. Like all the other reports that slandered him to death, this one is without a shadow of truth.

Mrs. Bentley has, since the trial, stated that to her knowledge as well as that of several members of her family, Mrs. Kirwan was fully acquainted with Mr. Kirwan's intimacy with Miss Kenny before the expiration of one month after the marriage, more than 12 years ago. Ellen Malone, since the trial, said that about three years ago a little boy called on Kirwan and Mrs. Kirwan said that he was Mr. Kirwan's son and he had two or three more of them. The medical gentleman who attended Miss Kenny on her lying in was aware of the fact and has since the trial so publicly stated and Teresa Kenny has also deposed that both she and Mrs. Kirwan knew of this intimacy for the last ten years.

Independent of this conclusive evidence, surely reason would dictate to ordinary observation that it was impossible the convict could leave his house and have a family by another woman without, as it was alleged, his wife knowing it, they living within a mile of each other.

Pat Nangle Left Howth at Half Past Seven

The chief witness examined upon trial was Pat Nangle who swore that Mrs. Kirwan directed the men to come at eight o'clock in the evening and then at half past seven o'clock he and the men left Howth for Ireland's Eye, which they reached about eight o'clock and when they reached it they saw Kirwan standing at the landing place and that he had a bag, book and stick. It is most important to take the evidence of the witness in detail. In reference to the direction given by Mrs. Kirwan, that the men should come at eight o'clock, it was proved before the coroner that she was much annoyed at the men coming before their time on their former occasions on visiting the island.

The usual period in fine weather for rowing from Howth to Ireland's Eye is about fifteen minutes, which puts the period of time when Kirwan was at the landing place at about a quarter before eight o'clock.

The phrase "standing by the landing place" was calculated to mislead the jury into the belief that Kirwan was closer to the boat when the men came over, and that he was actually stepping onto it. It was not so; the spot where Kirwan stood and which has been shown to many is on a high bank, 15 feet above the sea, having rugged rocks between it and the shore, and distant at least 60 feet from the boat.

The Bag
The bag which this witness examined was examined by the coroner's jury. It contained knives and forks, soiled plates and the remains of ham etc. It was stated in court that it did not appear what [items] Kirwan had in the bag and it was suggested to the jury that he might have brought over the bathing dress, an inference not warranted by any proof, and which told strongly against the prisoner.

Kirwan advanced a few paces on the bank with the bag, which he gave to Nangle. This circumstance has been magnified into an intention on his part of leaving the island without Mrs. Kirwan. Now, if he had the folly to go back to Howth without her, we appeal to the dispassionate judgement of every man, would he not on the instant of his arrival, be questioned; suspicion would be aroused, and on the body being found, he would have been instantly arrested as a murderer.

The Sketch Book: Kirwan at the Martello Tower Ten Minutes after Seven O'Clock

The sketch book was produced to the coroner's jury, after Kirwan had given evidence at the inquest and had told what he was sketching. It contained numerous sketches and among others one which Kirwan told the inquest he had just finished of an evening sunset effect of the Dublin Mountains and part of Howth Head tinted in colour. This effect would have been impossible to obtain unless about sunset, which was twenty minutes before seven. It can be proved that Kirwan, while he was residing at Howth, was in the habit of sketching at other islands, and was seen so occupied at Balbriggan and Skerries.

It may be fairly inferred that Kirwan remained for some time to secure the effects while fresh in his memory, this being the usual habit of artists; he also required time to put up his paints, colour box, sketch etc. Now allowing him to paint only until sundown, and then giving him but half an hour for the performances detailed, it fixed the period when he must have been presumed to have quitted the Martello Tower, for the purpose of committing the alleged murder, at about ten minutes past seven and then he had to transverse the island through rank grass and fern nearly 3 feet high and then return and be standing on the bank before eight o'clock.

Discovery of Body and Sheet

The same witness Pat Nangle proved that he heard Kirwan when they were searching for Mrs. Kirwan moaning to himself and crying "Oh Maria, oh Maria" and that getting down to the Long Hole the second time he found the body of the lady, who was lying on her back. The deceased had a bathing suit on her and it was "gathered up about her waist, leaving the rest of her person exposed. There was a sheet under her back which was wet, and so was the bathing shift." This witness deposed that when he came to the part about the sheet, he was interrupted and put back by Kirwan [at the inquest]. This statement which tended to convict Kirwan, was, since the trial, been proved to be totally untrue, and is contradicted not only by the coroner, but also six of the coroner's jury.

The most important feature in the whole of this case is to the alleged finding of the sheet, "this horrid sheet" so eloquently impressed on the minds of the jury. The first evidence to refute this statement is that of the witness, Michael Nangle, who was the only other person with Pat Nangle when the body was discovered. He contradicted Pat on the inquest, and swore positively that the sheet was brought down by Kirwan himself from the rock; and at the trial he did not state there was a sheet or any other white thing under the body, but asserted that Kirwan brought down something from the rock, something white like a sheet in which the body was wrapped up.

Mrs. Tate has since the trial sworn that the day after the alleged murder, she spoke to Pat Nangle and said to him: "But Paddy, what about the sheet? People say it was under her." He replied: "God bless you, ma'am, it was the poor gentleman got the sheet to cover his poor wife and no wonder, she was quite stripped."

Mr. E. Jackson has stated since the trial that he had frequent conversations with the Nangles, and so had Mr. and Mrs. Hill, and that Nangle informed him that Kirwan had exhibited much grief on finding his wife drowned, and that in reference to the sheet he said that Kirwan seemed ashamed on seeing his wife so exposed and ran for a sheet to cover her.

The coroner and six of the coroner's jury, all gentlemen of position and standing in society, have pledged themselves that Pat Nangle gave more materially different evidence at the trial from what he gave at the inquest. Their statements have long since been sent to the Castle.

Swords, Wounds, Blood etc.

Pat Nangle gave some extraordinary evidence about wounds and blood flowing which he said was from a sword cut, and when asked how did he know there was a sword cut, his reply was that he saw it. The fact in evidence on the trial was that Kirwan had a walking stick, which he carried with him, and which the witness actually swore was a cane with a sword in it and thus his examination expanded into the belief that Mrs. Kirwan was murdered by a sword. To place any reliance on it or that the jury should have been told to give it any credence is the strongest possible proof that Kirwan's character was his ruin. Having failed to state these circumstances on inquest, it is impossible to believe he ever saw what he related in this respect on trial.

Mrs. Kirwan's Clothes

Pat Nangle also created a great prejudice against Kirwan by reason of his statement in reference to the finding of Mrs. Kirwan's clothes. He says that Mr. Kirwan told the witness to go and look for the lady's clothes; the witness did so and could not find them; that the clothes were not in the place where he searched, where they were afterwards found; and then when the witness came back after his unsuccessful search for the clothes, Mr. Kirwan rose up from the body to seek for the clothes. He came back in a few minutes and told the witness they were on top of the rock.

The Top of the Rock

The large rock, upwards of 20 feet high and on the edge of which (and not on the top) Mrs. Kirwan's clothes were deposited, is at high water completely surrounded by the tide, and the spot on which the clothes were laid is covered at high watermark; so Mrs. Kirwan could not possibly have stripped unless at half tide, and the rock must have taken some time to dry. The rock on which the clothes were admittedly found is but a few feet above the strand, not on top of the rock, but on the edge and there is no doubt but the phrase "go up to the rock" and "top of the rock" led the jury to infer that Kirwan must have placed them on top of the rock.

Arrangement of Mrs. Kirwan's Clothes

The appearance which the clothes of the deceased presented is of paramount importance. The basket which Mrs. Kirwan had with her, and which was found on the rock beside her clothes was produced by the police at the inquest and on examination, its contents were as follows: in the bottom a large shawl pin, a pair of garters laid together and a pair of lady's stockings on the top, carelessly one inside the other. Now is it likely that if Mrs. Kirwan was first murdered and then stripped by Kirwan, that Kirwan afterwards made all these arrangements which are peculiar to the female sex alone and which no man would dream of doing?

Mrs. Tate swears that Pat Nangle described to her the natural position of the clothes, her dress and petticoats, to use his own phrase: "Just as she had stepped out of them, her boots as she had taken them off, one partly under her clothes, the other a little distance." These facts, coupled with the admission that there was not the least appearance on Kirwan's person of his dress having been disturbed, are in themselves powerful evidence of Kirwan's innocence.

It is a universal belief that the murderer shuns the body of his victim. In this case Kirwan lay on the body in a lonely isle upwards of an hour. Michael Nangle differed from Pat Nangle on the sheet. On the coroner's jury Michael positively stated that Kirwan brought the sheet to cover his wife and on trial (having previously undergone the process of tuition) he still fairly admitted that Kirwan brought back something like a sheet.

The Long Hole
It was Michael Nangle who asked Kirwan where the mistress was, to which Kirwan replied he had been looking for her; and that he had been up the hill for that purpose; and when asked what way she went, Kirwan immediately pointed to the Long Hole as the direction in which she went. The act of Kirwan pointing to the Long Hole was not the act of a murderer who would have pointed in another direction to elude the discovery of the body.

Motive for Nangles' Evidence
Searching for a motive for the extraordinary discrepancy of their evidence before the coroner's jury and the trial, particularly Pat Nangle's, this is it. They demanded a large sum of money for their services in bringing over the body of Mrs. Kirwan; they stopped the hearse when coming into town and but for the police would not have permitted the body to leave Howth.

They assert that Kirwan paid but £2 among them and spoke of his shabbiness etc. Mr. Robert Jackson declares that the Nangles offered obstructions and demanded payment before the corpse would be permitted to pass. Catherine Brew swears that she heard Pat Nangle say: "If I am called again I will pinch him." Now if Kirwan had been conscious of having committed the murder, would he not have paid these persons liberally and thus silence their reports?

The Time of the Supposed Murder
A central consideration and contrast of the period of time when Kirwan was at the Martello Tower waiting for the boat and the period when the alleged murder is supposed to have been committed, is of the greatest importance. Hugh Campbell, in his information sworn on the 15th of September, 1852 states: "On Monday evening the 6th of September he heard a call from the island of Ireland's Eye between the hours of seven and eight at a place which could not be far from where Mrs. Kirwan's body was found."

As near as the evidence of this witness and the others can fix the time of Mrs. Kirwan's death it must have been between seven and half past. Kirwan, admittedly, was standing on the bank near the tower at about a quarter before eight. If the convict had murdered Mrs. Kirwan he must have remained at the Long Hole some time to dispose of the body. There was also between him and the Martello Tower a half a mile to be traversed over land, the entire surface of which was covered with thistles, nettles and fern and which in summer grows to the height of 3 feet. It is therefore extremely improbable, if not impossible, that he could have perpetrated the murder and be found waiting on the bank a quarter before eight o'clock.

Kirwan Painting at Seven O'Clock

When Kirwan was asked by the coroner's jury what he was doing he replied that he was sketching and taking the evening appearance towards Dublin. The sketch book was then called for and on it being produced, the sketch showed a tinted, coloured sketch of the sunset effect which could only be obtained at sundown. Now supposing that Kirwan, being occupied until seven o'clock, sunset being twenty minutes before, and allow him as before mentioned some time to arrange his colours, palette etc and to secure his effects, while fresh in his memory, is it unreasonable or farfetched to say that he may be supposed to have been at the Martello Tower at quarter after seven o'clock?

Is it not within the limits of reason to believe that he could have between a quarter past seven and a quarter to eight traversed the island to the Long Hole, committed the murder and returned, all within half an hour and with not the least appearance of disorder on his person or his clothes, although if he committed the murder in the interval he had to contend with a strong and able young woman struggling for life, who the jury supposed had neither hands, nails or teeth.

207

Father Hall

The body was removed to Howth and when it was made known that Mrs. Kirwan had drowned, it caused a great sensation and Sergeant Sherwood of the police, with his men, proceeded to the boat to take charge of the deceased.

Father Hall, the Catholic clergyman was there and he openly stated his suspicion that she was murdered by Kirwan and pointing to him said to Sergeant Sherwood; "Keep your eyes on that man." We hesitated for some time to make this fact public, but think it was best to do so for this reason: the whole of the evidence on which Kirwan was convicted was of the humblest class in society; every person at all conversant with this social condition of this country must know what influence the word of a priest has with the people. It is not only probable but morally certain that when Father Hall fixed on Kirwan the suspicion of murder, every fact which could be elicited and brought forward against Kirwan on inquest would be proved to make good the priest's suspicion.

The Cries

The first witness examined about cries was Hugh Campbell who said he heard three cries. In his information to police on the 15th of September he said he heard a call. Thomas Larkin proved he heard cries as he was sailing into Howth, though the wind was blowing in a direction from the boat against the spot whence the cries are supposed to have come. By Larkin's own statement he was sailing at some distance from the tower where Kirwan was painting. Kirwan was looking for his wife, and may not his calling "Maria, Maria" have been mistaken by Larkin for cries from the Long Hole?

It certainly seems a more probable solution to the matter, than to believe that he heard cries against the direction of the wind. In reference to the possibility of hearing cries at all, it has been severely tested by several gentlemen who tried whistles, rifles and halloing and found it impossible that any cries could be heard from the Long Hole, either near the

Martello Tower or at Howth. The jury were told that if Kirwan was standing near the Martello Tower when the supposed cries of Mrs. Kirwan were heard at Howth and by Thomas Larkin he must have heard them too. This has been practically found to be impossible and when the formation of the island and the relative positions of the Martello tower and the Long Hole are considered, on every principle of acoustics, it is impossible.

The island of Ireland's Eye is a mountain 324 feet high, its side on the north presenting a bold and rugged coast with crags and rocks nearly 200 feet high. The mountain slopes towards Howth and part of the high ground lies between the Long Hole and the Martello Tower. If a line be drawn from the spot where Kirwan stood to the Long Hole, it would intersect at about one-third the height of the mountain, descend into the hollow ground and rise again near the Long Hole. The Long Hole is open to the sea on the north side only and on two sides are precipitous cliffs, 80 feet high.

Thus the voice should ascend first over the cliffs, descend to the church and then rise over the mountain before it could have reached Kirwan, which is thus practically shown to be impossible. It appears the court had forgotten that there is always on the sea side, even on the calmest summer's evening, a noise created by the flowing or rippling of the sea upon a shingled and gravelly beach. One of the women, Abernethy, swore at the trial that she told Sherwood, the police sergeant, of the cries she heard the morning before the inquest. It is strange if she did so that Sherwood did not bring her forward. There was not a word about cries at the inquest.

Bloody Appearance

It is quite evident that the testimony that convicted Kirwan was that of Pat Nangle about the sheet, which has been totally refuted, and the evidence of the two women who washed the body. Reference to the bloody appearance was noted and testified to by Anne Lacey. The statement by her that the belly was flat to the backbone was evidently suggested by what Dr. Hatchell told the people about the post-mortem examination. It is wholly untrue: the belly was full and firm. [Boswell is either confused or being deliberately misleading: Dr. Hatchell referred to the stomach, not the belly, being "empty and contracted" and said the abdomen was distended with gas.]

Depth of Water at the Long Hole

The next branch of this case is the evidence given by the Crown in reference to the depth of water in the Long Hole, which has, since the trial, been proven to be altogether erroneous. It was proved that it was high water at Dublin bar at half past three p.m. and at 7 p.m. the tide was one foot 9 inches over the rock where the body was found, the rock being one foot high, thus making the depth of the water at 7 p.m., 2 feet 9 inches. It has since the trial been incontrovertibly established that the gentleman who made the calculation erred, and that his measurements were incorrect. It can be proved to demonstration that the tide, instead of being only 2 feet 9 inches deep at 7 p.m. was nearly 6 feet deep; and Nangle swore at the trial that it was 5 feet deep at half tide. Nangle also states that when he first went into the Long Hole, he could not see the body, which must have been covered by the tide and which was long after 7 p.m.

Mr. Foakes, an English engineer of considerable experience, having had his attention directed to the evidence, went to Ireland's Eye on the 17th of December (high water at Dublin bar being 3.30 p.m.). He found the depth of water over the rock where the body lay to be 6 feet 3 inches, the depth of high water the same day being 10 feet.

He says: "Being anxious to test if there was any current receding towards the sea, Mr. Boyd and I undressed and went into the water, a little after half tide; when I arrived at about 50 feet from where the body was found, the water being then up to my breast, I was swept off my feet; and had I not been able to swim I have no doubt I should have been carried into deep water and against the rock which lies across the channel. I had a thick staff with me, but the current was so strong that even with its assistance I was unable to keep my feet where the water was only 4 feet 6 inches deep. I swam as hard as I could but made little or no way against the receding waves, when Mr. Boyd ran in and gave me the end of a staff he had with him, about 8 feet long, to help me out."

Mr. Foakes goes on to say that on the 22nd of December last, he again went to Ireland's Eye, for the purpose of checking the levels he had previously taken, being convinced from the forward position of the Long Hole that the effect of the wind on the sea causes greater variation in the height of the tide there than it does in less exposed situations.

He found the water at half tide to be 4 feet 8 inches deep over the spot where the head and shoulders lay and 5 foot 8 inches over the feet and that the level of low water on the day was about 6 inches vertically below the former place. The day was perfectly calm and scarce a ripple was on the sea. Several scientific men in Trinity College have proved the inaccuracy of Mr. Jones' statement and Mr. McArthur of Capel Street, an engineer who published a map of the Long Hole and who made several examinations of the tide levels, has established that Mr. Jones' calculations and measurement were altogether erroneous.

Sometime previous to the 6th of September the wind was S.E. creating a ground swell which forced a greater amount of water into the Long Hole and which swell continues for two or three days after the wind changes; such swell gives an increase of a foot upwards to the height of the tides in Dublin Bay. The Long Hole from its formation and situation is for this reason subject to great variation in the height of the tides. The receding tide, when at about half-tide, becomes a rapid and dangerous current.

It is a singular fact that there is scarce a particle of evidence on which Kirwan was condemned that has not been found erroneous or capable of contradiction.

There follows a letter from the coroner, repeating his evidence at the trial and rejecting criticism of his handling of the inquest.

Washing the Body

Kirwan is claimed to have asked Mrs. Campbell to have the body washed and policemen present said there was no reason to wait for the sergeant. Had Kirwan said what was alleged it would argue for innocence rather than consciousness of guilt. Had he been guilty, he must have known that there were some marks on the body which washing would have exposed to view. It is impossible to account for the silence of these women at the inquest.

The Lodgings were Taken till November

It was most improperly put to the jury that Kirwan contemplated the commission of the murder just as he was about to leave his lodgings at Howth. The fact is not so; Mrs. Campbell swears that both Mr. and Mrs. Kirwan told her that they would stop until November, and they paid her by the week only because Mrs. Campbell, who was a poor widow, required the weekly money to support her; and in evidence of the truth of this statement, Kirwan was actually at the time altering and cleaning down his house in Merrion Street, which now lies in an unfinished state.

The Wetness of the Grave

It was also stated to the jury that Kirwan provided the wettest spot at Glasnevin for the burial of his wife. Mr. John Leeson has, since the trial, deposed to the fact that he, without Kirwan's knowledge, selected the burial place, and that Kirwan knew nothing whatever of the arrangement. And that it has since been ascertained that the grave in which Mrs. Kirwan was buried was in the driest part of the ground;

but at the time the grave was opened the season was uncommonly wet.

Kirwan's Wet Trousers

A great point was made of Kirwan's sitting at the fire at twelve o'clock at night and drying his trousers. The jury were told that he could have not wet his trousers up to his knees in the Long Hole when he accompanied the Nangles and therefore he must have wet them when he murdered Mrs. Kirwan and carried the body as far as he could walk into the water up to his knees. If Kirwan had really wet himself with salt water at about from seven to half past seven o'clock, the time Mrs. Kirwan is said to have been murdered, he must have been dried long before twelve o'clock at night.

This fact will strike anyone that was ever wet with salt water and fishermen know well that it would be impossible that "drops of water" (as sworn at the trial) would come from trousers nearly five hours after the wetting by salt water.

The fact was given in evidence at the trial, that when Kirwan was searching with the Nangles for Mrs. Kirwan, he had to walk through the high fern, nettles, and briers wet from a heavy shower which fell between five and six o'clock; and so conscious was Kirwan of innocence, that he actually turned up his trousers to dry his drawers and called for a dry pair of stockings before the police; and a boy named Carey took off Kirwan's wet stockings. Yet this circumstance has been relied on as evidence of the murder.

Mrs. Kirwan's Health

Mrs. Kirwan, being subject to a scorbutic affection, was in the habit of bathing for many years, and frequently twice a day, and would remain for half an hour in the water at a time, as appears by her mother's evidence; and it was at her instance that Kirwan took lodgings at Howth, for better salt-water bathing.

Seaweed

The fact of bits of seaweed having been found in Mrs. Kirwan's hair is quite probable, because bits of seaweed are always floating on the surface of the water, especially in a receding tide; had there been no seaweed in the hair, it might naturally be said that there was indication of the body having being left where it was found after the tide had altogether receded; but the fact of seaweed in the hair negatives the statement that Kirwan carried the body and left it on the rock.

Epilepsy

The important question in this case is, did Mrs. Kirwan die of epilepsy, having taken the fit in the water? The following important evidence goes to establish the fact that she had a tendency to apoplexy or epilepsy during life:

Mrs. Bentley, a lady of respectability, and on terms of intimacy with Mrs. Kirwan, in her declaration made on the 22nd of December, 1852, states that "About two years and nine months ago, Mrs. Kirwan told Mrs. Bentley she had quite suddenly been attacked with trembling of her entire frame, her knees knocked violently together, her teeth became clenched, she lost all power to move and when she recovered, she was unconscious how long she remained in that state; that subsequently she told Mrs. Bentley that on Mr. Kirwan going into the bedroom, he found her suffering under a similar attack, and he was just in time to catch her in his arms etc.

Anne Maher, who had formerly lived with Mr. Kirwan and his wife as a servant, in her declaration made on the 16th of December, 1852, states that she was attracted by loud screaming upstairs and when she went up she found Mrs. Kirwan working in a fit, her arms and hands working violently, as if in convulsions and froth coming from her mouth. And that during her stay with them they lived on very affectionate terms.

The next evidence is that of Arthur Kelly, who in his declaration made on the 16th of December, 1852, declares that he remembers Mrs. Kirwan to have been attacked by two fits; he saw the deceased lying on the floor, working in a fit. This witness also deposes to the convict's kindness to his wife.

The next evidence is that of Mr. Thomas Harrison and his son, who in their declaration made on the 22nd of December, 1852, state they were on terms of affection and constant intercourse with Mrs. Kirwan and that the deceased often complained of dizziness of sight, confusion of ideas and always spoke of her husband in the kindest of terms.

The last witness is Ellen Malone, who had been in the service of Mr. and Mrs. Kirwan. In her declaration made on the 24th of December, 1852, states that one occasion six months before she left Mrs. Kirwan's service, while she was sitting in a tin bath of lukewarm water, Mrs. Kirwan told her that she felt her senses leaving her and "I perceived her face turn suddenly very red and she became insensible."

Medical Opinions

The medical portion of the case is conclusive upon the point that Mrs. Kirwan died of a fit of epilepsy while in the water; and if a reasonable doubt existed on the matter, it has been set at rest by the paper of Dr. Alfred Taylor, of Guy's Hospital, London, the author of a standard work on medical jurisprudence, quoted in all criminal courts in the Empire and who is considered the greatest medico-legal opinion in England.

Another Man on the Island

It has been ascertained that there was another man on the island at the time of Mrs. Kirwan's death, and that he got secretly to Howth, one of the fishermen having brought him across. By his own account, he next day went to Liverpool with cattle and from Liverpool to Waterford. This man was traced by very singular means, unnecessary to detail, and was found living in Nicholas Street; and when discovered said that Kirwan was as innocent of the murder as the child unborn; and when asked why he himself had absconded, he said that he was afraid of being implicated himself. This man has since left Dublin, and no trace whatever can be found of him. The man, John Gorman, in the presence of others Messrs Smith and Bentley and subsequently Rev. Mr. Malet, made a statement to the effect that he was on the island on the whole of the day of September 6th and after the body of the late Mrs. Kirwan was removed. This information was passed to the police at College Street. The informant left his lodgings in Nicholas Street and was never seen again.

Letters from the Jury

Two letters have appeared since the trial, purporting to have come from the jury, one of them signed by Mr. Dennis, the foreman, on behalf of himself and ten of the jury. There are some remarkable passages in these letters.

The following extracts have been selected from the letter signed by Mr. Dennis, which appeared in *Saunders Newsletter* of the 13th of January, 1853, evidencing what had been passing in the minds of the jury.

Mr. Dennis says: "Seeing the two men, Patrick and Michael Nangle, and hearing the evidence, we could form no reasonable doubt of the truth of either of them. They are both elderly men. Michael appears older than Patrick, nor is he by many degrees so observant or intelligent a man. Patrick Nangle's account of finding the body with the sheet partly under it and his tying it across the chest and knees is perfectly consistent with all the circumstances of this particular period."

If the jury had before them the statements of the coroner and six of the coroner's jury, the facts disclosed in the affidavits and declarations herein alluded to in reference to Pat Nangle, it is not probable that they could possibly have formed such an opinion. Mr. Dennis asserts that "some of Kirwan's innocent offspring and the partner of his crime were living in the house where his deceased wife had resided within a month after her death". If Miss Kenny had been examined at the trial, this circumstance would have been fully explained, and the mind of the jury disabused of such belief.

Miss Kenny stated in the Crown office that she was obliged to bring her sick child into town for a few days but that she did not sleep at the house. Like all the reports about Kirwan it was a shameful falsehood. It was also publicly stated that Kirwan had married Miss Kenny a day or two after the alleged murder and this report evidently weighed with the jury.

Again Mr. Dennis says: "True, it was not sworn that the body of Mrs. Kirwan was the body of a murdered woman. Proved to have been murdered, she must have been murdered by Kirwan."

With every respect of the just privileges of the jury box, it was going too far to say she must have been murdered by Kirwan. Five hundred men might have been secreted on the far north side of the mountain hid under rocks, some of which are nearly 200 feet high, the mountain itself being 324 feet high, and there were several fishing boats becalmed off the Long Hole at the time of the alleged murder.

Again, Mr. Dennis says: "We do not believe that Mrs. Kirwan died of a fit of epilepsy, nor do we believe that had she so died she could have uttered such repeated screams as were heard at Howth; therefore all this special pleading falls to the ground." As has been said, Mrs. Kirwan had fits of epilepsy during life and Kirwan noted the fact before the trial in one of the briefs now in the possession of a gentleman and ready at any time to be produced.

The following extracts are from a letter from one of the jury published in the *Freeman's Journal*, 20th January, 1853: "It was evident that about that hour (five minutes after seven o'clock) the unfortunate lady had been decoyed to the spot where her bathing cap was found and then thrown down, the damp sheet held forcibly down upon her face whilst her murderer knelt upon her belly and in her struggles to tear the sheet off her mouth, she tore the earring out of her ear and scratched her own face and neck. As soon as the resistance ceased, he [*Kirwan*] stripped the body, attiring it in a bathing shift and then carried the body into the water in the Long Hole, as far as the depth of his own knees, and committed it to the ebbing tide."

The Earring

It is lamentable that the jury should have fallen into the error that the earring was pulled out of Mrs. Kirwan's ear, for the earring, before the coffin was screwed down, was taken out of the ear of the deceased at the request of Mrs. Crowe, her mother, who was present, and given to her. The other earring was found by Dr. Hatchell in the ear, one month afterwards, at the post-mortem examination.

The Long Hole

In reference to the Long Hole and the ledge of rocks which goes nearly halfway across, and where the body was found; the first time Mr. and Mrs. Kirwan went to Ireland's Eye, Mrs. Kirwan asked the men to go round the island which they did, and landed in the Long Hole; and it may reasonably be presumed that Kirwan knew of the rocks, because the boat was steered so as to avoid them. Kirwan, knowing that rocks were there, is it likely that he would have carried the body to a place where it must have been stopped?

Mrs. Kirwan's Clothes

One would almost incline to the opinion that the jury lost sight of the fact that Mrs. Kirwan had on her bathing boots. Did Kirwan put them on and lace them?

If Kirwan first murdered Mrs. Kirwan and then carried the body as described by the juryman, what an admirable arrangement he made of the clothes: "just as she stepped out of them", to use Pat Nangle's phrase; and with the exquisite care and nicety he arranged all the smaller articles of her dress in the basket! But though this foresight and cunning

218

were great, they were nothing in comparison to the activity he displayed; for all the acts of tragedy must have commenced and concluded in less than twenty minutes.

No Marks of Strangulation

That Kirwan could not have strangled his wife is evident from the fact that Dr. Hatchell found nothing to warrant the assumption from any appearance, and the supposition of her having been stifled with a wet sheet is inconsistent with her cries; for it is impossible that anyone could cry out with a wet sheet pressed on the mouth, either wet or dry. Again we find the following [*from one of the jury in the* Freeman's Journal]: "Kirwan was a bad husband. Nobody but a fool and a knave could pretend that such appearances were compatible with death by drowning or epilepsy." This latter opinion is not very complimentary to Doctors Taylor and Rynd who signed the certificate. And from the statement it must be evident that Kirwan's character and the slanders that were circulated against him, charges of wholesale murder etc, which Mr. Butt in his able speech properly observed had poisoned the public mind, led to his condemnation.

If Miss Kenny had been examined, and had admitted that her brother wrote for her to go to America in 1847, and that Kirwan wanted her to go and offered to give her money to support and educate the children (then four in number) or that he would keep them here, would it not have given a different colouring to the case?

The question now really is, and it is one of great public importance, had Kirwan a fair trial? And was the evidence on which he was found guilty (having reference to the facts herein disclosed) so free from taint or suspicion as to justify his conviction?

The most remarkable feature in this case is the fact that the judges who tried the case were the parties who applied to the executive for commutation of sentence. Kirwan is either guilty or not guilty. If guilty, such a monster should not have been permitted to encumber the earth. If innocent how terrible his doom! And that no murder had been committed we have the evidence of Dr. Taylor and of many able and talented medical gentlemen of England and Ireland; their opinion being, that the medical evidence is wholly irreconcilable with death by violence, and that goes to rebut such a case.

It is perfectly clear that the executive found itself placed in a difficult position, in consequence of the interference of the judges who tried the case and induced the Crown to extend to the convict the Royal clemency. Under such circumstances, it would be more consistent had the sentence been altogether remitted, and it is quite clear that had there been a Court of Criminal Appeal, the judges should have granted a new trial; and it is equally clear that if Kirwan was tried again he must be acquitted. In the annals of criminal jurisprudence it was never known that a party was murdered by violent means, where no marks of violence were found either on the body of the deceased or on the person of the alleged murderer.

The public mind of Dublin has been so prejudiced against the convict, by means of false and slanderous reports circulated by the Dublin press, who denounced Kirwan as a wholesale robber and murderer, and who, with the exception of the *Warder* newspaper, refused publicity to his vindication, a circumstance unparalleled in the history of the press, and such we trust may never again occur. The circulation of these libellous and cruelly false statements has made it a hopeless effort to obtain sympathy or even a patient hearing for the wretched man in the city. An appeal is therefore made to English justice, not altogether on behalf of the convict, but on public grounds to vindicate the constitutional laws of England. Kirwan's case is the case of Everyman; for who is safe against the combined effects of slander and conspiracy?

◄○►

A voluminous appendix was added to the document which purported to prove the innocence of the prisoner including two self-serving statements from the Dublin County Coroner Henry Davis and Alex Boyd the foreman of the jury that conducted the inquest, attempting to justify the incompetence of their conduct of the inquiry and stave off some trenchant criticism from the media. There was also a letter to the *Daily Express* on the subject of the commuting of the prisoner's sentence: a letter from John Wynne, the Under Secretary to the Lord Lieutenant, Earl of Eglington, to the *Daily Express* on January 25th, 1853, correcting erroneous reports, pointed out that Lord Eglington acted on the recommendation of Judge Crampton and Baron Greene with the concurrence of the late Lord Chancellor and that he neither solicited nor received the advice of any other person whatsoever.

More pertinently there was a declaration signed by Teresa Kenny and the complete opinion of Dr. Alfred Swaine Taylor on the medical evidence presented at the trial which are vital to the case for the innocence of Kirwan and therefore worth considering in full. There are two points to bear in mind in considering the evidential value of the post-trial declarations. One is that Miss Kenny had clearly a vested interest and did not turn up to give evidence at the trial and the second was that Dr. Taylor in spite of his high qualifications – one of the foremost experts in medical jurisprudence in Britain – had not attended the trial and was relying on second-hand information.

Teresa Kenny's Declaration

I, Teresa Kenny of Dorset street in the city of Dublin, spinster, do solemnly and sincerely declare that I was examined by Major Brownrigg in his office, Lower Castle Yard some time about the 6th of October, 1852, and previous to the trial of the Queen *v* Kirwan and that in reply to one of the questions put to me, *viz* "If I was married to William Burke Kirwan?" I distinctly told him I was not. I declare that I was not married to said William Burke Kirwan, and that I knew of his marriage

221

with the late Mrs. Kirwan for the last ten years. I also declare that the deceased Mrs. Kirwan, from my own knowledge, was aware of his intimacy with me for the last ten years. I declare that when said William Burke Kirwan was first put on his trial sometime in November last, I attended pursuant to the summons served on me, and remained in court during the latter part of the day, when the trial was postponed.

I declare that the first day the trial came on in December last, I went to Green Street but could not get into the court and that I was most anxious to be examined; I was then suffering from a severe cut across my thumb, which bled until I fainted. I declare that during the trial of the said William Burke Kirwan I was in the house of Mrs. Bridget Casey of No. 19, North Anne Street, who generously gave me shelter and I was suffering from the effects of such cut, which threatened me with lockjaw, and that this wound and my agitated state of mind produced a low fever, and that for two days I was in bed almost wholly unconscious and insensible, and at which time one of my children was dangerously ill.

I declare that since my name has been brought before the public in connection with Mr. Kirwan, I have been hunted and persecuted, and almost driven to madness, not knowing where to find shelter either for myself or my seven helpless children. I declare that I have been obliged to leave my abode. I succeeded in obtaining lodgings in the house of a Mr. Matthews in North King Street and that I went there with my furniture and children between the hours of seven and eight o'clock of the 31st of December last, being New Year's Eve, and that the greater portion of my furniture having been brought up the stairs, Mrs. Matthews came to me and told me I could not remain; she gave me back the money I deposited and sooner than be subject to exposure I left the house; and that I and my children were obliged to remain in the street until almost two o'clock in the morning; and that but for the shelter of a covered car my children would have perished from the cold.

That having engaged lodgings in my present abode, a person of the name of Mortimer Redmond of the detective force called on me on 14th of January inst., in company with another man and a Mrs. Bowyer. He said he had a warrant against me for felony of papers and made search for them, and also for property alleged to have been stolen from Mr. Bowyer in the year 1837. He asked me if I knew anything about the murder of Mr. Bowyer; to which I replied I did not. He also went to the inner room and in the presence of my son Edward and my servant Mary Ann Rochford said: "Was I not a foolish woman not to have taken away some of the feather beds from Kirwan's house?" To which I replied that I never took anything, either papers or property, from Mr. Kirwan's house, save two newspapers.

I declare that about seven o'clock on Sunday evening the said Mortimer Redmond a second time called on me and against my wish intruded himself into my room. He said he came from Colonel Browne to inform me that Mr. Kirwan's property was to be sold on the following Friday, and to know if I had any legal claim and was I not married to Mr. Kirwan? He said he had evidence in the Castle of that marriage and that all he wanted was the name of a witness; and if I would I tell him and admit I was married, I would be restored to my position in society, and be entitled to Mr. Kirwan's property. I replied that I was not married to Mr. Kirwan and that I had told Major Brownrigg so. I then requested the said Redmond to leave my room, which he refused.

He sat down on the sofa and said that he would not stir until I told him when and how I was married; and when I insisted on his quitting and not terrifying my children, he then in a threatening tone and manner said: "Since you will not give me the information I want I now tell you that Colonel Browne will put your children in the poorhouse" to which I replied "My children are not begging; do with me as you like; but you shall not touch my children except over my dead body." I then insisted on him quitting and threatened to make him if he would not, when at last he did so.

223

I solemnly declare that sometime in the year 1847, my brother who resides in America wrote for me to go over to him; and that Mr. Kirwan begged me to go, and offered the means I required, and that he would either provide for the children here (then four in number) or I might take them with me and he would give me ample funds for their support and education, which I declined doing; and I do solemnly declare in the office of Mr. Kemmis the Crown Solicitor, that the responsibility of my intimacy with Kirwan was mine and not his. And I will make this solemn declaration at the request of Mr. John Knight Boswell, solicitor, conscientiously believing the same to be true and by virtue of the provisions of an act made and passed etc.

TERESA KENNY

Declared at Capel St. Police Court, Dublin, 26th January, 1853

Second Declaration on 28th January

I, Teresa Kenny, of Number 16 Lower Dorset Street in the city of Dublin, spinster, do solemnly and sincerely declare that it is not true that I and my children went to reside in the house of Mr. William Burke Kirwan in Merrion Street, shortly after the death of the late Mrs. Kirwan. I declare that sometime after the death of Mrs. Kirwan, my son William being very ill, I brought him to town to Mr. Kirwan's house to obtain medical advice, and for three or four days I remained in the house until four o'clock each day, attending on the child and returned to my family in the evening. I declare that the only other of my children who came with me was my son Edward who was in the house when Kirwan was arrested. I solemnly declare that after Mr. Kirwan was arrested I came into town and slept in his house for two nights, for the purpose of securing his property.

Dr. Taylor's assessment of the medical evidence was given to the supporters of Kirwan in time for John Knight Boswell's file and published in the February and May editions of the *Dublin Quarterly Journal of Medical Science*.

After the trial and conviction of W.B. Kirwan at the Commission Court in Dublin in December last, for the alleged murder of his wife, an appeal was made to me by several gentlemen of good professional standing in London and Dublin, to state my opinion regarding the validity of the medical evidence against the prisoner. The subjoined paper embodies that opinion. It was not written originally with a view to publication in a medical journal, but to aid in bringing about a revision and consideration of the medical evidence upon which the conviction seems to have taken place.

In considering the whole case, it seemed to me, notwithstanding the moral and circumstantial evidence against the accused, the learned judges who presided at the trial considered the medical proof of violent death to be absolutely necessary to conviction. The jury, by their verdict, came to the conclusion that the cause of death was violent, and from the hands of another; but the appearances of the body, so far from supporting, rather tended to rebut this view. Such, at least, if I am rightly informed is the conclusion to be drawn from the medical facts. But for the moral circumstances adduced against the prisoner, it is not possible to suppose that, in the absence of any marks of murderous violence on the body, to bear out the theory of the prosecution, of any marks of violent struggling or resistance, and in the absence of any of the special signs of drowning or strangulation on the body of the deceased, this man should have been convicted of murder.

A question then arises whether any amount of moral evidence can compensate for a deficiency of proof of the cause of death? From a sentence extracted from the charge of the learned judge, and placed at the head of the subjoined paper, the answer to this question must, I apprehend, be in the negative. The proof of a violent death is an essential part of the proof of the alleged crime; and in Kirwan's case this proof, medically speaking, is deficient. Had the signs and appearances of the kind of death (drowning and suffocation by pressure) by which the deceased is alleged to have been destroyed, been properly placed before the jury, they must, in my opinion, have been led to entertain a rational doubt whether death in this case was so clearly traced to violence at the hands of another, as to justify a conviction of murder.

Different degrees of evidence satisfy different minds; but a medical witness is bound to base his opinion on medical circumstances, and when these are not forthcoming, he cannot be allowed to supply their place by moral circumstances. It may be that some criminals will escape by strict adherence to this rule, but it is of small importance to society, compared with the punishment of one who is really innocent. Looking at the unsatisfactory nature of the medical nature of the medical evidence in the violent death of Mrs. Kirwan, it would certainly have justified a verdict of Not Proven.

Now, interrupting the flow of Dr. Taylor's assessment for a moment, "Not Proven" is a singular aspect of Scottish law which allows a third finding apart from guilty or not guilty. The accused may be guilty but if the jury have a problem with the production of sufficient evidence to prove guilt then that option is open to them. It does not mean that the accused is innocent but the prosecution have not persuaded them so. William Roughead, writing on the case much later, concurred with this view, with qualification, finding the medical evidence unsatisfactory: "Had the trial been held in Scotland, our national *via media* of Not Proven would have probably have followed." His qualification we will return to later.

In the charge to the jury by the learned judge, who tried the case, I find according to published reports, the following remark:

"But if you are unable to satisfy yourselves as to whether this was a *violent death* or a *natural death*, you ought to give the prisoner the benefit of your doubt, your rational, well-founded doubt, and to acquit him."

The jury seems to have been satisfied from the medical evidence that it was not a natural but a violent death, and to have returned a verdict accordingly.

With deference to the medical witnesses who gave evidence on this occasion respecting the death of Mrs. Kirwan, I beg to submit that the appearances of the body did not justify the inferences drawn, that these appearances fail to prove that the deceased died a violent death, and that they are quite reconcilable with the view that the deceased died, while in the water, from a sudden attack of apoplexy or epilepsy.

Dr. Taylor went on to agree with the defence view that the deceased died while in the water from a sudden attack of apoplexy or epilepsy and accepted the inquest evidence of the medical student Hamilton that there were abrasions of a small extent about the right temple and eyelids; a white froth, untinged by blood, issuing from the mouth; the countenance rather pale; blood on the cap coming from the ear; no wounds or marks of violence about the body. He then dealt with the details of Dr. Hatchell's post-mortem examination.

Taking these statements to represent the condition of the body of the deceased, I would beg to observe, that there is nothing here of a medical nature to prove that the deceased died by drowning, or by any form of asphyxia such as suffocation or strangling.

The most important and well-marked appearances of drowning are:

1. The presence of a frothy mucus and fluid tinged with blood in cases of great congestion during life throughout the air tubes of the lungs.

2. The presence of water (salt water if in the sea) in the stomach.
3. Congestion of the lungs with a full and distended condition of the right side of the heart and of the great blood vessels connected with it.

In dealing with the appearances observed by Dr. Hatchell at the post mortem thirty-one days after death Dr. Taylor concluded that there was no inference presumptive of death by drowning or any form of suffocation.

> In so far as the appearances can be relied on, they actually prove that the only certain signs of death by drowning were absent.
>
> The froth observed by Hamilton as issuing from the mouth recently after death may as well have been produced by a fit causing death while a person is in the water, as by actual drowning. The froth was not tinged with blood, a fact quite adverse to the theory that there was such congestion in the respiratory organs, from great pressure exerted during life as to cause oozing of blood from the ears. When well-marked appearances are wanting, there is an entire failure of medical evidence respecting the species of death.
>
> I believe that the only appearance which Dr. Hatchell relies on, engorgement of the vessels in the lungs, may have been due to post-mortem changes; it is not of the least value as medical evidence of drowning unless observed soon after death; and unless attended with other appearances which, upon the assumption of death by drowning, or by some other form of asphyxia, ought always to accompany it. One of the most striking characters of asphyxia including death by drowning, hanging, strangulation and suffocation is a distension of the right cavities of the heart, and of the large blood vessels connected with these cavities, with black fluid blood.
>
> Cases have been met where the lungs have not been found gorged and the cavities of the heart empty; but I cannot call to

mind a case where the lungs have been found engorged as a result of asphyxia and the cavities of the heart empty.

Dr. Taylor has now asked vital questions of the medical evidence of the post mortem on which first the investigation of Mrs. Kirwan's death was predicated and on which the conviction of her husband was achieved, saying in lay terms that she neither was forcibly drowned nor subjected to the pressure of suffocation. He has, however, to provide a cause of death and deal with one other hugely important observation not just by witnesses after the death but also by Dr. Hatchell at the post mortem: the bleeding from the vagina, an appearance which could equally question the eminent physician's assessment if not scientifically explained.

But thus far his opinion is simply stated: that with the highest degree of probability Mrs. Kirwan did not die either from drowning or suffocation. But in fairness to the doctor there was a qualification:

> But it may be said that that frothy mucus may have existed in the air passages at the time of death, so also the heart may have been distended with blood, and the stomach may have contained water, that in fact decomposition may have led to the obliteration of these conditions.
>
> Nonetheless when no marks of violence were found on the body to indicate death from asphyxia, it would be equal to declaring a man guilty of murder, not upon scientific proofs, or upon data confirmed by experience but upon mere conjecture. The theory of death therefore assumed by the prosecution is not only not proved but actually disproved by the appearances found on the body.

Had the dead body of Mrs. Kirwan been found inland, at some distance from the water, her clothes removed and no appearances of wetting about the body or hair, it appeared to Dr. Taylor impossible that any medical man in examining the body, and finding only the appearances described by Dr. Hatchell, could have arrived at the conclusion, that death had taken place from forcible drowning, or from asphyxia by compression, as a result of manual violence.

In dealing with the cuts and abrasions on the body, again Dr. Taylor relies perhaps too heavily on the observations of the medical student Hamilton who viewed the body after it had been washed the previous evening and said that these could have been caused by the deceased falling on her face and her struggles in dying. The bleeding from these parts including the ears could have been caused by the fact that the body was warm and the blood was prevented from coagulating by reason of its continual removal by water.

In regard to possible compression of the neck he states that this would result in not only bleeding from the ears, effusion of blood or frothy blood from the mouth and nose and a bloated and livid condition of the face, but also permanent marks of compression on the head, neck or chest.

He next moved on to the matter of bleeding from the vagina which Dr. Hatchell had stated was not caused by any wound to the area. He had not known it to occur in drowning and not in the murder of two females by strangulation in a very violent form which he had examined. There was violent constriction in both cases but no effusion of blood from the vagina.

The doctor posited to this having been as a result of delayed menstruation following from shock but he added that as far as cause of death was concerned, because there was no wound in the area, this proved nothing. It is as difficult, he observed, to reconcile this effusion of blood with the theory of death from violence, in a case like this, where no indication of violence from constriction or compression is apparent on the body. He did however admit that it is a rare condition in asphyxia and not a constant accompaniment or sign of the suffocation or strangulation of females. In other words it had been observed in such cases.

The fact that the genital organs were found vascular and injected, amounts to nothing; because the observation was

230

not made until thirty-one days after death and decomposition in the abdomen had advanced so far as to cause great distension and a pushing up of the diaphragm. Gravitation as well as the mechanical effect of this compression on the blood contained in the abdominal and pelvic viscera, might account for this increased vascularity. As it was not observed when the body was recent, it is a sign of no value as an indication of the cause of death.

This last sentence is in fact incorrect and clearly Dr. Taylor has not been made aware of the fact that the bleeding from the vagina had been noted by Patrick Nangle immediately after the body had been found, and later by the nurse tender Anne Lacey who was able to definitively state that the blood was not a result of menstruation. Thus his finding about it was capable of contradiction later by another medical examiner.

He disagrees with the prosecution contention that the deceased was suffocated by the placing of a sheet over her head as it would not prevent violent struggling, swallowing of water, marks of great resistance or injury to the back and arms of the victim where rocks and shingle were beneath. The prisoner would have wet his coat as well as trousers in such a struggle. If it might be suggested that the cavities of the heart were emptied by the process of decomposition, then it would only be fair to comment that the post mortem threw no light on this matter.

I assert, as my opinion, from a full and unbiased examination of the medical evidence in this case, that as far as the appearances of the body are concerned, there is an entire absence of proof that death was as a result of violence at the hands of another. Persons while bathing, or exposed to the chance of drowning, are often seized with fits which may prove suddenly fatal. The fit may arise from a stroke or epilepsy, and either of the conditions, would in my opinion, reconcile all the medical circumstances of this remarkable case.

In Dr. Taylor's twenty years' experience the commission of a murder usually required a lot more violence than anticipated and the lack of external wounds on the body of Mrs. Kirwan indicated that the death was not a result of homicidal drowning or suffocation, but most probably of a fit, resulting from natural causes. But had there been a post mortem within forty-eight hours of the death then there would have been better data and less need of speculation in relation to the cause of death.

> I have always regarded it as a necessary condition to support a charge of murder, that the evidence of the cause of death from violence should be distinct, conclusive and satisfactory. In this case, the medical proofs utterly fail to make out a violent cause of death.

He instances the appearances, the emptiness of the heart, the absence of salt water in the stomach as conditions adverse to the cause of death assigned by Dr. Hatchell. Their absence threw much doubt on the allegation necessary to prove Kirwan's guilt. Dr. Hatchell was placed in a difficult position by having to give an opinion on the cause of death from an inspection made, the body having been placed in a wet grave and decomposition advanced to a considerable extent.

> He would have acted more wisely and more in accordance with the rules of science, had he referred the infiltration of the lungs and vagina to post-mortem changes.

Dr. Taylor concluded by saying the post mortem either proved nothing with regard to the cause of death, or from the state of the heart and stomach it proved that death could not have taken place in the manner in which the witness supposed and asserted that it did take place.

That Dr. Taylor's expertise and qualifications were of the highest standard cannot be disputed so for the supporters of Kirwan's innocence his findings provided the most important element in their criticism of the circumstances surrounding the event on Ireland's Eye and the conviction of the husband for the murder of his wife. A more definitive stance from a medical expert they could not have hoped for and it was seeming vindication for all their efforts which were, it has to be said, energetic and exhaustive.

But like every aspect of this extraordinary case, this interpretation of the medical evidence was capable of both criticism and indeed contradiction for in the words of that well-worn cliché: Doctors differ and patients die.

That Dr. Hatchell's evidence was somewhat unsatisfactory was true but it was not his fault that the body was buried in unfavourable conditions and it was his opinion that, despite the state of decomposition, the internal organs were well preserved and thus capable of supplying a cause of death that at the very least were grounds of suspicion.

Needless to state, except as a reminder, that suspicion is not proof, but it would transpire that there was available to the prosecution a scientific opinion that went much further than that supplied by the police surgeon but inexplicably was not put into evidence. It was also available to the defenders of the prisoner but was given scant attention because the findings could have the effect of scuttling their campaign and the most important elements of the report were suppressed.

To justify its true importance in providing an answer to the guilt or innocence of Kirwan, it will be dealt with in detail later and in the proper context.

CHAPTER 8

THE ARGUMENT

Boswell's defence is thorough, detailed and impressive but in a number of instances providing an interpretation which was both self-serving and inaccurate – in other words, deserving of further analysis, which is the concern of this chapter.

The divergence of opinion between the Crown witness and engineer Alfred Jones and the engineer Mr. Foakes, solicited on behalf of the supporters of Kirwan, is remarkable. Mr. Jones' calculations were decided by the latter to be highly erroneous. Could such a difference be so radical and could either be considered credible? It would be up to a third expert to decide but he would not publish his findings until almost a decade later. This was the Reverend Samuel Haughton F.R.S., a fellow of Trinity College, who delivered a paper on the subject to the Royal Academy on Monday, May 7th, 1861.

The paper was entitled "On the true height of the tide at Ireland's Eye on the evening of 6th of September, 1852, the day of the murder of Mrs. Kirwan" and is as follows:

The following facts relative to the tide at Ireland's Eye were ascertained by me in December 1852, in consequence of the reports of Mr. Kirwan's trial, published in the Dublin newspapers, containing statements as to the time and height of the tide on the evening of the 6th of September which carried with them internal evidence of their inaccuracy. For example, it was given in evidence that the hour of high water on the evening of the day was half past three o'clock, and that the range of the tide was 9 feet.

I knew from the tidal observations of the Academy, of which I had the custody, that both these statements were erroneous; and, as they both seemed to be considered of importance in the trial, I resolved to make the measure requisite to ascertain the truth, with precision. I have never made the results I arrived at public as they did not affect the result of the trial, for a reason which will be stated; and I now bring them before the Academy as an illustration of the importance of the tidal observations made by that body, and to show the valuable uses to which those observations may be applied.

In bringing forward this subject, I have no wish to accuse those who conducted the prosecution of any negligence in procuring the best scientific information available, not to express any opinion as to the course adopted by the Lord Lieutenant, in commuting Mr. Kirwan's sentence after conviction for the murder of his wife.

On the 18th of December, 1852, low water occurred exactly at 10 a.m. (Dublin time) at Ireland's Eye; and on the same morning, by simultaneous observations on the tide gauge at Kingstown, it was found to occur there at 9 h 53 mins, showing that the tide at Ireland's Eye is seven minutes later than Kingstown. By careful levellings made forward and backward by Professor Downing, it was found that the top of the "Body Rock" was 1.26 feet higher than the zero of the tide pole used on the 18th of December. The following table contains the quarter hour observations made on this occasion at Ireland's Eye and Kingstown:

Hour	Height of Tide at I.E.	Height at Kingstown	Difference
9 a.m.	0.60 ft	6.25 ft	5.6ft
9.15	0.43	6.00	5.57
9.30	0.21	5.82	5.61
9.45	0.20	5.85	5.65
10.00	0.20	5.75	5.55
10.15	0.18	5.80	5.62
10.30	0.21	5.85	5.64
10.45	0.44	5.95	5.51
11.00	0.56	6.20	5.64

Mean average 5.60 feet.

The interval from high water at Kingstown to that at Ireland's Eye being thus found to be seven minutes, and the zero of the tide range at Kingstown being ascertained to be 5.64 feet below the zero of the tide pole at Ireland's Eye, we have, since the top of the "Body Rock" is 1.26 feet above the zero of the tide pole the following result:-

Height of zero of the tide pole above zero of the gauge:

5.604 feet.

Height of "Body Rock" above zero of the pole:

1.26 feet.

Height of "Body Rock" above zero of the Kingstown gauge:

6.84 feet.

On the day of Mrs. Kirwan's death the moon's age was 21d 9 and her declination 20°1.8N. Calculating the times of high water, low water and half ebb, from the Academy's observations at Kingtown for the 18th September 1851, find that on the evening of 6th September 1852:

High water at Ireland's Eye occurred at   4h. 37 p.m.

Low Water   10.14 p.m.

Half Ebb   7.25 p.m.

Time	True Height	Height in Court	Difference
High Water (4.37 p.m.)	+4.84 ft	+ 7.00 ft	+ 26 inches
6.30 p.m.	+3.11 ft	+2.50 ft	- 7.3 inches
7.0 p.m.	+2.37 ft	+1.75 ft	- 7.4 inches
7.15 p.m.	+1.85 ft	+1.375 ft	- 5.7 inches
7.30 p.m.	+1.34 ft	+1.00 ft	- 4.0 inches
Low Water (10.15 p.m.)	-1.86 ft	- 2 .00 ft	-1.7 inches.

Fortunately for the interests of justice the time of Mrs. Kirwan's death coincided very nearly with the time of half ebb of the tide at 7.25 p.m. when the real height of the water above the Body Rock only exceeded that alleged on the trial by five inches. Had the critical moment been nearer the tide of high water, the evidence given would have been in error of upwards of 2 feet; and as the exact height of the water was considered of great importance by both the Crown and the prisoner's counsel a substantial injustice would have been done to one side or another by the admission of erroneous evidence on a scientific question of so great delicacy and importance.

The Reverend Haughton's entirely objective assessment of the tidal conditions that prevailed on the evening of Mrs. Kirwan's death contradicted Mr. Foake's calculations to a degree that does not brook argument and suggests that they must have been living on a totally different planet in that regard. But the fact that the former, a world-renowned expert on tides, took so long to reveal his findings only serves to underline their veracity. And that Reverend Haughton found that the Crown witness only erred by a matter of five inches goes to prove in some way that Kirwan's defenders were capable of subjecting the truth to suit their purpose. That was not the only example.

It was not within his remit to say whether the height of the tide of the water over the Body Rock assisted Kirwan in the commission of the crime, but his calculations had that precise effect. It meant that the commission of the crime could have been effected by wading into the water landwards of the Body Rock and placing the corpse on the rock without the immediate consequence of it being moved by the receding tide and perhaps with the expectation that it might later. It suggested that the perpetrator had become familiar with the height and movement of the tide before the time chosen for the act and some little time afterwards.

Certainly the Reverend Haughton's assessment had the potential to prove that accidental falling on the rock as a result of a natural death was improbable. If someone, for example, was seized by a fainting fit while swimming it would be natural to seek a place that was bare of the very element that might ensure their demise and that would hardly be a rock that was at the time covered by almost 2 feet of water. On the other hand it would be natural for a perpetrator who had despatched the victim in more shallow water to place it on an elevated position with the hope that the tide would dispose of the body either further down the creek or out to sea.

It is a common aspiration of killers that the longer the period elapses from the act of murder to the discovery of the body the less chance that the sword of justice will fall upon them.

The next question that arises is the presence of the bathing sheet under the victim.

The boatman Pat Nangle was found by the trial jury to be a man of intelligence and good powers of observation. During the second search on the island for Mrs. Kirwan he discovered the body and was unequivocal about what he saw: the deceased had a bathing shift on her which was gathered up under her arms leaving the rest of her person exposed. There was a sheet under her back which was wet as well as the bathing shift. Under no circumstance could or would this witness of such an awful sight be induced to invent the conditions in which he found the body, nor being an experienced sailor should whatever shock he felt affect his judgement. He saw what he saw.

The significance of the wetness of the sheet has been overlooked. However dark, it was not a matter that the witness could have mistaken. Had it been left with the clothes on the rock above the high watermark, it would also have been dry.

His cousin Mick Nangle, when he arrived on the scene with Kirwan, appeared to think that the husband had brought down something white from the rock, in which the body was subsequently wrapped. It was dark and he might have been mistaken about this property, most likely being a chemise. Kirwan's supporters relied too heavily on the truncated proceedings of the inquest to refute Pat Nangle's observation.

This is not an uncommon phenomenon of direct evidence when witnesses seem to see different things. Mick Nangle's evidence was as uncertain as Pat Nangle's was consistent. Pat stated that it was the wet bathing sheet that he wrapped around the body to preserve some dignity for the exposed corpse. This detail is all the more telling as this evidence was given at the inquest the morning after the death, when Maria Kirwan was presumed drowned, and there could be no reason at this juncture for inventing evidence. Thus it must and should be accepted that Pat Nangle did see the presence of the bathing sheet under the body of Mrs. Kirwan on the rock, providing evidence that asked a huge question about the circumstance of what happened on the evening of the 6th of September, 1852.

Boswell was apt to exaggerate the importance of so-called prejudicial evidence against Kirwan such as the confusion about the clothes of the deceased. Pat Nangle felt that when Kirwan went up for them and he retrieved them that they had not been there when he had searched before. What was far more important, as far as inference went, was how Kirwan had any idea where the clothes were in the first place as he was not, according to his account, at the Long Hole at the time of the death.

It is then suggested that the rock is completely surrounded by the sea at high watermark and the spot where the clothes were found is covered at the same time. But that was at 4.37 p.m. almost two and a half hours before the screams were heard. It was of no consequence in the larger picture whether the husband or the wife placed them there (most likely the former) but of some consequence how the husband came to know where they were after the boatmen had failed to find them.

The appearance of the clothes and the contents of the basket found beside them are rightly suggested to have been more likely to be the work of a woman as opposed to a man. So, if it was posited by the prosecution that Mrs. Kirwan was first murdered and then stripped of her clothes, that theory was problematic. It would have placed an unusual and highly difficult task for a killer to strip the victim and attempt to put on her bathing clothes and then place her in the water and on to the rock where she was found. It simply makes no sense.

But it proves nothing in itself in relation to the ultimate method of the carrying out of the crime. It would have been far easier and more efficient in terms of time and the possible finding of the cause of death to attack when the person was in or about to get into the water in the bathing shift, cap and boots. That, as it will be later proved, is precisely what occurred.

The time of the supposed murder is quite rightly to be held as of great importance by Boswell and he admits from various witness evidence it must have been between 7 and 7.30 p.m.. Kirwan, he states, admittedly as he put it, was standing on the bank near the Martello Tower at about quarter before eight and if he had murdered his wife would have had to have time to dispose of the body. The weakness of this argument is that only one person knew where he was at the time and there is nothing to prove that he had been at the bank at the time suggested. The first thing that is heard of him is at eight and the screams were heard some time nearer to and after 7 p.m.

On this time sequence it would have given him close to thirty minutes to traverse the half mile to the bank above the landing stage, however rough the terrain, and sufficient light to accomplish the journey. A strong and fit person, as Kirwan was described to be, could have made it in half the time allotted.

Again, on the subject of where Kirwan was at the crucial time, Boswell relies on his statement to the inquest that he was sketching an evening appearance towards Dublin, which could only have been obtained at sunset. He allowed him time to put his utensils together and then get back to the Long Hole in time to meet the boat. An impossible task perhaps but only if based on two conditions. One that Kirwan was where it was suggested and also that he painted the scene on that evening. Allowing for the fact that this was the case, this version is predicated on a highly skilled artist having to wait until sundown for the effect and then taking an inordinate period to gather his effects. The sun began to set at 6.36 p.m., so he is allowed, say, fifteen minutes, to get to the Long Hole, all downhill and then say forty minutes to return to the bank. This would have given a very tight but not quite impossible window to commit the crime. He would have had to leave his bag in the spot where he had painted and collect it on the way back. Not entirely impossible but unlikely as the element of chance would have been greatly increased by the pressure involved.

Now the alternative scenario might have been that, given that he had spent two days with his wife on the island but a short few days before, on one of which Mick Nangle had seen the couple returning from the Long Hole, that he had completed the sunset sketch in advance. He could have completed it either day but to most effect on the previous Friday when the sun set at 6.43 p.m., giving him more than sufficient time to gather the tools of his trade and meet the boatmen at the arranged time on the nearby strand at 7 p.m.

Under such circumstances on the fateful evening he was under neither time nor location constraint. He had been to the Long Hole in advance and also had the opportunity to sketch the sunset appearance. No forensic process, even if there was such a suspicion could have proved when exactly that picture was completed or dismantle a somewhat tentative alibi, as a canvas can give no evidence other than what the painter desires.

The campaign to prove Kirwan's innocence veered from somewhat strong challenges to pure absurdities. One of those related to an alleged statement of a Father Hall, the local Catholic priest in Howth, who it was stated on the occasion of the arrival of the body at Howth openly spoke of his suspicion that Mrs. Kirwan was murdered to Sergeant Sherwood. That might or might not have been true but on two levels displayed a most uncomfortable prejudice, given that Kirwan was a Protestant and his wife a Catholic. The statement that Kirwan was convicted by evidence of the humblest class in society was not only a display of rank prejudice but compounded by the assertion that in doing that they would be influenced in the conviction of an innocent man by the word of a priest, as if they would manufacture evidence in a concerted manner as a result. When John Knight Boswell spoke of the slander of Kirwan with some justification, it was equally matched in this instance. To suggest that witnesses who withstood expert cross-examination would, because they came from a lower class and were Catholics, perjure themselves at the behest of a priest was an opinion beyond contempt. Perhaps also, it spoke of desperation to prove the unprovable; at the least it was a kick well below any acceptable belt.

The next matter the defender addressed was more acceptable of interpretation but not without the same facility of twisting the facts to suit a particular view.

The cries from the island he deals with, complaining that one witness heard one call when first giving information to police and then three in the trial, and that the most credible witness, acknowledged by the defence, Thomas Larkin, on the boat with the wind against him, nowhere proved he might not have mistaken cries from Kirwan when looking for his wife for cries of distress. Another absurd notion, considering the time difference involved and the fact evidenced by witnesses that there was no wind on that evening.

In relation to the time, Hugh Campbell's evidence was that he saw the boat leave Howth Harbour in or around half past seven which disposed of the theory that the cries could have been those of Kirwan or the boatmen while searching for the wife.

It was beyond all reason that five witnesses could have conspired or acted in concert when delivering such dramatic and unusual evidence, all in different locations at the one time. As William Roughead put it: "And those dreadful screams, heard over the water by five witnesses, re-echo across the years in a very ugly and suggestive manner for such as have ears to hear."

There follows a complex attempt to prove that Kirwan, when near the Martello tower sketching, could not have possibly heard the cries from the Long Hole despite the fact that five witnesses in Howth and on the passing boat had heard them. What the defender forgot or chose to forget was that Mick Nangle, in the company of Kirwan, heard Pat Nangle shouting from the area of the Martello Tower when they were right next to the Long Hole. Kirwan stated that Pat Nangle could not hear Mick Nangle's reply, something Pat had never said in evidence.

Also the first scream was heard by the fisherman Larkin when his vessel was but a short distance from the Martello Tower. If Kirwan was sketching nearby, he could not have failed to hear the same scream.

That demolished the defender's argument because there could not have been a possibility on a calm, windless evening that cries that were actually heard could not have been heard in the reverse direction. The only possible barrier, a wind, was not present in either direction. The cries heard could not have not been heard on the island, save by ears that did not want to hear them.

The washing of the body was brought up. Kirwan, it was claimed, asked Mrs. Campbell to have the body washed and then later in no uncertain terms the direction was given to Catherine McGarr. This, the defender says, is more redolent of innocence than guilt. The act seemingly or more alarmingly interpreted as to suggest that by covering up would attract suspicion. That it happened could not be contradicted and the motive could not possibly be any other but to wash away the wounds that were found on the body of his wife. He was told by one of the women attendants that this should not be done and still he insisted.

Suppression of evidence might not have been far from the mark. What other reason could there have been apart from a weak purpose of preserving the dignity of the corpse? If a servant girl could have known the inappropriate nature of the act, what could been going on in the mind of a man who had many dealings with top surgeons in supplying them with anatomical drawings, highly sophisticated in renderings of internal organs and representations of case histories of a wide variety of human disease?

With regard to Teresa Kenny's two declarations, again not sworn, in the first instance they provide a pitiable account of the persecution she and her children suffered at the hands of the landlady who ejected them on to the street and also the unwarranted attention of the constabulary putting her under pressure to admit that they were married. She appears to have been a lady of strong character, though somewhat misguided in taking all the blame for her relationship with Kirwan.

Her statement in relation to the crucial matter of the knowledge by Mrs. Kirwan of that intimacy is weak. "From my own knowledge", as she puts it, is less than definitive and translates more like "as far as I know". There is nothing to back it up – for example, some contact with Mrs. Kirwan that might prove it. In fact the calling of a woman to her door, mentioned briefly at the trial, is not addressed. The probable explanation is, perhaps, that Kirwan to suit his own purpose told her that his wife was aware of it without that having been true – a not unusual phenomenon in a triangular connection.

Her explanation for not turning up to give evidence has a ring of truth but speaks more of a woman beset by terrible anxiety who, understandably, could not face the extreme ordeal of appearing at the trial and being made a public show of in the witness box. It is obvious from the detail of her ordeal in the wake of Kirwan's arrest why she took this course of action, believing, quite correctly, that the ordeal would continue, though in a more apparently civilised fashion, in the full view of the public and the slavering attention of the press.

She does admit to have been in Kirwan's house for legitimate reasons after the death of his wife and after his arrest but somewhat underestimates the impact created by that presence, amplified by staying overnight to protect his property. Even to the unsuspicious and unprejudiced mind that was not a clever move and does not explain why medical attention could not have been administered at her own abode.

It is clear that under Boswell's direction the statements are narrow and selective but throw no meaningful light on nor contradict in any convincing way the prosecution theory in regard to motive. The confrontation between Teresa and the lady who was certainly Maria Kirwan, mentioned but omitted from evidence in the trial, is similarly omitted in her declaration which tells its own story. In both cases, the omission was favourable to the accused.

It was not the only one. What occurred, for example, between the couple during the time of the sojourn in Howth, when Kirwan for the first month or six weeks travelled to and stayed three nights a week with Teresa and the children? And how did he explain his permanent absence after that? Did he explain it by promising her that he was about to deal with the problem of Maria once and for all? Was the infamous row between Kirwan and Maria a result of the mysterious confrontation at the house of the second "Mrs. Kirwan"?

There is an undertone of depression and desperation in the declarations that even from the most hardhearted could elicit no less than sympathy for her plight. Teresa Kenny was also a victim. Victorian hypocrisy demanded that no heartfelt plea on the behalf of her children could be made in court, no appeal to the jury not to deprive seven children of the support of their father and literally throw them on the streets. The concept of Family was enshrined in the hearts and minds of the Victorians but Teresa and her children did not qualify and hence had no rights at all.

William Roughead was beyond harsh when he described her as a chronic concubine. As future events would demonstrate, she loved Kirwan, and her position was entirely a result of his despotic ways. Independent witness she could not have been.

While the campaign in favour of William Burke Kirwan's innocence was more notable for its vigour than an accurate interpretation of the facts, it gained great credibility for many years afterwards and the consensus of opinion was that the artist had been a victim of a miscarriage of justice. For any proponent of the opposite view and there were few if any, with the possible exception of William Roughead, a dispute over circumstance would not be sufficient to definitely prove the case, however compelling the argument.

The consensus of the advocates for miscarriage of justice was that William Burke Kirwan had been convicted for the crime of moral misbehaviour as opposed to the destruction of his wife. R.S. Lambert, a proponent of this view, writing on the case many years later summed this up: "For it proved in mid-19th century Ireland, a man could receive a life sentence for adultery combined with suspicion of murder, neither of which offences, in themselves, does our law recognise as punishable crimes."

There was a bit more to it than that rather simplistic summation. As Roughead noted: "Despite the famous dictum of Mr. Justice Stephen in the Maybrick case, adultery, of itself, is not necessarily an incitement to murder. If it were so, I am afraid our criminal courts would be sadly congested and the hangman would be worked to death."

All argument would, in most commentators' opinion, have been settled by a Court of Criminal Appeal which did not exist at the time, the outcome of which under such circumstances can only be a subject of speculation. Certain absent evidence for both sides might have been ventilated. For example, some of Boswell's in relation to the previous history of Mrs. Kirwan's health, but of course this time sworn statements as opposed to declarations. Others perhaps with reference to any previous knowledge by the wife and mistress of each other's existence.

But the danger for the defence, even in the event that an appeal process was available and successful and a retrial ordered, would be that Teresa Kenny would have no excuse to avoid the witness box and "from my own knowledge" would not be accepted by a tough cross-examiner as an affirmation. There would also be no excuse not to bring up the visit of a certain lady to Miss Kenny's abode. Worse still, if certain medical evidence canvassed but not used by the prosecution was introduced, the success of the appeal would have been placed in great jeopardy.

For 160 years this evidence has been in a medical journal housed in the library of the magnificent building of the Royal College of Physician's on Kildare Street. It provides the key to the secret of Ireland's Eye.

CHAPTER 9

THE CRIME

In the summer of 1852 and probably for a number of months before, William Burke Kirwan was under emotional, social, work and quite possibly financial pressure. It is evident from the diversity of his professional endeavours that he was an extremely hardworking man. He described his profession in Thom's Directory as miniature artist and watercolour painter. His creative urge must have craved singular attention but the remuneration would not have been sufficient to maintain one household in his neighbourhood not to mind the addition of another containing his mistress, seven children and a servant.

His stated profession could not have been anything but part-time, competing with anatomical drawings, picture cleaning, map-making, all related to the basis of his talent but hardly as satisfying in an aesthetic sense. Professionally he was being dragged in several directions and like all artists he would have desired recognition. This was inevitably related to his personal life and the financial implications of his choice but also the emotional ones.

The chances of a peaceful co-existence with such a division of affection and care are very slim and in Kirwan's case further complicated by striking fecundity in one woman and apparent

248

barrenness in the other. Quite apart from that fact, whether a wife, whose beauty was commented in life and death, would acquiesce to such an arrangement can be judged by some basic tenets of human nature.

But if secrecy provided a burden for Kirwan then exposure would bring with it a whole new set of problems and stresses. Jealousy, retribution and demands of faithfulness to mention a few. And justifiable threats without a doubt.

Prevarication or procrastination on Kirwan's part would have added to the mix, most especially under pressure from his wife who from a personal and social position was the woman betrayed, and it can only be speculated what impact the presence of children, when she had none of her own, had on Maria Kirwan. It is unlikely that she would give her husband an easy passage, given the extent and length of the deceit.

If it had not weighed on his mind before, and he would have been particularly arrogant and unfeeling had it not then in the secret phase, in the open was a different matter. It would inevitably have brought all sorts of unwelcome turmoil and a demand by his wife to make his choice for once and for all between her and his mistress. As time would prove, this so-called arrangement had not managed to make its way into the public domain and the possibility of that happening would have had many negative consequences for Kirwan, not only socially but also professionally.

The best possible outcome for the artist, as his wife would hardly have insisted on allowing Teresa Kenny and her children to starve, would have been to stick to his marriage and provide for his mistress and family. But the sensible thing that men might embrace in such a situation is often not what they want and the alternative, however ruinous in the long run, retains its attraction.

However, there is little doubt that a promise was made and it is not hard to imagine the nature and terms of that promise. If Kirwan was capable of loving anyone other than himself, in this scenario Teresa Kenny, for him the pressure and stress would have been magnified as opposed to alleviated, however well experienced he was in the practice of deceit.

Therefore, if Kirwan adopted this course, he would have been infected with anger and resentment towards his wife for forcing him into this position and not maintaining the status quo. There is no doubt that there was a massive confrontation, acknowledged by defence counsel Isaac Butt and called by him a reconciliation. Whether this referred to the row in Howth is a moot point. There would have been a prelude of a prolonged pain for both parties and not for the gaze of the marketplace or the subject of idle gossip for the servant.

While there was little known or attested in relation to the personality of Maria, she was a healthy, beautiful, finely built woman, a strong and brave swimmer, which indicates a strength of character, and who would not easily submit to the whims of her husband. His mistress may well have been more accommodating in that regard but she had her own pressures, not least a large family with no secure future on the horizon. She had her own worries and must have expressed them to the man of her house, irrespective of what she knew about the other household he occupied.

Kirwan may well have suffered from a form of melancholia, deeply depressed by the continual stress and the lack of acceptable resolution to the dilemma he faced. He would be later described as a gentle man and caring of his wife. The history of domestic violence is littered with previously quiet gentlemen, who for one reason or another adopt homicidal tendencies.

Nothing else would explain the vicious and dangerous nature of the row at the lodging house during which Kirwan threatened Maria's life and subjected her to a beating. The fact that it took place in a small lodging house within earshot of the occupants provides an insight into the lack of restraint demonstrated by Kirwan. He could not disguise or put reins on the depth of his anger. There were a number of other confrontations, this the worst, and all within the first month of their stay. Then all seemed well – for the moment. It was curious, however, that

Kirwan never even acknowledged or apologised to Mrs. Campbell for the inconvenience of the disturbance. Arrogance it may have been, shame it was not. Or perhaps someone of Kirwan's status would not stoop to save face to a social inferior.

He continued to travel to Dublin and stay there but later confined his trips to the daytime, returning to Howth by train for the evenings and sleeping exclusively at the lodgings. His behaviour in this regard was probably conditional on whatever strictures his wife had imposed but in no way meant that Teresa Kenny occupied a different place in his affection, proof of which would be provided many years thence.

It is not uncommon for men in the throes of such a dilemma to harbour ideation of the wife's death, a death from natural disease more than likely entertained, but some men are prepared in the absence of that to take it further. But on the surface, and to any prying attention, it appeared that the Kirwans were getting on well and people who had word of the earlier altercation which was certain in such a small community, could be forgiven for feeling that it was an isolated incident that was out of character. It could have been an uneasy peace or something more sinister.

The weeks passed and then in the early part of September there was a curious change of routine. On two succeeding days, Thursday the 2nd and Friday the 3rd, the couple took two long day trips to Ireland's Eye. On the Thursday the Nangles collected the Kirwans at 6 p.m. and on the following day at 7 p.m. as the sun was setting. This provided the artist the opportunity to sketch a sunset scene on a spot near the Martello Tower close to the landing place for the boat.

It also supplied an ample window for Kirwan to make a reconnaissance of the small island, check the timing of walking distances from one location to another in rough terrain and to observe the movement of the tide and sea in the Long Hole, all in the guise of sketching, lunching and walking with and without his wife while she was engaged in reading or bathing. If Kirwan had murder on his mind then this was the ideal preparation, made without the possibility of drawing any suspicious attention to himself. He could also establish with reasonable certainty the usual last departure time for other visitors from the island. And even more importantly with three trips, over and back, exactly how long it took the boatmen to row over to the island.

With the return to Dublin on Tuesday there would be a final opportunity to carry out a plan and a plan there must have been, as the succeeding trips to the island in the last week of their stay was beyond the realm of coincidence. How many hours were needed to sketch a view of the setting sun for an experienced and accomplished artist? And or any amount of other views if that was the purpose.

On Sunday night the boat was again ordered for the following morning, Monday, September 6th, and this, the third all-day trip, would be extended until 8 p.m., over one and a quarter hours after the sun began to set and darkness began to send long cold shadows over the cliffs and craggy face of Ireland's Eye.

There is an element of chance that can aid or bedevil any plan but William Burke Kirwan would have made a calculated guess that any other visitors would not be enticed to stay on the island for a number of hours before sunset and certainly not beyond 7 p.m. He could afford to play the possibilities by ear and would be aided by information from the boatmen and his own observation. Time would tell.

And it proved generous to him as the Brews took the boat from near the Martello Tower at 4 p.m. He was alone with his wife on the island and all he had to do was stay calm and wait for as near as possible to the hour that would cover his representation of the setting sun towards Howth from the spot he had already chosen near the Martello Tower, already finished and in his bag. And with a pretext to induce his wife to the Long Hole between six and seven.

That would not be difficult as she had been disturbed by the approaching boat earlier in the day when bathing near the Martello Tower and the Long Hole would provide more shelter at the later time in the evening. The day and the sea were calmer than he had expected and the power of the receding tide would be less than in more windy conditions. But that was a minor matter that he could find a way of dealing with without cluttering his brain or shredding his nerves. He'd had enough unwarranted suffering in the past months and all he wanted was for it to end together with the confusion of spirit and the constant nightmares. He had cursed himself enough and it was now the moment for her to take the brunt for her refusal to compromise. His procrastination made it worse, paralysed him even more as a result of her inviolate decision which had brought him to the brink. He had loved her once and was surprised when hatred replaced it in his heart and then ice-cold resolve to obliterate this pestilence from his life.

She was now no more than an object, the source of his wounded pride who had as a result of her recalcitrance reduced him to a common abuser, his delicate painting hands transformed to the fists of a drunken lout. A Punch and Judy Show for the poor widow and the servant girl. And now the impossible gulf between him and his former self, the glorious artistic spirit replaced by the trembling criminal mind.

But now there was no turning back and he was well aware that any such comparable crime is incredibly difficult to commit without leaving a signature, a simple clue, one small miscalculation that can instantly expose the guilt of the perpetrator. For all the meticulous preparation, the element of chance was always present, the matter of risk in such an undertaking could never be erased.

All he hoped was that the tide would take her out to sea and her body be soon disposed of by its natural inhabitants, not to be returned but taken away by the currents into the bay. Then there would be little explanation needed of him, other than the one he had rehearsed. *She left me to bathe and would walk around the island and meet me at the landing place.* He looked for the weakness in that and could find none. The darkness of the hour would hamper and delay the search. The less he said the better, for he knew well that a man could set a trap for himself in half a sentence.

Within the precipitous cliffs of this darkening hole he could do his worst with no one to see or hear and just pray that the sea would do the rest. Everything else augured well except the calm – there was hardly a breath of wind. Too much time to think, the quiet played on his nerves, this mountainous isle now with the demeanour of a sleeping whale. He tried to distract his confused thoughts by sketching but he found it increasingly difficult to concentrate. He had to for he would have to produce something for all the time spent on the island.

He had made all his calculations with meticulous rigor; he was a map-maker after all. The location was the best but not perfect. The entrance to the creek was narrow at the entrance but wider towards its head and a little beyond the middle landwards it was divided into two channels by a large and elevated rock. One hundred and fifty feet from the head a low barrier of rocks stretched across the channel about 12 feet above low watermark. The channel at this point was about 28 feet in breadth.

For the practical purpose of providing the sunset-sketch as proof that he was in the vicinity of the Martello Tower at the time but more importantly to be back at the landing place in time for the boatmen, he would have to strike no later than 7 o'clock and whatever complications arose have more than enough time to make the half-mile journey back. His observations of the movement of the receding tide approaching half-ebb gave the impression it was more than capable of pulling the body along the channel between the rock barrier and seawards.

There was always the possibility that it could get blocked by the barrier, but it was a chance that he would have to take, not having the time to overcome this obstacle and at the same time immerse himself above the waist to achieve that end. But to his advantage the depth of water on the landward side of the rock barrier would be relatively shallow. Two feet in depth would be more than sufficient.

He brought her to the Long Hole for the last time, the one last time to bathe before they left for Dublin and a new life, the one she had looked for and that he had agreed on. He looked at and consumed her beautiful body in his mind but it meant nothing to him any more.

There was nothing but hatred for her burned into his soul. Her looks and good character counted for nothing either but he did not dwell on how what beguiled him once upon a time now revolted him to the very heart of his murderous intent.

She decided to go for one final swim. It was getting late and in over half an hour the sun would set. He had suggested that he put her clothes on a sheltered part of the elevated rock in case there was another shower. She then walked towards the shallow water in her bathing shift, cap and the boots to prevent her feet being cut by the gravel. The bathing sheet he kept back from the rock so that she could dry herself when she got back to the strand.

She had noted his rather nervous silence but paid no attention; he was like that when he was sketching and painting, the moody concentration of the artist. His aggression had gone after that awful row; he had begged her forgiveness and given her the promise that was her marital right: to end that adulterous relationship. He had returned to being attentive and kind. She could and would experience happiness again.

Their love had subsided, but that was the ways of things, passion takes a second place after time, companionship takes its place and that has its own rewards. Her hurt and anger had also subsided but she knew that it would take a long time for the deep cut of betrayal to heal.

The sky was beautifully clear, the water not too cold. She turned to wave to her husband. He waved back. He was holding the bathing sheet in his hand. How comforting, she thought – he would wrap it around her when she got out of the water. She moved towards the barrier of rocks that traversed the channel.

Since the idea of murder had first entered his consciousness as the only solution to the threat of the disruption of his relationship with his mistress and ultimately separation from his children, his soul had been plunged into a dark chamber of conflict, despair and depression. He had been plagued by ideation of violence and transformed into a state of heightened anxiety. He felt trapped and hopeless. His normally ordered routine had been turned upside down and his self-esteem stripped to the bone.

His wife's steely determination not to accept the sharing of his affections had both surprised and angered him and he was incapable of truly understanding the depth of her hurt and shame. If he could not accept the terms of monogamy he would have to leave and he could not countenance that possibility. His sleep patterns utterly changed and however long he postponed his bedtime he awoke abruptly every morning at four on the hour as the sounds of birdsong welcomed the dawn.

Those signals of the entry of a new day, for one of a creative temperament, were now a form of torture, the onset of another chapter of conflicting thought, emotion and spiritual paralysis. He could hardly paint or sketch without a sensation of artistic revulsion. The anatomical drawings to which he applied such skill and care appeared to be grotesque far beyond the awful clinical detail. Everything in his life was flat, stale and unprofitable.

The pleasure he formerly derived from his work melted into ether and instead became a burden. He hardly recognised himself: a grey pallor had installed itself on his once sallow skin, his eyes were dull and lifeless and bordered by purplish black crescents.

His tangled emotions swung between suicidal and homicidal ideation, the latter prompted by the fact that *she* was blooming, powered by the exultation of *her* victory and his humiliating promises of sinning no more. The result was that his breaking of the sixth commandment was pushing him to the same of the eighth. In early August he had decided that the spiral must be halted and he pulled back from the brink of self-immolation and concentrated on the destruction of his wife.

He contained the wild horse of his hatred and swapped it for ice-cold determination. He realised that in this new phase that he must carry out the commission of the crime with as much care as he practised in his art. Otherwise the consequence would be simultaneous self-destruction, a possibility he must avoid at all cost. The sudden realisation struck him that his wife, being a strong swimmer who had been chided by her mother for taking risks, could be like many people in a coastal and fishing community, a victim of accidental drowning.

He was also aware from his many dealings with the medical profession that this rarefied breed was replete with many highly educated and clever men who, in the matter of deciding the cause of any death, most would not be found wanting. The drowning would of course be anything but accidental. Therefore the force applied should not leave the slightest appearance on the body of violence and equally no signs on the perpetrator.

The most perfect circumstance to avoid both suspicion and detection would be if the body was washed out to sea, either never to be recovered or exposed to the attentions of fishy predators who would inflict extensive damage to a corpse already exposed to the effects of tides, immersion in water and collision with rocks or other hard objects of every nature and size.

Most perfectly, the absence of a body would equal the absence of a crime.

But one way or another, he knew that if for some reason of chance the tide did not do its work, he must avoid inflicting any marks of external violence that might attract the attention of a medical examiner and lead to a suspicion that drowning might not be obviously the cause of death. He had to create conditions and a modus operandi that could not lead to the creation of any suspicion directed towards him. This had to be the perfect murder and carried out like no other before.

As an artist he had total visual recall and he trawled in his mind through the countless clinical records that he had been provided with while working on the drawings for the surgeons in The Royal College, the Meath and Jervis Street hospitals. He was working on a number of new commissions and on his day trips back to Dublin he had time to consult the records; his medical masters had given him complete access to them.

They had total trust in him and valued his work which had become part and parcel of their clinical work, adding a hugely important visual dimension which they could study and absorb without constant recourse to the patients. The drawings also provided a visual chronicle of the physical progress of the patients and the aftermath of successful operations.

He was no fool; there is an element of risk in every human endeavour but it must be reduced to a minimum. In that regard, the location of their holiday, if that could be so described, was propitious and more so for the elimination of possible witnesses, the island that lay off Howth Harbour, Ireland's Eye. As always time was pressing, there had been some idle talk about staying until November, but that was one of those aspirations that were but fleeting. It had been decided that they would return to Dublin on Tuesday, September 7th.

Although the iron had set in his soul he was still surprised by the strength of his reason and will. The plan to destroy another human being had never entered his mind before, not to mention that the planned victim was his wife of twelve years who he loved once upon a time and possibly still would have but for her obstinate nature. She was responsible for this catastrophic reality, after driving him to the brink of a nervous breakdown. No more.

But he was no different than any killer with intent in the frame and knew that such a crime is not easy to commit without being caught. The average and not-so-average murderer inevitably leaves too much to chance and always leaves clues. Intelligence provides no immunity to this experience. He could but do his utmost and hope for the best outcome, but nothing could or would be certain other than his determination to end the source of his overstrained irritable condition, his self-absorption and his misery.

In the event of a so-called accident he would have to be placed at the approximate time in another part of the island so he hatched the idea that he would be sketching a sunset scene towards Dublin which could only be achieved near the Martello Tower. Therefore the accident would have to happen at the furthest distance possible from that location and in a secluded spot. To that end and aware of his wife's knowledge of his punctilious methods of pursuing his art, he persuaded her that several trips to the island were necessary to achieve his objective.

The first two were planned for Wednesday the 1st and Friday the 3rd of September.

On those days he could utilise the long time spent on the island to minimise the risk of the enterprise and carry out a careful reconnaissance of the distances over the rocky and brambled terrain, the movement of the tides and choose the location of the crime. As for the tides, he would have to rely on his eyes. The days of mental rehearsal caused him some nervousness but when he concentrated on his sketching and drawing he was calmed.

The provenance of the nervous reaction was the constant introduction of extraneous possibilities of what might go wrong, for a variety of reasons he knew he had to accept, he could not control. These were but practical material difficulties that apart from the basic plan he knew would be best put aside. He had to concentrate on what he could control and stick to the chief point.

But that, he found at times, was easier said than done. On occasions his hands trembled when the enormity of what he was planning loomed in his thoughts. It was against everything that he was brought up to believe, and he, an intelligent and creative man, knew that it was against nature other than that of the jungle and no animal of that kingdom would slaughter another on the basis of inconvenience.

Then at other times, it all seemed like a trifle. What did one life matter, when set against the slaughtering machine of war? If the masters of the battlefield could justify their mass acts, so he should be able to also in a tiny insignificant case. He realised that the constant and invasive doubt must ultimately be banished, and he must believe in it all. Insofar as the moral question came into play, that had been settled. Despite the myriad of complications it was a simple act. So he told himself with increasing conviction.

And he had to maintain an outward appearance of calm and civility, at all times, especially in the wake of the evening that he lost all control and abused his wife mentally and physically. That had been a result of the mental and emotional pressure he had been undergoing but that was no excuse for allowing his emotions to cancel out all proper restraint. When reason fails the devil steps in. He knew with utter certainty that the devil in his psyche must be contained or he would either finish his life on the end of a rope or amidst the ghastly hardships of a convict colony in Australia.

But nature always has a way of reflecting what is hidden in the heart. On the Friday, shortly after 6.30 p.m., the sun had begun to set as he sketched towards Dublin and the clouds seemed to turn blood red. He was startled for a minute but continued and finished the work and was ready for the boatmen when they arrived at the landing point just before 7 p.m., but that night he had a troubled sleep and in his dreams the sky above the island began to weep blood. He would have liked to have incorporated the colour into a final finish on the image but knew that every artist left a print of his mind on the canvas. He could not afford such an indulgence in a work that was primarily intended as a form of inanimate alibi.

By mid-afternoon on those days the island was emptied of visitors and Monday should prove no different. But to be utterly sure this would be the case and to allow darkness to fall he had pushed back the collection time to 8 o'clock.

They had lunched and she had bathed at the Long Hole, which for him would be the ideal scene for the killing as it was on the opposite side of the island from the mainland and surrounded by cliffs. The rock barrier did provide a disadvantage but one which could be overcome depending on the strength of the tide going back out to sea.

The day had passed in a bit of a haze as he went through the motions of sketching, painting and being a civil and attentive husband, a role that he was well used to but not under this special circumstance in which every detail of the demise of his wife had been worked out in minute detail. If successful, no suspicion would lie on him nor could it.

He could have selected no better location for the committing of murder, or, in his opinion a better method, in many ways a unique one, fiendishly clever in its conception and hopefully matched by the execution. It had to be, to allow him to live and breathe again and to be in control of his destiny and not subject to the whims of his wife whom he had objectified as a vile and unforgiving woman in order to maintain the motivation and provide the justification for her death.

The thunder clouds of his confusion had drifted away and he was feeling stronger and more resolute and less bothered by the spectre of God's justice as opposed to earthly law. The latter he had no fear of as he had discovered that the legal punishment for such a crime frightens the potential perpetrator much less than the lawmakers anticipate once he has set his mind on the course of action.

The former he had reduced to a concept and not a matter of faith. He could hardly have justified all these years of illicit sex and adultery while being a believer. And he recognised in his sexual relations with his mistress, the animal within him that was sent to the kennel in the company of his wife. Because such flagrant satisfaction of desire was foreign to both her nature and status. He was addicted to that desire and could not contemplate a complete existence without it.

It was not all carnal. He loved his children and enjoyed their companionship and feared for their future. His wife had only herself to concentrate on and that selfish view could not be tolerated and could far easier be sacrificed in the complicated scheme of his life. These thoughts had concentrated his mind and hardened his heart as he sketched. She had brought the brute out in him; it was all her fault and she must pay the price.

There had been the shower sometime around six and then they had moved on to the Long Hole. She was reading and he was idly sketching on a pad. In reality he was running the plan over again. He would wrap the bathing sheet around her head and shoulders to prevent reactive wounds to himself and then submerge her in the water with the expectation that with slight loosening of his grip some of the sea water would seep into her mouth, stomach and lungs. He would then tighten his grip and push her to the bottom, holding the knotted sheet in place with one hand and pushing her chest with the other.

It should take no more than two to three minutes. He would then place her body on one of the rocks, which he noticed were still well covered with water, and the tide should take her down the channel and into the sea. It would be more certain if he could go beyond the rock and guide the body but it would mean being submerged above the waist, a risk he could not afford to take as he was supposed to be on dry land at the time. That would have no rational explanation other than he was attempting to rescue his drowning wife and that was not in the plan.

He took off his jacket and folded it carefully, leaving it on a rock, and pulled his shirtsleeves up beyond his elbows. She was accustomed to seeing him painting in his shirtsleeves and would think nothing of that.

She had changed out of her clothes and got into the bathing shift, put on her cap and boots. He offered to put her clothes in a sheltered spot on the elevated rock in the event of another shower. It made perfect sense to her. He kept the bathing sheet and told her that he would hold it for her when she came back from the swim. She smiled and gave him a kiss on the cheek.

This had the effect of unnerving him and time seemed to slow down and sound seemed to be elevated. There was a buzzing in his ears; he felt isolated and alienated from the immediate surroundings. She had turned and was walking through the shallow water towards the rock barrier. Now was his chance, to take her from behind, and the shock could help hasten her death. But he was frozen, his fingers gripped the sheet and he was paralysed with a fearful attack of nervousness.

Time passed without his notice, she had been in the water beyond the rocks and was now on her way back, the tide was beginning to recede fast, he had to pull himself together and act now or never. He pulled off his boots and socks and, rolling up his trousers, walked through the shallow water to meet her, keeping his eyes on her legs as they pushed towards the strand. He held up the bathing sheet as he did so. The brute returned and he kept walking, now raising his eyes to look in her face. She stopped and looked quizzically at first and then with a dawning cloud of fear. She had already begun to untie the upper strings of the bathing shift.

He rushed at her and with a swirling movement of his hands on the upper and lower ends of the sheet, covered her face and head. He tried to hold it firm but she fought with all her strength and managed to dislodge the upper end and uttered a piercing scream. Briefly, he caught a glimpse of her eyes, which were wide and bulging with fear. His blood was now boiling and he snarled and wrapped the sheet once again around her head and face and with a push of his chest and shoulders forced her back into slightly deeper water.

He had underestimated the speed of the tide, there was still more than enough to drown her but the shallowness would create the necessity for greater effort on his part. He had to be careful all the same to leave no marks of human violence on her that could provide a different interpretation of the event than he intended. He tried to force her downwards but she fought and fought, increasing his frustration and anger.

He wanted to abandon any restraint and strangle her with his bare hands while he looked into her eyes but he had to resist that path of self-destruction. The sheet was loose again and she let out another bloodcurdling scream. It did not matter, there was no one on the island to hear it. In one swift movement he secured the sheet and pushed hard on her chest until she fell backwards into the water. Again he pushed downwards and succeeded in submerging her head in the water. He held her down for a while and felt her body relax. The fight had gone, perhaps she was unconscious. He relaxed his grip on the sheet and then she rose up, pulling the sheet back again and for a moment he was frozen then brought back by another more mute scream. He could see she had been weakened by this effort.

He pulled the sheet back over her head and tightened it round the neck, pushed her chest and deftly turned her body about and pushed her downwards in the water until he could feel her head on the bottom. She wriggled like a dying fish and then went limp. Finally it was over. His heart was racing and every nerve in his body was jangling but he experienced when he stopped shaking a great sense of relief. He let go for a moment.

The light in the sky was beginning to fade and soon the boatmen would be preparing to make the journey back to the island. The sheet had been dislodged from the head in the final struggle but was still tight on the neck. He unwrapped it and placed it on its back on the nearest rock in the barrier. With a sinking feeling he realised that there was blood on the face and ears. The bathing cap had been dislodged in the struggle and he could not see it anywhere. With further dismay he noticed one of the earlobes was injured and there was a cut on the breast. He could feel the panic rising. He left the body as it was, while he recovered from the mental and physical effort.

All his mental rehearsals had not prepared him for this. It had all seemed so simple in his imagination: the sheet wrapped around the head, face, several submersions. Like a fool he had not accounted for her strength; every fish wriggles on the end of the hook. No being submits to expiry without a fight. He thought of leaving her where she was but that was now impossible. She must go to the sea.

He should not have turned her over: the shale on the sea bottom had cut into her. Anger and emotion had got the better of him and he just wanted to finish the task. He had no idea of how much time passed in the interim, he didn't care, he just had to have a clear thought. It was about a quarter past seven o'clock, he still had plenty of time. He quelled another wave of panic and got down to business.

He lifted the dead weight under the arms, pulled it the small distance to the small rock and placed it head towards the sea in the bobbing water. The shift had come up under her arms in the movement and he left it as it was in case the back might snag in the rock. He felt the comforting tide swirling around his lower legs under the instruction of the moon. He was overcome by a strange feeling: a mixture of exhaustion, depression and fear. Confusion followed and racing thoughts. In these moments reality took on the pace of a dream.

He retreated towards the strand in a daze. He looked up, the light was dying slowly in the sky, in one place it was a red streak. The central rock was right before him like a black inanimate monster, a witness to his foul act. It could betray him, the sea could let him down, already shale at its bottom had pointed the finger at him. He realised with another sinking of his mood that the reason that had driven him to this point had been nothing but the slave of his passion. And passion recognises no boundaries of logic.

And then calm. It was done; it was to time to go.

The fear had been substituted by the return of his vanity and conceit, a move to the real and comfortable side of his divided self. He was convinced that from this moment nothing would impede his path to happiness and contentment with his beloved Teresa and their children.

He had to move fast to get back to the landing spot and felt confident the fast-moving tide would complete the rest of the plan. If that did not work then it would be perceived as a tragic accident, a result of accidental drowning.

The encroaching darkness matched that of his soul. But he felt no pity for the woman he thought he had once loved, just the comfort of the prospect of being in control of his life again. He turned away from the strand and left the earthly remains of his wife to the waves. As he made his way back with his bag in hand to the Martello Tower he experienced a sense of elation but knew that he would have to be now careful about every utterance in regard to the tragic death of his "much-loved" wife.

He had played a number of roles in his life thus far and the latest was to be that of a grieving husband. As far as William Burke Kirwan was concerned, he was now a free man and his future happiness was assured. But a killer could very easily condemn himself with his mouth and he decided to be economical with everything he said. He was determined not to trip himself up. He had his story, he would stick to it and the less said after that the better.

He had a legal right to silence and thus could hold his tongue but not even a restrained man can account for the impact that the swirling tide of chance or change of circumstance can have on his self-possession. There is an art to concealing the mind's construction in the face and the act of depriving another human being of life has haunting consequences that the architect could never anticipate.

Kirwan would be aware of those truths all too soon.

The brutal extinction of his wife was only the beginning of a nightmare that began almost immediately that night. His procrastination at the landing spot started the torment, followed by the uneasiness of his first lies and the chiding of his social inferiors the boatmen. Their insults tore at him but he knew that he could not respond. He should have shouted from the bank, but no, they got in first. He should have affected some sense of panic, but he could not, that would only come to pass with a genuine threat to his self-preservation.

He dreaded the search of the Long Hole as they moved through the malignant shroud of the island, his cries for his wife stuck in his throat like an errant chicken bone, rendering them meaningless and unconvincing. What if the tide had not done its work, what then? As they approached the creek for a second time, his stomach became a knot of nervous anticipation. He stumbled twice in his confusion and fear, anything to stave off the inevitable.

The boatmen transformed to monsters in his mind, punishing him for leaving his wife to make her own way back in the dark. He was filled full of loathing for the situation and the weak position he was playing against the strength and determination of the searchers to find his missing wife. He should have admired their fortitude in the face of danger to themselves but he didn't – he resented it. He hoped against hope that full fathom five his wife would lie.

The nightmare continued in connected images that both taunted and repelled him. His worst fear was realised when he heard the shout that the body had been found. She lay on the rock where he had placed her. He feigned distress but it was more for himself and may have appeared genuine. Her blood was freely flowing and he was seized with an internal convulsion of terror; this was not what the records described on the body of the drowned.

He stayed while they went to bring about the boat. He tried to think straight, to be calm in the face of what lay before him. His homework had all been for nought. She was weeping blood triumphantly and there was nothing for the moment he could do about it. He would have to wait until they returned to the lodging house. For some reason he had made a mistake, the cause of which he did not know. There was no evidence of a struggle on him; the scratches on her could be easily explained. But the rest?

He had now become a horrified witness of his own action that seemed to mock and taunt him in a hideous dream, the end of which would be certain retribution. He felt no pity for his victim and no remorse, for if he hanged it would be even. It was more the emerging futility and self-defeating nature of his deed that disturbed him. He hardly remembered the journey back but once on dry land his self-possession must be restored; for a man, grief must be a brief visitor and he must take command or he would be lost.

The first thing on the way was to withstand the boatmen's demand for compensation and he stood his ground. The next was not an act of bravado but a vital necessity. The wounds and bleeding had to be modified as long as there was no intervention by the constabulary. He ordered Mrs. Campbell to have the body laid out and washed. Despite a mild protest which he slapped down, it was achieved. He was in control once more and was determined to say as little as possible at the inquest.

He had probably, he thought, used too much force in the execution of the crime but felt the tide had turned in his favour. He would take his chances and there would be no more mistakes. He dried his wet trousers in front of the open fire. His shadow flickered on the wall, he ignored it. The hauntings evaporated. He was William Burke Kirwan, a person of substance, a resident of a favoured neighbourhood, a spouse who had lost his wife to a tragic accident and above all an innocent man. His life, in time, would return to normal.

As he had already discovered, when one ceases to believe in oneself, anything of awful nature is possible.

CHAPTER 10

THE PROOF

William Burke Kirwan or more accurately his reputation had been the subject of a reversal of fortune in the wake of his conviction and the commuting of his sentence. There was an intense campaign to prove his innocence and prove that his trial and conviction had been a miscarriage of justice, backed by men of expertise and reputation. As already discussed, the issues raised contained many valid points and just as many absurd notions, contradictions and highly selective interpretations of the evidence and circumstances of the event and the case.

Conveniently and rather sadly, the victim Maria Kirwan and the real nature of her brutal death received scant if any attention. The rights of the perpetrator, sacrosanct in law, are always perceived to be superior to those of the victim. One of the remarkable aspects of the case, taking into account his right to avoid self-incrimination, was the paucity of the statements of Kirwan, first at the inquest and secondly in his address to the court after conviction.

The other was the failure of the one other person who could have thrown great light on the subject to turn up in court to give evidence. If Teresa Kenny had appeared and said what the defence proposed, that she and Maria Kirwan had all along known and approved of each other's existence, then there would have been no credible motive for the murder and Kirwan might well have been acquitted. Her lover's life was at stake and yet she could not help him in his hour of need, later giving the lame excuse that she had cut her thumb and one of the children was sick.

The more likely explanation was that if she spoke the truth, the motive would have been copper-fastened, and in any event, to be fair to her, she was not prepared to commit perjury. And/or her lover persuaded her not to appear. One way or another it did not reflect well on a plea for innocence for Kirwan and left a gaping hole in the process of establishing the truth.

As William Roughead put it: "In hearing, reading and writing about these cases, I always feel how much there is behind the scenes that one ought to know in order to arrive at a fully informed judgement and how much that, by reason of sundry rules in the game played by counsel with the prisoner's life at stake, is never allowed to come out in court."

Kirwan's address to the court is quite remarkable, unintentionally revealing and not redolent of the expression of an innocent man who is about to be condemned to death. His demeanour was utterly composed throughout and he showed not a scintilla of emotion.

For a start there is no mention of the issues at the heart of the trial and he refers to the tragedy as an unfortunate affair. There is no reference to love of his wife or grief or regret for her passing, or an attempt to confirm that she and his mistress were aware of each other, no plea for mercy for his children who will be left without a father.

He eschewed a perfect opportunity, however late in the day, to stake his claim of innocence; instead he offered his account of the fateful day in September in which he unwittingly removed one of the main planks of the defence case. After their arrival on the island Mrs. Kirwan went to bathe near the Martello Tower but a short time later approached him "partly dressed, and told of the arrival of a boat with another party". This must have been the Brews arriving at midday. The boat, he observed, was travelling rapidly with the wind behind it.

There are two elements of sub-text here. Firstly he claims Mrs. Kirwan will henceforth be uncomfortable bathing at this strand because of the likelihood of interruption by outside parties. Did "partly dressed" mean she threw on some clothes as she was not dressed at the time, or was she undressing? This detail was meant to explain why she would choose a different location later, one not usually used by women. He weakens this explanation further by offering a different excuse to Michael Nangle, saying that his wife did not like to go to bathe where he told her to "because there was a bad smell".

The second element of subtext suggests that there was a wind from the Howth direction helping the boat travel faster than usual, though the advantage for him in that fact he did not make clear.

They walked about a bit and went to the old church ruins where he made a couple of sketches and remained for "some considerable time". His wife read and walked about. They left the ruins before the departure of the Brew party at 4 p.m. Previous to that they went to another part of the island and under the shelter of rocks ate the dinner they had brought with them.

This was hugely significant because it must have been between 2 and 4 p.m. when Mrs. Kirwan spoke to Arthur Brew as the party was leaving the landing place. The defence theory that Mrs. Kirwan entered the water with a full stomach, bringing on an epileptic fit, was thus dismantled in an instant by her husband and completely corroborated the post-mortem finding that the stomach was empty and contracted. And of equal importance Kirwan did not tell the court that she suffered from or had any history of such affliction.

He made no reference to this only explanation offered for the accidental demise of his wife at the inquest and again at trial where the subject was exhaustively examined and proposed to save him from the scaffold. Again he was avoiding the substantive issues which landed him in this extreme predicament.

He then said that they went to a place where he was making a study or sketch towards Howth Harbour. He left out Mrs. Kirwan's strand encounter with the Brews and the Nangles, so it is to be assumed that this is much later.

What is also striking about this account is the lack of specifying some of the locations, which coming from a man who had been there already twice before within a short period, smacks of deliberate vagueness. The condemned man, even at this fateful juncture, was treading very carefully through his rambling narrative.

For example, the best shelter of rocks for the meal would have been the Long Hole but he avoids locating it by name. Similarly, the spot where he was supposed to be sketching.

Next comes the most incredible arrangement. From there Mrs. Kirwan leaves, saying she would go to bathe, taking her bathing dress with her and she would walk around the island and meet at the landing place. She does not specify where she is going to bathe and he does not ask, an understandable omission, given the facts.

But later he will be able to point the direction she took. He has an aversion to mentioning the Long Hole. The time is presumably after the shower at 6 p.m. So Kirwan, who knows the small island like the back of his hand, allows his wife to go to bathe in a location which with the fall of night has many hidden dangers and then traverse rough terrain in darkness to meet him at the landing place? Is it likely that any sensible person, man or woman, would assent to such an arrangement?

Hardly, so why would an innocent man concoct such a story?

He continued his narrative, sketching for more than a couple of hours, "till it was getting duskish". He then washed his brush and colours and put them in his bag. On the basis of the sworn statement to the inquest, his wife left to bathe around 6 p.m., but this account now puts him gathering his art utensils after 8 p.m. and then going to the landing place where he saw no sign of

Mrs. Kirwan. Next he walks towards the high ground to see if she was coming and called out her name saying that the boat was approaching.

But by this time-scenario the boat had already arrived. So his story does not tally with that of the boatmen. How could a man who is telling the truth get so mixed up? "A liar needs a good memory" comes to mind and exposes the complete fallacy of the so-called arrangement. He next plays the role of concerned spouse. He calls out to the men.

"I called out and asked them what delayed them and to hurry and make haste." Apart from the fact that none of the men heard this entreaty and could not have failed to do so on the calm night, there had been no delay as they arrived perfectly on time. But the convicted man gave the impression that the boat was late, a version entirely at odds with those who would defend him later. Now, having been untroubled by his wife's absence in another part of the island for a number of hours, he was beset by anxiety for her welfare.

Here he elects himself as the guiding hand in the search which was patently untrue. That Kirwan could play this role is without debate; his professional masks were many and his personal ones had been effective for a considerable time. But he had a big problem when it came to credibly explaining what happened on the fateful day.

Pat Nangle came up unannounced, he says, and picked up his things off the bank. Not from him, he added, as he had not got them in his hands. The boatman, on the contrary, testified that he responded to Kirwan's direct order to come to relieve him of the bag and sketch book.

Kirwan then told the court that Michael Nangle approached and that he "advanced a few steps" to meet him. Nangle then asked him where the mistress was and he "immediately told him she went to bathe after the shower, that I was looking and calling for her and that we would go and look for her".

The boatmen, however, obviously found it strange that Kirwan was mute on the matter of his wife until they demanded her whereabouts. There had been several inferences made about this apparent silence, the principal interpretation from the prosecution being that he intended going to the boat, which his defender Knight correctly said was patently absurd. But not even he could account for the silence. Perhaps Kirwan was collecting his thoughts, wondering what to invent next.

Apart from exaggerating his role for self-serving purposes, the rest was close enough to what happened. But again, in recounting the search, he let slip a detail of prime importance but of damning implication to himself. He had of course neither at the inquest nor in his address referred to the matter of the screams that had been heard by people on the shore and on the passing boat. His counsel Isaac Butt offered no explanation for this failure on his client's behalf and concentrated on trying to undermine the evidence of those on the shore.

There was no wind blowing from the direction of Howth; it was so calm a candle could have retained its flame. He first falsely claimed that after seeing nothing in the Long Hole he suggested to "this man", being Mick Nangle, that they should retrace their steps – maybe Mrs. Kirwan might have hurt herself and was delayed by it. "At that time we heard the cries of Pat Nangle from the bank." This was the bank that was above the landing place, so the boatman's cries could be heard from beside the Martello Tower by the two who were beside the Long Hole. Mick Nangle also heard his cousin's voice but felt no need to reply. There was no natural impediment to hearing cries in the opposite direction, though this seemed to have been the point of the next statement. "Pat Nangle states that he did not hear Michael Nangle answer his replies. I told Michael Nangle to answer and expressed my gratification that Mrs. Kirwan, I was sure, had come to the boat." The first part of this is pure invention to create the impression that Pat Nangle could not have heard cries or shouts from the vicinity of the Long Hole. An absurd proposition in itself as there was no impediment whatsoever except to deaf ears. The second part is possibly true as, if they had returned to the landing place, there was a further stalling in the search and the possibility that they would not return to the Long Hole.

Judge Crampton then interrupted and that was the end to Kirwan's statement about the "unfortunate affair".

CHAPTER 11

THE MEDICAL PROOF

The following paper published in the *Dublin Medical Press* on Wednesday, January 26th, 1853, is deserving of a full treatment, as it not only supersedes the medical opinion of Dr. Alfred Swaine Taylor and the other medical witnesses at the trial but also in its punctilious medical and forensic detail proves with little shadow of doubt that William Burke Kirwan murdered his wife on September 6th, 1852. The author, Dr. Thomas Geoghegan, a professor and fellow of the Royal College of Surgeons had the benefit over his esteemed English colleague of not only visiting the scene of the crime on a number of occasions but also sitting through the whole trial.

Of all the medical witnesses in the trial none was better qualified than Dr. Geoghegan to properly assess the vital appearances and come to a conclusion as to the cause of death. Since 1835 he was Professor of Medical Jurisprudence at the Royal College and also held the chair of Forensic Science, and his professional acumen and qualifications were so well recognised that he was consulted in many complex murder investigations in England. He was, in addition, an expert in toxicology. At the time of the trial he was, at 45 years of age, a man at his prime both humanly and professionally. His paper would provide more than adequate confirmation of the fact.

Why his findings were not admitted into evidence is one of the mysteries of the case. That they were dismissed out of hand by the prisoner's defenders without qualification is indicative of their power as they defeat conclusively all previous medical opinion on behalf of Kirwan.

Geoghegan's colleague Dr. Hatchell's evidence may have been adjudged to be wanting but his post-mortem findings, however barely expressed, were found to be not too short of the mark. Delivering medical evidence in court is an art in itself and Dr. Hatchell did not match it with his scientific ability. Nonetheless it is the foundation stone on which Dr. Geoghegan builds his case. The basis of the professor's findings is based firmly on medical science but also and properly, as forensic science demands, combined with the circumstances surrounding the death.

What failed to definitively emerge in the trial was a firm interpretation of the appearances on the body that would satisfactorily account for the cause of death. This is precisely what Dr. Geoghegan provides and thus eliminates the doubts that persisted about the efficacy of the conviction of Kirwan. It will also be seen that his victim suffered a brutal and violent death at the hands of her husband.

"An Examination of the Medical Facts in the Case of the Queen v Kirwan; with Medico-Legal Observations"

The extraordinary interest that has attached to the late trial of William Burke Kirwan for the murder of his wife has been sufficiently evinced by the protracted discussion of the subject in the public prints. What may have been the qualifications of the persons engaged in the controversy is no part of my purpose to enquire; nor shall I comment on the dangerous consequences which are apprehended, if, in future, solemnly and deliberately conducted judicial inquiries should become subject to the revision of popular clamour.

These topics have been handled with much force by those whose province it is to discuss them.

I have been induced to attempt an exposition of the medical facts both in consequence of my having observed that the majority of the profession appear to be, and (for obvious reasons) necessarily must be but imperfectly acquainted with them; and also as the inferences to which they lead appear of considerable moment in a medico-legal point of view.

Having been consulted by the Crown at an early stage of the case, and having been present through the entire trial, I have the opportunity of becoming fully acquainted with its medical relations. I shall, in the first instance, state the medical facts, both as they appeared in evidence and elicited by the Crown previous to the trial. It will, however, be necessary to premise such observations on the locality where the death occurred, and also on the general facts, as may render the medico-legal details more clearly intelligible.

Dr. Geoghegan then goes on to give a detailed account of the geography of Ireland's Eye and then comes to the discovery of the body.

Just within the barrier of rocks and immediately at the base of the south-eastern wall of the inlet, which is here 31 feet in height, the body was discovered a little before 9 p.m. It lay on the back, in a direction parallel to the course of the channel. The head, placed towards the sea, hung backwards, resting at the base of one of the barrier rocks 3 feet in height.

The body lay on a low rock (9 inches high), the arms were extended, the knees bent, the feet lay in a small pool of water. A little below the feet was another rock, 16 inches in height. These rocks were covered partially with seaweed and scattered limpets. The deceased was found clad in a wet bathing dress with loose collar and bathing boots. The former "was gathered up towards the arms". A wet sheet lay beneath the body. The head was uncovered and the hair filled with seaweed and gravel. The bathing cap was discovered at high watermark a few weeks afterwards.

The clothes of the deceased, the situation of which was pointed out by the prisoner, were found at an elevation of 5 feet and a half on a steep part of a large rock, already described as dividing the channel and at a distance of 72 feet from the body. From the place the clothes occupied to the "Body Rock," the bottom of the Long Hole declined towards the sea by a gradient of about one in 18 feet.

It appeared from the concurrent testimony of five witnesses (one at sea) that several screams identified by one witness as female, were heard to proceed from the direction of the island at 7 p.m. at which time, according to the carefully checked measurements of Mr. Jones, there was a depth of but 21 inches over the "Body Rock", and a total depth of 30 inches *beside* it. The water's edge at this time was about 60 feet beyond the "Body Rock", and 16 feet below the spot occupied by the clothes. The tide was receding, the water and the weather perfectly calm.

When discovered the body was warm and flexible, and presented other conditions, to be afterwards described. Having been wrapped in a sail, it was conveyed to Howth at midnight, at which time the limbs were still pliable, but the surface cold. It was washed shortly afterwards by the peremptory direction of the prisoner, despite the remonstrance of one of the assistants, who suggested that it should be first inspected by the police. The recent external appearances were observed by an experienced nurse tender, who had lived at Howth forty years, and who had, during that time, externally examined numerous drowned bodies and was in the habit of laying out the dead.

They were also witnessed for the most part by the boatman who discovered the deceased's body, and by the assisting women. They were, as follows:

Intense and dark livor of the right side, extending from the axilla to below the knee. Eyes much injected; the right one closed, the left open. Considerable swelling of the lips, especially the upper. Thin white froth about the mouth and nose, recurring in quantity after removal from the scene and still observable on the second day, at which time the body was free from putrefaction. This was evidenced by the fact that the neck, shoulders and abdomen were still rigid indicating that rigor mortis was still present. The belly flat. Blood flowed freely from the ear-passages for a considerable time despite repeated cleansing with a towel. Blood flowed rather freely from the genitals and was found coagulated on the sheet when the deceased was about to be put into the coffin. It was not, according to the nurse tender, like the natural discharge but thick and black.

There were superficial cuts or scratches on the eyelids, cheek, forehead and right temple, and blood is stated to have flown from the left nipple, all of which were bleeding freely while the body was being washed. The edges of the ears were rubbed and the right lobe nearly detached. The nose was crooked, the neck a little twisted but otherwise showing nothing unusual. In addition to the above, the following conditions, not elicited in evidence, had been ascertained: lividity of the face; bluish blackness of the nails; considerable swelling of the external genitals.

A coroner's inquest was held, and although no post-mortem examination had been instituted, and notwithstanding that the general facts were of a character to awaken strong suspicion, a verdict of accidental death was returned. The attention of the authorities having been subsequently directed to the case, an exhumation was ordered and took place on the 6th of October, thirty-one days after death and twenty-six after burial, the mean temperature of the interval having been 55 degrees.

Dr. Geoghegan then reproduces Dr. Hatchell's post-mortem examination given in evidence in court.

It appeared that the deceased had been seen late on the day of the fatal occurrence, apparently, quite well walking and reading on the island. The woman with whom she lodged considered her to be in good health; and that she really was so, is rendered highly probable by the circumstance, that during her stay in Howth that she was known as a most adventurous swimmer. No evidence was adduced at the trial to show that she had been the subject of any previous disease, and the prisoner on examination at the inquest, made no allusion whatever to the subject.

An attempt, it is true, was made through one of the witnesses, to establish that she had a hereditary predisposition to epilepsy; this was coupled, however, with the admission that the information was derived from a deeply interested party. This same matter of hereditary tendency is also alluded to in a singular document bearing the signatures of Dublin practitioners, privately circulated in Dublin and afterwards published in a London paper.

The document alluded to, if genuine, would lead to the conclusion, that the subscribers believe, that a certificate, which they do not profess to have seen, and to the effect that a certain person "died of a fit" (the kind not stated), is to be received as evidence that his daughter died by epileptic drowning!

Another less refined species of evidence, however, was thought desirable; accordingly, two witnesses (an artist and a servant maid) sometime after the trial made declaration (not oath as erroneously stated by the subscribers of the above document), that the deceased had been seen by them on two occasions in a fit, and that the prisoner was present. On this evidence every person of common sense may be left to form their own conclusions.

It would be drawing too largely on human credulity to demand the belief that prisoner's counsel or his experienced solicitor should not have been aware of these facts; nor of the above witnesses having been in attendance; nor again, of the views of the medical witness who entertained the epileptic theory of death, and who was present and in communication with counsel on both days of the trial. How far the admission of their truth should have influenced a decision on the cause of death, we shall presently consider.

The medical facts, the import of which we are about to examine, are of threefold kind: first, the important external conditions noted by several persons while the body was still quite recent; secondly, those observed at the post-mortem examination; and lastly, and in connection with the two preceding, the medical history of the deceased, and such collateral circumstances as are closely interwoven with the medical data, and appreciable in their true relations with the medical inquirer only.*

[*Geoghegan's footnote: *It may be desirable here to examine a question on which much misapprehension prevails; I allude to the influence which putrefaction exerts both on the morbid condition of internal organs and on the external signs of violence. In the document to which I have already alluded, and in one appended to it, and which, as bearing a solitary signature, is I presume, considered a cheval de bataille by the prisoner's friends, the doctrine is maintained that a month's (in reality 26 days) interment in a moist place renders it impossible to determine the existence of morbid changes or signs of violence. This statement is not only refuted by the dissection, in which some of the external signs of congestion and violence were found to have remained unaltered, but is opposed by the experience of Orfila, the highest authority on legal medicine.*

Of the brain he writes: "Pendant plusieurs semaines á moins que la temperature n'ait ete forte elevee le cerveau conserve assez toutes ses properties normales pur qu'on puisse y reconnaître les diverses parties que entrent dans sa composition et constater les traces épanchements, ce dependent il tend de bonne heure a devenir d'un gris olivatre clair." ["During many weeks unless the temperature has been very high, the brain conserves almost all its normal properties so we can recognise the various parts of its composition and note the traces of effusion, that tend early on to become a light olive grey."]

From the latter fact the inference that the brain was congested at the time of death appears to have been a sound one.

Of the lungs Orfila says: "Ils conservent leur aspect natural pendant long-temps; on peut meme au bout de quelque mois reconnaître leur structure, et constater s'ils sont le siége d'un lesion pathologique." ["They retain their natural aspect for a long time; one can even after a few months recognise their structures, and note if they are the seat of a pathological lesion."]

In a body, the exhumation of which I superintended at Mount Jerome, by direction of the Government, and which had been three weeks buried in a very wet grave I had no difficulty in determining the cause of death, or in recognising the conditions of the thoracic and abdominal viscera. In conjunction also, with Dr. Hatchell, I lately examined two cases after a month's interment, under similar conditions. The inner organs had undergone remarkably little change. The chief alterations in such instances arise from the accumulation of gases in the abdomen, and the influence this exerted through the diaphragm on the right side of the heart.

There are other interesting effects of gaseous accumulation which are generally little understood, but of such moment in practice. One of these is the protrusion of the eyeballs, which occurs in putrefaction under water, or in rapid putrefaction in the air, and which was witnessed in the present case. In a celebrated criminal trial here in 1842 (The Queen v Byrne), I stated and (still more to the point) proved the occurrence of such a condition; which depends, as I have found by dissection, on the accumulation of gases in the back of the orbit.

As protrusion is the opposite condition to that observed in slow putrefaction of the dissecting room my statement was received with incredulity by that portion of the profession which, inexperienced in medico-legal questions assumes, notwithstanding, on important occasions and almost exclusive right of deciding on them. My view on the subject, in the trial alluded to, was fully concurred by a gentleman, Mr. Robert Adams, as well known to surgical science as he is respected for his sterling integrity and worth.

Protrusion of the tongue may be similarly produced. The second effect of gaseous accumulation is the expulsion of the contents of stomach and rectum; and hence the presence of portions of food in the mouth, fauces [passage from back of mouth to the pharynx] *and air passages in persons who have lain for some time in the water. The absence of food in these quarters in Mrs. Kirwan's body, and the contracted state of the stomach clearly prove that the organ was empty at the time of death.*

Dr. Hatchell and myself have found by experiment that the saline ingredients of sea water are not sufficient to prevent the expulsion of the latter from the stomach by gas pressure in the abdomen. As respects the influence of putrefaction on congestion of the lungs, it is certain alike, as a matter of fact and theory, that the latter condition cannot be produced by decomposition.

It is true, as Orfila remarks, that congestions, which in the recent lung, under the influence of gravity, occupy the most depending parts, become more diffused when decay takes place. But in such cases, the nature of the congestion must be determined, as in that of recent origin by the amount of the accumulation and the collateral facts. Exclusive weight is too often attributed to the influence of time and other extrinsic circumstances on the putrefaction process. The intrinsic conditions of the body, though more obscure, often exert a much greater effect. Thus I have seen a body, thirty-six hours after death, in cold weather, in state of extreme decomposition, with enormous extrication of gas.

The influence of decomposition on the blood is also much misunderstood. If coagulated at the time of death, it remains so, often for several weeks. The fact, to which I think Bernt first drew attention, that the condition of the blood, as to fluidity and coagulation, varies in the same body, is often overlooked. Thus in the spinal and cerebral veins, it is often fluid while coagulated in the heart. I have constantly observed that it differs in these respects in the heart and lungs and even in the auricles and ventricles of the heart. When the heart is empty in a body in which the abdomen is distended with gas (if the organ were not empty at the time of death), the blood may be assumed to have been fluid at that period. I have found firm coagulation in the heart after three weeks' interment in wet ground.

Another circumstance deserving of notice is the coagulation of the extravasated blood where it remains fluid in the vessels. Thus, I have sometimes observed the blood which has flowed in a fluid state from drowned and other bodies to coagulate by exposure. Dr. Munro observed the same in hanged persons.]

In the case which forms the subject of this communication, a careful consideration of the *entire series* of *appearances* in connection with the fact that the deceased had been immediately before in good health, that the body presented no sign of organic disease capable of suddenly terminating life nor of other modes of violent death (as wounding etc) clearly proves that the fatal event was the result of asphyxia.

Thus under the circumstances above described were present, intense congestion of the otherwise healthy lungs, dark and fluid condition of the blood* [*see footnote below*], intense livor of the dependent parts of the surface. To these were superadded the signs which are present where suffocation is a result of incomplete exclusion of air, and consequently protracted struggle, namely froth about the mouth and nostrils, injection of the eyes, considerable swelling of the lips, and lastly, those local haemorrhages which sometimes occur when asphyxia has been combined with compression of the neck or chest.

The defence adopted by the prisoner's counsel, based on the views of some of the medical witnesses, was that the deceased had been seized with epilepsy while bathing shortly after a meal and had thus been drowned in shallow water. No attempt was made to show that she had perished either from epilepsy alone or apoplexy. Independently of other considerations, the latter view might have been refuted, simply by reference to the situation of the body when discovered; for had the deceased been attacked by either, or where the water was so shallow as not to have covered the mouth and nostrils, the body could not have been afterwards wafted to the "Body Rock" by the receding tide even had it (in the absence of any assisting cause) immediately after death.

[*Geoghegan's footnote: *The intensity of the livor of the right side of the body, the colour of blood discharged from the genitals and the persistent bleeding of the superficial wounds sufficiently attest to the above character of the blood. The empty condition of the heart also afforded a presumption to the same effect; for I have found that when the organ contains coagula, these are not expelled by the pressure of gases in the belly.*

It must, however, be remembered, that in some cases of asphyxia, the heart has been found altogether empty (as in the celebrated case of the Prince De Conde, who hanged himself during the revolution of 1830); and in some of Devergie and Orfila's dissections, the left heart contained more blood than the right. Such exceptional conditions, however, would be likely to be mistaken only by those who fall into the error too common in medico-legal inquiries, of forming a judgement from individual and not from combined appearances and medical facts.

In Mrs. Kirwan's case the recent condition of the heart is unknown. The very free flow of blood, however, on the section of the great veins at the base of the neck renders it probable that the right auricle was loaded. Any objection to the evidence of asphyxial death, on the above score, applies with equal force to the epileptic theory of death. In the case of Ferrari (London 1831), the heart was quite empty and the lungs not congested.

Here the death, according to the confession of the prisoner, was by smothering. The characters of the body were chiefly negative. The organs generally were healthy. The conviction was had entirely on circumstantial evidence.]

The phenomena of drowning present themselves practically under two distinct forms: firstly, where the submersion is continuous from its commencement, and where asphyxia is consequently produced in its most rapid form; secondly, where the drowning person in possession of consciousness and volition maintains a more or less protracted struggle, rising and sinking for some time beneath the surface of the water. A corresponding and marked contrast exists in the appearances of each.

In the former, the face is pale and placid, lips unswollen, and froth is absent from the mouth. *Internally* the signs of congestion are comparatively light and not unusually altogether wanting. Such are the results of numerous practical investigations on the subject by the most eminent medical jurists. Several very careful observations and dissections of the drowned, have led me to the same conclusion.

It is almost superfluous to observe that the epileptic who falls senseless into the water is placed in the former of the above named conditions. Hence the ordinary phenomena of epilepsy which depend on partial closure of the aperture of the windpipe and prolonged expiratory effort are at once superseded by those of rapid drowning.

A good illustration is afforded by the following case, for an opportunity of examining I am indebted to my friend Dr. McDowell: a lunatic female subject to modified epilepsy was found dead and lying on her back in a trough, in which she had been in the habit of washing, and in which the water was about 18 inches deep. The face was pale and perfectly calm, like that of a person in sleep. There was no froth at the mouth, [*bloody*] injection of the eyes or swelling of the lips. The lungs were but slightly congested. A few trivial contusions were on the posterior part of the body. A person who falls insensible into the water from any other cause, presents the like appearances.

Fodere notices the absence of froth in epileptic drowning and Dr. Ogston's experience, as he informs me is the same.

The appearances of the countenance and those of the lungs in the Kirwan case were therefore altogether opposed to those of epileptic drowning.

The previous history of the deceased (as we have already seen), the posture of the body as compared with the external marks of injury, and the absence of any exciting cause, were alike in conflict with the above hypothesis. Had the deceased been seized with epilepsy, and *fallen on her face*, she would have remained so, as the convulsive motions (either of the disease or of drowning) could not have sufficed to have turned the body which the presence of scratches would indicate to have lain in contact with the adjacent rock.

An attempt was made to show the marks were produced by crabs. This is refuted by both the character of the injuries, by the evidence of the nurse tender, who from long observation of drowned bodies, was familiar with such, and also by the fact that no crabs were discovered near the body, with which they must have been very busy in order to have produced the injuries observed *so soon after death*.

Had she, on the contrary *fallen on her back*, there should have been no scratches on *the face*. Lastly, the assumed exciting cause did not exist. The stomach, on dissection, was found empty and *contracted*. From the latter circumstance, it is manifest, on the grounds, already stated, that at the time of death the organ contained no food. The discussions relative to epileptic screaming, were alike superfluous and absurd, inasmuch as screams could not be repeated by a person lying, as it was assumed with the mouth *under water*, and as on the occurrence of the fit, the sufferer falls at once.

Had those appearances alone, which have already been considered, been present, it is evident from preceding facts that the deceased, *if drowned at all*, must, during no inconsiderable period of the process, have been in possession of consciousness and voluntary motion. Suicide in shallow water being out of the question, both from the medical and general circumstances, the question therefore would then have presented itself for the jury: by *what obstacle* the escape of the deceased from shallow water had been prevented. I can state from very minute examination of the Long Hole, that none existed in the nature of the bottom.

An answer to this might perhaps, with difficulty, have been found in the moral facts.

The Dublin medical dictum is not only in conflict with the well-ascertained facts of legal medicine but ignores or *eludes* the circumstance, that the decision of juries in questions of homicide, is based not merely on the *medical evidence*, but on the *entire body of facts* submitted to them. Were this not so, the function of the jury would virtually cease. Daily experience shows that in cases where two or more hypotheses as to the cause of death are left open by the medical witness, a jury may determine from the general evidence which is the true one.

The question, however, must now be entertained: Was *drowning at all concerned* in the production of the fatal result? The post-mortem conditions, taken in their integrity, were, in my judgement incompatible with drowning in its simple forms; for, after a careful and extended examination of the subject, I have been unable to discover a *single case* amongst the numerous instances of drowning on record, in which either bleeding from the ears or genitals (independent of wounding) has been noticed, or even any general statement to the same effect.

I have been equally unsuccessful in the inquiries I have instituted amongst those most competent, from medico-legal experience, to elucidate the subject. One of the city coroners informs me that out of about 270 cases of drowning which had fallen under his notice, nothing of the kind has been observed. From equally careful inquiries I arrive at the same result with epilepsy. My venerated friend Dr. Marshall Hall known throughout the world as a profound physician and physiologist and who has devoted, as it is well known, especial attention to epilepsy, has favoured me with a note to the following effect: "My dear sir, I have never seen bleeding from the ears or vagina in epilepsy. Bleeding from both ears and vagina occurs in hanging." I have received similar statements from other distinguished members of the profession.

Exclusive of bleeding from the ears and genitals, the medical facts are obviously reconcilable with either strangulation or the protracted form of drowning. Thus, the conditions of the countenance are common to both, as are the state of the lungs, stomach and blood.*

The above haemorrhages, however (occurring, independent of mechanical injury), have only been observed in asphyxia resulting from either strangulation (including hanging) or compression of the chest. This subject appears not to have sufficiently attracted the attention of medical jurists; yet it would appear that vaginal bleeding has been frequently noticed in hanging and strangulation. Thus Dr. Cooke recorded three cases of suicidal hanging in lunatics which have fallen under his own notice, and in two of which the subjects had passed the period of menstruation.

It seems to have been frequently noticed in executed criminals; so much so that as Dr. Cooke and others state, it has been the practice in some prisons to place straw under the drop in female executions. I learn from a gentleman who was present at the dissection of Butterly and Ennis, hanged in this city some years ago, that he observed their drawers copiously stained with blood. This condition, which formed a subject of controversy some years since, has been described as menstruation.

By whatever title, however it is designated, it is equally important if present as a consequence of strangulation, and not other forms of asphyxia. In Mrs. Kirwan's case, that the discharge was neither a result of menstruation nor of wounding, was evident from the careful dissection performed by Dr. Hatchell.

No fluid of any kind was found in the uterus; the *healthy pus* covering the *ulcer of the cervix* was unstained, a thin *bloody* fluid coated the walls of the vagina, which with the interior of the labiae, were highly congested. The blood discharged from the genitals was also observed by the nurse tender in clots upon the sheet. Further, had the deceased been menstruating on the day of her death, it is most improbable that she would have bathed. Finally the nature of the discharge is corroborated by the co-existence of bleeding from the ears.

It is to be expected in those cases only where from a concurrence of favouring circumstances, the congestion is extreme. The source of the bleeding probably varies. Littre found the membranes of the ears ruptured in a case of manual strangulation but probably such a condition is by no means indispensable. The occurrence of aural bleeding in strangulation and its absence in drowning, are, I conceive, readily explained.

In the latter the obstruction to the return of blood from the head is to be sought for in the loaded state of the right heart, and in the great impairment of the respiratory motions. In strangulation an additional source of obstruction is furnished by the pressure on the jugular veins, while the arteries continue to deliver blood to the head. In drowning again, the entire tract of the venous system of the head and neck, and downwards to the heart, is open to receive the accumulating venous blood; while in strangulation *all that portion below the seat of compression* ceases to be available.

The occurrence of haemorrhage from the vagina, in the latter form of death does not admit of this explanation. It seems to be produced by the same conditions which occasionally give rise to bleeding into the cavity of the stomach, sometimes observed in hanging. The fact of the absence of vaginal bleeding in drowning and its not uncommon presence in hanging, is not the less incontestable. An analogous fact presents itself in the male subject, in the erection and seminal omission of the hanged, a phenomenon which obviously depends on the accumulation of blood in the organ.

The greater rapidity of death by drowning as compared with strangulation, and which, according to Sir B. Brodie, is perhaps due to the concurrent influence of the cold, may assist in explaining the differences in the amount of congestion and consequent haemorrhage in the latter form of violence. The nature of the medium may also have its effect.

Bleeding from the ears also occurs in *compression of the chest*; it was observed in three out of twenty-three persons suffocated by pressure in a crowd at the Champs De Mars. Where other circumstances are favourable it is probably adequate to the production of bleeding from the vagina also.

Although froth was not discovered in the air-passages on dissection, it unquestionably existed there at the time of death. No other view can explain the abundance of recurrent froth while the body was still fresh. Thus, on the second day, notwithstanding the previous cleansings, it was present in abundance around the mouth (Hamilton). There appears no reason for refusing the presence of asphyxia froth in the latter situation, the same weight which is attached to its existence in the windpipe, provided that its characters are equally well defined, and that it is supported by consistent train of collateral appearances, and in harmony with the rest of the medical facts.

If an opposite view has gained some credence, it has probably been in consequence of the servility with which some of late have adopted the opinions of the French writers on legal medicine. I have also observed in the drowned, that movement of the body (by acting on the walls of the chest) causes the expulsion of froth, so that while an abundance was found around the mouth and nostrils, little was discovered in the windpipe. Where the inspection is delayed or the body has lain in water, Orfila has shown that the froth of drowning is generally absent.

The preceding considerations, will I think, suffice to show that the entire series of medical facts leads to the following conclusions:

That the death of Mrs. Kirwan was not the result of apoplexy, or of epilepsy, nor yet of epileptic or suicidal drowning.

That the *combined* conditions of the body (both external and internal) were incompatible with drowning unattended with other violence.

That the appearances observed may have been produced by strangulation alone or combined with compression of the chest, or with partial smothering.

That they are also consistent with a mixed process of strangulation and submersion, in which the latter condition was not continuous from its commencement.

The chief circumstance which tends to render the last named view more probable, are the nature and quantity of the froth observed.

In strangulation, froth is not uncommonly absent, and when present, usually mucous or bloody, smaller in amount and of coarser structure.

The absence of any mark upon the neck is perfectly consistent with strangulation with a broad and soft material. Duchesne inspected the body of a man who hanged himself with his drawers; there was no discolouration, and even the mere trifling depression of the skin was scarcely visible. I examined in 1848 a similar case of suicidal hanging with a pocket handkerchief. The depression just described would be at once obliterated by mere motion of the neck.

The scratches and abrasions noticed on Mrs. Kirwan's face and body and the lacerated wound of the ear most probably resulted in her struggles to procure freedom for the face and neck.

As to the precise details of the mode in which the destruction of the deceased was effected, it would be, I conceive, impossible to offer a satisfactory opinion. On the whole, the conditions of the body, with such of the general facts that are intimately connected with them, as the special depths of water and the nature of the locality, are most consistent with the view that the deceased had been strangled at the land side of the "Body Rock" in very shallow water. Whatever may have been the precise spot where the purpose was effected, it seems clear, from the position and clothing of the body, and from other circumstances, that the deceased must have been placed after death on the rock where she was discovered.

In determining the person by whom the homicide was committed, the jury were of course, guided, as in other cases, by the moral facts. Had the medical details been elicited in a fuller and systematic manner, even that question might have been limited within a much narrower compass. The general evidence showed that in addition to maltreatment, the accused had threatened the destruction of the deceased; that he had maintained an adulterous intercourse with another woman who became an inmate of his house shortly after his wife's death; that although his wife had been parted from him for some time on a lonely island and had not joined him after nightfall he did not even mention her when about to depart for Howth.

When to this is added, his having caused, as far as might be, the removal of the signs of violence; his suppression of evidence on the latter head; and, that, when he himself examined as a witness at the inquest, he made no allusion to the fits of epilepsy, which were afterwards urged as the cause of death, etc.

With these data to aid their decision the jury probably felt that the view which assigned to the prisoner the murder of his wife, was more consistent with the evidence than that which referred to an agency of fishermen or pirates. In its medico-legal relations, the present case is one of interest and importance; and should the foregoing, the imperfection of which I fully recognise, tend to a more correct estimate of its real nature my object will have been attained.

This is an extraordinary paper which through the medium of medical examination, medico-legal inquiry and forensic science proves beyond all reasonable doubt that William Burke Kirwan not only murdered his wife Sarah Maria Louisa but did so in a clever and particularly brutal fashion. It is equally extraordinary that Dr. Geoghegan, who had assisted the investigation, had made a minute examination of the scene of the crime and had attended the trial, was not called as a medical witness for the prosecution.

All this information was in possession of the prosecution in advance of the trial and, if utilised with Dr. Geoghegan as a witness, Mr. Hayes would not have had to admit that their medical evidence was not what they had expected. Worse still, had William Burke Kirwan been acquitted as a result of such a shortcoming, a real miscarriage of justice would have resulted and it was probably only because of Mr. Hayes' skilful cross-examination of Dr. Adams that this did not happen.

It was no coincidence that the first thing the jury looked for before making their final deliberation was the evidence of Dr. Adams.

It is little wonder that the supporters of the campaign for Kirwan's innocence completely ignored Dr. Geoghegan's findings as they also exposed the fact that the eminent members of the medical profession in Dublin who subscribed to it simply did not know what they were talking about and however well qualified in their own disciplines had no expertise in the very specialised medico-legal field.

The thoroughness of his examination of the medical facts of the case is hugely impressive and he literally leaves no stone unturned, utilising not only his own considerable forensic skill but backing his analysis with investigative power and reference to the opinions not only of top contemporary professionals but also some of the greatest practitioners such as Orfila.

He dismantles the medical theory put forward on behalf of the defence that the cause of death was an epileptic fit brought on by immersion in the water after a meal and consequent drowning. In the first instance there was no evidence of a history of the condition and secondly, with the support of experts on the subject and his own analysis of the possibility, the doctor proves that the medical appearances of the body and its position on the rock could have never been consistent in any small detail with the theory.

The appearances of the body were entirely at odds with those of epileptic drowning. Even in the event that she had a fit and had fallen on her face, she would have remained in that position and in the opposite case, fallen on the back, there would have been no scratches on the face. The further absurdity of the defence theory the doctor highlights was that, if the fit was brought on by a meal shortly before bathing, why was the stomach found empty and contracted at post mortem and no sign of food particles in the air passages which would have been diffused by the gaseous process of decomposition? Dr. Geoghegan's point was unwittingly corroborated by Kirwan in his address to the court when he placed the time of eating the meal in the mid-afternoon.

Even in the matter of circumstance there was no explanation offered by the defence, assuming their theory was credible, exactly how the body came to be lying on a rock, which on its landside had such shallow water that the tide could not possibly have carried it there not to mind deposit it in such a position. If the tide had been high enough, the rock was so low that it would not have provided an impediment to it being carried further down the channel.

If that was a calculation Kirwan relied on, which is probable, his study of the tide was either deficient or his action was predicated on other factors. Reverend Haughton's calculations put the height of water over the rock at high watermark, which was 4.37 p.m., at 4.84 feet. Given that this was only close to forty minutes after the Brew party had departed the island, Kirwan probably was not prepared to take the risk that another party might arrive. On the other hand, this logic would dictate that closer to the time of sunset would eliminate such a risk. But still, at 6.30 p.m. just a half an hour before he must have struck, there was 3 feet of water over the rock, more than sufficient to carry the body with the tide. When he did strike, the level of the water towards the landside of the rock was so shallow that it could not possibly have deposited the body on the rock. And also complicated the commission of the crime. This was the first slip-up on the murderer's part.

Sarah Maria Louisa, the professor attests, with no credible contrary medical opinion, was a very healthy woman and a strong and adventurous swimmer at the time of her death, a fact confirmed by the post mortem in relation to the health of the internal organs found by Dr. Hatchell also, remarkably well preserved despite the external state of decomposition accelerated by the water in the grave and coffin.

Killers frequently underestimate the force required to subdue the victim and the Kirwan case provided a classic example. The fact that his wife was able to emit three screams over a relatively prolonged period confirms this. Dr. Geoghegan proves that in the circumstances those screams could not have been emitted from a person suffering from an epileptic fit and during the period of the process the victim must have been conscious and fighting back. Again this was confirmed by the scratches and abrasions on the face and body and the laceration of the ear, which the professor says were caused by Maria's struggle to free herself from the sheet which was about her face and neck. Although the professor declined to go into the mode of killing, some of those injuries could have been sustained while the head was pressed downwards against the bottom under the shallow water.

The damage to the right earlobe is a telling pointer to the ferocity of the struggle. It may have been caused when the bathing cap was ripped from the head. Whether this was a result of a defensive act by the victim or an aggressive act by the attacker is impossible to say. When the cap was found two weeks after the event, the strings were tied in a tight knot.

The assumption that he could execute the crime with some ease was Kirwan's second slip-up.

It can be safely assumed from the highly unusual, not to say unique modus operandi employed by Kirwan to murder his wife, that he had carried out some research into the medical implications and appearances involved in drowning. There can be no dispute that he had free access to the clinical records of his medical employers. It cannot and did not escape his attention that forcible drowning had the potential of producing somewhat different appearances than accidental drowning. But it would have afforded him some comfort that accidental and suicidal drowning could produce a variety of appearances depending on such factors of temperature of the water, the location of the event and the period of immersion in the sea and whether the process was rapid or prolonged.

But while the killer's focus was on the external appearance of the body, he apparently forgot or did not know that the internal appearances would provide a far more accurate indication of the cause of death. That was Kirwan's third slip-up, with the potential to cause him most damage. But maybe he reasonably felt that if an inquest came to a verdict of accidental drowning any internal signs would be academic and disappear during the process of putrefaction.

As Dr. Geoghegan illustrates, the consequences of the process of putrefaction are much misunderstood by members of the medical profession, never mind a potential murderer with some forensic knowledge.

His fourth mistake was simple and understandable. In the heat of the problematic struggle to keep the bathing sheet over the face and neck, Kirwan omitted to ensure that sea water entered the victim's mouth. And that was his undoing, not so much the matter of water in the stomach and lungs as there is such a phenomenon as dry drowning. It was as a result of his panic when he effected with the sheet a combination of strangulation by tying it hard about the face and neck and then compressing the chest of his victim in the act of submerging her in the water.

It was those actions that produced unmistakable signs of asphyxia which are completely absent in drowning.

All the medical facts and appearances both external and internal, most notably, the lividity on the face; the bruised fingernails, the froth on the mouth, the swollen lips, the congested lungs, the bleeding from the ears and vagina provide the proof that Sarah Maria Louisa Kirwan was murdered by her husband.

It is a view also shared by a friend of William Roughead, Dr. Devon, a medico-legal examiner for the Crown in Britain, whose opinion he canvassed for his essay on the case. This is his opinion:

> In this case it was suggested that the deceased had an apoplectic stroke but there was no evidence in the brain of haemorrhage. Syncope was also put forward as a cause of death; but the appearances pointed to death from asphyxia. Epilepsy was also advanced as a cause but there was little evidence to support it. Granting that the deceased fell into water from fainting or an epileptic fit, and was there drowned, how could she have sustained the injuries she had received and be found lying on her back?
>
> If she had fallen forward against projecting rocks or stones might she not have cut her face and breast and bruised her right side? Possibly, but if she fell forward and got injured and drowned, how did she fall backward on a sheet with her clothes up under her armpits? I am unable to imagine any accidental or suicidal drowning in which the deceased would be found in the position and with the injuries of Mrs. Kirwan.
>
> And how might it have occurred? If the sheet on which she was found lying had been put around her when she was alive, in some such way as it was put around her dead body, before it was removed, she could easily have been submerged in shallow water. If she had been shoved in from behind, the injuries might have been received from the rocks and stones in the bed of the water.
>
> There was no evidence of throttling and there were no injuries on her back. The body seems to have been taken to the place in which it was found and in the process the bathing dress might have been drawn up under her armpits. It was a simple murder, clumsily carried out. If the body had been left in the water there would have been less room for suspicion, but it is a common thing for people under emotional stress to get exhausted mentally and behave with a degree of stupidity that is amazing.

Those remarks are apposite and concur to some degree with Dr. Geoghegan's analysis. The murder, was, however, anything but simple in its conception but Dr. Devon hits the nail on the head in a psychological sense and all murders involve that element. Particularly when he talks of the emotional stress involved in the commission which most often leads to the mistake or mistakes that inevitably lead to detection.

It would be a couple of decades until that most important aspect of the matter of murder would be translated into a form of science by the French forensic investigator Dr. Alexandre Lacassagne of Lyons University but just over a decade after the murder on Ireland's Eye it would be addressed in a fictional form by Dostoevsky in his classic work *Crime And Punishment*. In the great author's original proposal for publication in serial form he stated his ambition: "It is the psychological account of a crime."

If Dr. Devon's observations are to be believed, and there is no reason why they should not, Kirwan must have been visited with the same thoughts as Raskolnikov both before and particularly after the act. The dream or the imagining of anything rarely matches the reality. The author/main character explains it thus:

> At first, long before indeed, he had been much occupied with one question: why almost all crimes are so badly concealed and so easily detected, and why almost all criminals leave such obvious traces? He had come gradually to many and different and curious conclusions, and in his opinion the chief reason lay not so much in the material impossibility of concealing the crime as in the criminal himself. Almost every criminal is subject to a failure of will and reasoning power by a childish and phenomenal heedlessness at the very instant when prudence and caution are most essential.

The thought of the act is like a disease which reached its apogee just before the perpetration and continues apace at the moment of the crime, when all reason is abandoned and lasts for some time afterwards and then passes off like any illness. But

300

then there is no guarantee that some other form of consequent disease will return. Conscience, as the Bard noted, will make cowards of us all.

It will be remembered that the accused, all through the inescapable tension and pressure of the trial, at all times maintained his dignity and composure showing not the slightest ill-effect of the stress that might impress itself on a man accused of a capital crime with his life dependant on a positive outcome for his defence. This was soon to change.

While awaiting his fate in Mountjoy prison Kirwan went through periods of elation and self-possession followed by deep depression, a pattern of mood swings that obviously beset him prior to the commission of the crime and in its immediate aftermath. After the commutation of the death sentence and with transportation facing him he was seized by violent fits and descending into what was described by a dangerous illness requiring sedation by the prison physician Dr. Rynd, who had given medical evidence for the defence at the trial.

Contrary to what is often claimed, he was not transported to Bermuda, a fact that outraged those who believed he was a murderer. Instead he was sent south to Fort Westmoreland prison on Spike Island in Cork Harbour where he spent the next 24 years before being released. According to the prison physician Dr. O Keefe, Kirwan told him that he would be travelling to Liverpool and from there he intended to travel to America with the intention of joining and marrying Teresa Kenny, mother of his children. It is said that, faced with destitution, Teresa had thrown herself and her children at the mercy of the Crown which proved it had a heart after all – or at any rate a sense of fair play – and ruled that Kirwan's estate should provide for them. The older children were sent to school and Teresa and the two youngest, Edward and Mary, went to join her brother in America. Edward would be of age to fight in the American Civil War (1861-1865) while his father languished in prison.

But before going to Liverpool or Queenstown as was later suggested, he was found in Dublin, for a number of his anatomical drawings dated 1876 bear annotations by Dr. John Morgan, a surgeon attached to the Lock Hospital, recording information at the time given to him by Kirwan, recalling the circumstances in which they were made. Dr. Morgan was obviously giving the artist some work to contribute to his passage to America.

There is a story which may be a myth, but then again may be true, that a bent old man took a boat about that time out to Ireland's Eye. The locals believed that it was the murderer returning to the scene of the crime. Certainly in the pantheon of homicide, it would not be the first time that such a visitation occurred. For a certain type of killer the location of their foul deed proves a powerful magnet.

There was another story and that was connected to Teresa Kenny and the children, whose existence had been ascribed as providing the motive for the crime in the first place all those years ago. There must have been a powerful bond that survived the scandal, the shame and the life of a pariah that Miss Kenny had to endure in the immediate aftermath of the conviction. The passage of time should have properly buried that trauma but the love must have survived the rest. The tragedy was, that hate should have intervened and not only result in the brutal death of an innocent and the destruction of the meaningful lives of the other innocents whom the artist had drawn into his tangled web.

After going to America, nothing was ever heard of Kirwan again but some reports suggest that he was a broken man and died just a few years later. When one is burdened with the blood of another, as the proverb says, one is a fugitive until death.

Sarah Maria Louisa's remains still lie in a grave, unmarked by a stone, but numbered X D39 near the Oak Walk section of Glasnevin Cemetery.

Amongst a folio of Kirwan's sketches, paintings and drawings in the National Library of Ireland under the care of Honora Fall, there are a number, which in the light of this particular history, have the effect of raising a hair on the back of the neck. There is one from a seaward view of the landing spot and the Martello

Tower on the island. There is another of a woman and child bearing a strong family resemblance, grieving by a gravestone. It is not identified but it is more than likely Teresa Kenny and one of the children, on the death of one of Kirwan's sons.

There is a peculiar tenderness in the representation, which is different from the other quite cool objective feel in most of the works. As if an emotion has measured the eye of the artist. And there is one in which the cool eye returns: an elaborately attired woman, of handsome visage, which is coloured and strong of character, with no trace of vulnerability.

On the back is a caption in the handwriting of the artist: "*Mrs. Kirwan sketched by her husband.*"

There are a number of coloured sketches from the summer and autumn of 1842 obviously completed during a trip to Connemara, one of a fisherman's family, another of a young girl named as Mary Lynch, a stocking seller, and one of Bartholomew Costello, commandant of the Clifden Hunt. He must have moved around: there are portraits of a Wicklow rabbit-seller and a Tipperary milkmaid from the same period. Also in the collection are architectural drawings, ground plan for village buildings and a detailed map of a section of coastal land between Dublin and Howth. On the back of one drawing there is an extensive table of financial calculations, the nature of which is not clear but does make some references to drawing or painting utensils.

In an old R.H.A. catalogue under his name and title of painter and miniaturist is a list of his works exhibited between 1835 and 1846, dominated by portraiture. The first three works give an address at 14 Anglesea Street, some others 13 D'Olier Street and the final four dated 1845-46; 6 Lower Merrion Street. At least four of the works are in the NLI collection. In the same catalogue, coincidentally, among the exhibits of Howard F. Knee is a 1926 painting of Ireland's Eye from Malahide.

A large selection of Kirwan's anatomical drawings are held in that beautiful building of The Royal College of Physicians on Kildare Street in Dublin looked after by librarian Robert Mills and currently being restored by the archivist Harriet Wheelock.

And also more in the Royal College of Surgeons under the care of archivist Mary O'Doherty. The coloured representations of the physical manifestations of illness of patients, many of them young children, provide evidence of a great draftsman at work, whether under the circumstance of necessity or desire. For either reason, his medical employers must have been well pleased, as it appears long for before the invention of the X-ray the commissions would have been kept going for a considerable time. The artist, is seems, without much doubt, would have not been short of much more, in his working life.

There is one most affecting drawing of the body of a recently delivered and deceased baby with the umbilical cord still attached to the placenta. It inspires both a sense of horror and sadness, a reaction that the creator could hardly have avoided in the aftermath of the destruction of his wife. There are many of the ghastly physical effects of skin diseases and of syphilis commissioned by the great physician William Wallace who died tragically at a young age from typhus.

Almost without exception, his medical masters were men of great integrity, many who died prematurely as a result of their dedication to their profession. Men from whom Kirwan could have taken a lesson about the proper values in life but ignored, and men of a profession who would contribute largely to his undoing. An irony that could not have escaped him at his dying moment, which might or not have been more deeply stressful than that of his wife.

On the evidence, perhaps not so, but who knows what conscience might deliver to a killer on the cusp of eternity.

The whole cast of this haunting drama have long gone to that bourn from which no traveller returns, their deeds of life left in the form of one legacy or another. In this case, the central characters were beautiful but became the damned as the devil in one created hell for all.

CHAPTER 12

EPILOGUE

He remembered the shock that had gripped his body and mind when the Clerk of the Court delivered the verdict of the jury. Nothing in his life had prepared him for such a moment of absolute terror. All his composure evaporated in the utterance of the word *Guilty*. He had gambled and lost. He had taken every cut and thrust of the prosecution counsel and the damnation of their witnesses with the upright attitude that he believed was the right of his status and position in society. He did not flinch once while his moral reputation had been torn to tatters. The witnesses were his social inferiors and who would listen to their evidence with anything but doubt?

They had an agenda and why would the respectable members of the jury side with them against him? That possibility never entered his mind. He was confident throughout the proceedings that his top-class defence team would deliver him from the nightmare of public examination. The stabs of the leering spectators he could survive and the absence in court of his mistress gave him great hope. He knew that she would never let him down. And she did not and after it was all over he would make all his promises to her be true when he was vindicated from these foul attacks on his character.

Of course it was unimaginable that he occupied a solitary prison cell under the eyes of the turnkeys and was brought, handcuffed, to the disgusting cell in the bowels of the court, but he could put up with all that with the expectation of the victory of being found an innocent man. Then all his troubles would be over. He would resume his industrious life with the respect of his medical commissioners, move on to be a proper family man and achieve the status of the talent he had as an artist already well established. But this time, no portraits, he would allow his proper creative talent to flow, no longer as a well-paid observer of the vanities of his fellow class.

The anatomical drawings would continue for he possessed a fascination for those less privileged of the fortunes of health and wealth that he had enjoyed. Some of his subjects were wealthy but had succumbed to the awful ravages of syphilis from the indulgences of their sexual inclinations and had come to the attention of Dr. William Wallace, one of his steady and loyal commissioners. Of such infiltrations of disease in the human body and mental condition he had long learned to be but a dispassionate observer.

He could not share the passion of his medical masters to find an alleviation, not to mind a cure for those terrible afflictions for he was just the eye on those, as only every trueborn artist could be. They desired representations of them, he provided them and all were happy. In no possible manner was he allowed or could allow himself, even if he was thus inclined, to empathise with the patient. Their bubles, their rashes, their tumours were and could not be of any concern to him. He was not the medical examiner but the reproducer.

Emotion, he knew with utter certainty, would never intervene in his professional life, but suddenly and awfully it did in his personal affairs. He regretted that deeply but he had no choice. All reason deserted him in a way that he could never have contemplated, the control of his life and destiny was being removed and he could not countenance that on any level. Why anyone could not accept that, he had no idea, but he was driven towards a fate that had escaped any imagination of his life.

He was born to be a winner and could never contemplate the loss of anything. But now the moment was upon him, he heard it with his own disbelieving ears: *Guilty*.

He longed for a distraction, which might bring relief from his constant restlessness. But there was no distraction possible in the hell to which he had been condemned, other than the dull, boring unrelenting routine that is the lot of the prisoner. Not even of conscience which was superseded by self-pity and a growing loathing of the world and its ways. He had always been over-sensitive to how others viewed him and affected an air of superiority. That was now gone, he was nothing more than a common convict. The thought repelled and overwhelmed him.

In the cell of Mountjoy Prison, afterwards, he fell into a sick delirious state, vomiting into that awful thing beside the harsh bed, half-conscious of everything that meant anything of the situation that surrounded him. All that came to him, including people, disappeared into a haze. He heard their voices, mocking in their tones of comfort and attempted consolation. There was nothing that could console him, facing as he did the hangman's rope. It was all over and could not be anyway otherwise.

He tried to remember everything and failed miserably. The details of the trial came up before him, interminably, in the sense of condemning every aspect of defence of his time on the island. He had perfect recollection of the event as he had rehearsed it – but then nothing. That oblivion of memory replicated that which he now faced. The walls of the home he now occupied, suffocated every particle of air from his lungs, only serving to remind him of the luxury of his previous abode. He moaned and cried and raged against the prospect of the oncoming terror.

He jumped out of the bed and ran to the door and banged and beat it to no avail. There was always an obstacle to his imagined escape. Through the slim aperture of the prison door human eyes observed him with equal disbelief. During the day there were seductive rays of light briefly alleviating his misery from the outside, but almost as soon as they appeared they faded and the darkness fell, just like on the island. But here there was no boatman to ferry him to freedom.

He was haunted by the failure of his murderous enterprise, all planned meticulously, as was every aspect of his previous life. It was like a work of art in his imagination; the method beyond the compass of any common criminal, unique in its fashion and meant to be in its execution. But, like the fool he was, he thought that the technique should be like that he exercised in his paintings and most particularly the anatomical drawings: removed, objective and concentrated.

He forgot that his subject was under no constraint to remain still, as all the others under his command and submit to his controlling hands. Worse still, he blindly underestimated his own strength and ability to adapt to any complication that might arise. He had misunderstood nature itself, the basic instinct of the prey for fight or flight when faced with the predator, the lust for life when faced with death. And that panic could paralyse the senses of the human predator and heightened emotion lead to careless decisions and mistakes.

Her face appeared to him, in that awful suspended hour between the fading of the night and the dawning of the day. Her widened eyes fixed on his from beneath the thin veil of the water before she burst through it screaming, the seaweed and gravel like a crown in her thick lush hair, her strong hands reaching up to grip his neck and her froth emanating from her mouth, choking his breath; the haunting exorcised by his wakeful silent scream. And so it went day after day until he could tolerate it no more.

The doctor eventually came and sedated him and gave brief relief from the torture. He had fallen apart already and so what did the future offer? Nothing but oblivion and that was welcome, now that his demons had been abated and fear was of no consequence. Far better than impotence, brought on by the eternity of memory. But that was never far away. When the effects of the drug wore off the hush returned again, that awful silence which marked the onset of another visitation. Whatever friendly moment that intervened was lost. There was not a single sound to be heard in the previously noisy prison. Then once again, on the cue of the hour she burst into his consciousness, projecting him into a state of fear, hopelessness and despair.

He looked forward to the short walk having been given the blessing of the parson, to the comfort of the gallows. It was the last opportunity to display bravery as opposed to abject cowardice. That chance was robbed from him by the misguided efforts of supporters of clemency on his behalf, most of whom he hardly recognised, not to mind having been acquainted with them. Instead he was condemned to relive that terrifying moment of visitation and recognition for the rest of his life.

It was, perhaps, no better, no worse or equal in some measure to the last moments of terror, fear and loathing that he visited on his innocent and unsuspecting wife. For those moments, however they might be perceived by the outsider, could well have lasted the equivalent of a lifetime for the victim. The haunting would last until his dying day and oblivion claimed him.

When someone is burdened with the blood of another, let that killer be a fugitive until death.

If you enjoyed
Murder at Ireland's Eye by Michael Sheridan
why not try
Game, Set, Murder also published by Poolbeg?
Here's a sneak preview.

GAME, SET, MURDER

MICHAEL SHERIDAN

POOLBEG

PROLOGUE

Nothing in his life had prepared him for this. His mind was a whirlpool of conflicting thoughts and emotions. Outside and inside the villa complex there was sunshine, laughter, enjoyment, eating, drinking, gambling, wealth, debauchery and all the other things that constitute the pursuits of human existence and expectation. Inside their apartment nothing but sheer fright and horror.

The dwindling of money, the panic that ensues when wondering where the next franc would come from, now seemed more a pleasure than a painful experience. There must have been a better alternative, a more civilised way of dealing with the onset of poverty. They could have promised, could have begged, stolen – anything but this with its terrible outcome that had for some reason previously escaped his drunken imagination.

Why had he agreed to his wife's plan? Because he was a weak, drunken, foolish man paralysed by his inadequacies. It had made no sense at the time and even less now.

The waft of cooking emanated from a neighbouring apartment, making him feel sick. But he knew he could not move to the bathroom.

He had carried out his part of the plan while his wife engaged the female visitor in conversation. A woman who was perceived to be the cause of their problems but was not. All their misfortunes were of their own making. He had downed another whisky while in the kitchen and then had taken the pestle in his hand. His hand was shaking, so he downed another drink.

Violence had never been part of his flawed nature. The only object he had ever hit with great intent and determination was a tennis ball in the great flush of his youth. The only person he had wanted to put away was an opponent on the court, and even that with the grace of skill rather than any aggression.

And now he was to hit an innocent woman over the head to stun her and to rob her of her much-vaunted jewellery and any cash she possessed. It made no sense. Even in their desperation. But his wife insisted and she had always got her way. He would have rather died in poverty, but she had other ideas and told him that he was responsible for the awful position they found themselves in. He had tried to argue. It was no good – he had lost all the arguments before, a long time ago.

It was no use. He staggered from the kitchen and quickly brought the pestle down as hard as he could on the back of the woman's head. The visitor fell to the floor, gurgling with shock, and then let out a scream. She was alive and tried to get up. He dropped the pestle on the floor. His wife was screaming at him but it was as if he heard nothing.

It was all happening a distance from him or, rather, he was distanced from it. He could and would do no more. He saw his wife as in a nightmare pounce on the unfortunate woman. They struggled and there were more screams.

"The dagger, the dagger!"

He walked in a waking dream to the sideboard, picked up the dagger and handed it to his wife who was punching the squealing victim and being scratched in return. He saw the flash of it as it was plunged into the chest of the struggling woman. He heard the slowly descending gurgle and saw the blood streaming from her nose. He ran to the bathroom and vomited the undigested contents of the whisky bottle.

"Come back here, come back!" His wife's order reverberated around the bathroom.

He rushed back to the living room. She handed him the knife. "Push it in, push it in!"

The woman was lying face to the ground. He shoved the bloodstained dagger into her back. It went through to the hilt.

"Pull it out!"

He did and, with a final gurgle and a tremor all over her body, the woman lay still.

He knew in that instant his life was over. The blood all over the carpet and seeping across the living room floor was evidence enough. He trembled from head to toe, ran back to the kitchen and put the whisky bottle to his mouth. He could hardly breathe with the shock of it all.

Tears rolled down his drunken face. What had his dissolute life been all about? Anything but this. The woman had done him no wrong. He wanted to join her in death right now. He was awoken from his instant remorse by a clunk on the kitchen sink. When he wiped away his tears a large knife and a saw came into focus.

"Now remember what comes next. She will be home soon. You know what we must do."

He did not want to go back to the sitting room. But now there was no choice. He did not want to look into those dead staring eyes that would haunt him for the rest of his life. But his wife said he must overcome such scruples. *There is nothing either good or bad, but thinking makes it so.* They would remove the body to the bathroom first, do the necessary and then plan the next move.

What did she mean by necessary? What next move? There would be blood everywhere and how could they get rid of those damned spots? Not to mind that damned guilt. He had no idea. All their time together, living on the edge, she had the ideas – as she would now. Maybe there was a way forward. He would listen to her suggestions and agree as he always had done.

As always there was no choice, no alternative. That had been the path of their lives. There was only one way forward, or backward. But he felt utterly sick in his heart and that had been the case for a very long time.

The rest was a blur of hacking, cutting and cleaning of a now inanimate thing that had once been a living human being. Blood provides the greatest challenge to erase after spilling in a variety of spots, splatters and formations from the body. Not to mind the soul which is beyond the constraints of the visible.

～～～

The sea was a dark shade of purple and blue under the scimitar moon. He looked furtively behind him and almost jumped at the small flat whale-like shape of Cap Martin. His nerves were shredded and he nearly let the bag slide out of his hand. From the white sand of the beach of Larvotto, the lights of Monte Carlo twinkled. From the direction of the seafront the warm wind carried sounds of gaiety. Their comforting timbre served only to mock him as he scuttled like a crab along the beach, fearful of encountering a human form.

He looked for an outlet that would carry the contents of his bag as far out to sea as possible. His glazed eyes were drawn to the moon from the shimmering reflection of its light on the calm surface of the sea. It watched him, unmoved, immutable. He trembled and trudged on, the sand tugging quietly at his feet.

The light reminded him of the streams of gold that flowed from the croupier's hands, and he could hear the dull thud of scattered coins on the table. It sent a shiver right down his spine. The cloying sense of greed that the image evoked was now a source of repulsion, for it was not a bag of coins he was carrying. The contents slid around as he stumbled on a mound of flotsam. Was it for this that he had stood around the tables, transfixed with trepidation? Always searching for something, a sign, a play, calculating, taking notes of the roll of the ball, the expression of the players, anything – even a hint of superstition – to lead to a reversal of fortune? But nothing turned in his favour and he was beset by more feverish thoughts and sudden false expectation that tomorrow would provide the break, and if not the following morrow. His chances were as good as being born all over again or rising from the grave given him by the dead hand of fate.

Of course he played the hand – it was his nature and nothing had ever changed that. It was copper-fastened by his companion in life, whose nature was the same if not worse. Without a check on that dual nature, nothing had even the remotest chance of improving their circumstances. Tomorrow it would all be ended. But now there was no tomorrow but certain ruin.

He slid across a number of small rocks beyond a turn in the beach. There in a modest gulf was a fast-flowing outlet. He opened the top of the bag, averted his eyes and slid the slippery stinking contents into the water. He heard a sickening plop and a gurgle. He dropped the bag in too and the current bore it away. He turned quickly away and made his way to the seashore and immersed his hands into the soft waves to wash them.

He gazed towards the moonlit horizon. If he walked towards that horizon it would be all over in a matter of minutes. But he lacked, as he always had, the courage of any conviction. Unlike his ancient ancestor, the crusader who had fought with distinction in Damietta. Unlike his domineering father, the resolute magistrate in Waterford who unflinchingly opposed the Fenian rebels.

The silent beauty of this place put the horror that he had left behind in the Villa Menesini into perspective. He shed some cowardly tears, for nothing or no one in particular, not for himself or the victim. He dreaded the return, and the dreadful aftermath of the awful act. He dragged himself to his feet and retraced his passage along the beach and onwards in the direction of Boulevard des Moulins.

The steps afterwards he did not dare to contemplate.

LE TRAIN

MARSEILLES, AUGUST 1907

In the early morning of August 6th, shrouded in steam, the 5.38 a.m. train from Monte Carlo pulled up at the designated platform of Gare de Marseilles Saint-Charles. It was the height of the tourist season and the platform was thronged with disembarking passengers and marked by the feverish activity of the overworked porters.

One, Beraud, was given the task of bringing a large trunk to the baggage section where it was due, according to instructions, to be forwarded to London. Sweat sprouting on his forehead from stress and effort in the heat, he brought it to the appropriate section where he placed it on the last existing space on the bottom part of the large wooden rack. He noticed an unpleasant smell emanating from it and wondered what it contained. He then speedily returned to the platform to retrieve more luggage and suffer extra punishment for his now constantly aching bones.

Meanwhile station commissaire Louis Pons, famous for his punctilious follow-up and examination of his underlings' work, was doing his rounds of the room, making sure that every bag and item of luggage was in the right section and placed correctly for quick and efficient removal. His devotion to duty was much lauded and he was personally proud of the performance of the service under his tutelage.

318

His team of porters did not resent or hate Pons because he was considered tough but generally fair. Everyone knew the lie of his land and knew never under any circumstance to get on his wrong side. So respected was he by his employers that his judgement was final. Beyond him there was no court of appeal.

His life outside his work was equally regimented. He tolerated no excess and in his life there was no room for the unexpected. When it turned up he dealt with it quickly and firmly, thereby keeping it at bay.

He noticed the recently delivered trunk and re-adjusted its position slightly to his own satisfaction. As he approached the next rack, he stopped in his tracks. Some instinct which he could not explain at the time, or afterwards, made him turn his attention to the trunk once more. The perennially prepared superintendent was not ready for the grim scenario which was about to unfold.

As he stood over the trunk, within centimetres of his gleaming black shoes he saw a small dark-red spot and then another fell on it and then another, forming a small pool. The origin seemed to be somewhere on the underside of the trunk. It looked like blood. Pons instantly recognised that to investigate it was not his business and momentarily was paralysed by a wave of anxiety which went from his toes to his stomach and then to his head and back to his stomach again. For him a most disturbing, unusual and unwelcome sensation.

How, he thought, would whatever might prove to be the explanation for this aberration reflect on his well-oiled operation and his department, hitherto run to within half a centimetre of perfection? He was no fool. Like at a port, all life passes through a train station, and quite a lot of unsavoury things can and did happen. Many of sufficient interest to the newspapers. The congregation of travellers were under the constant attention of a gaggle of robbers, pickpockets, conmen and prostitutes. Who in turn were the subject of observation of Pons, his security personnel and the undercover police. But all those eyes and all the precautions could not stem the whole tide of criminal intent.

There had been numerous arrests made in the station, many unreported, and most of the rest attracting what could be described as cursory attention and a few paragraphs on the inside pages of the local newspapers. But a couple of incidents made the front pages – a stabbing after a row between two pimps, the arrest on a just-arrived train of a notorious fraudster. Pons winced at the memory and the perception that the wonderfully constructed station, so efficiently managed, accommodated within its august portals a den of iniquity.

In this instance, he recognised that if his dawning, anxious suspicion proved to be true, the local, national and the foreign press would come crawling like a plague of rats over his territory and, worst of all, his name would be dragged into reports. The object of newspapers, in his opinion shared by many, was to create sensation rather than further the cause of truth. It was of no comfort to Pons that he might be lucky enough to be portrayed in a favourable light. He detested the idea of such attention; his privacy meant everything to him. But as always, he knew, whatever his misgivings, he had to do his duty and properly. There was no question of cleaning up and disposing of the now-coagulating pool which had formed under the rack.

But of course, the thought had, even for an unacceptable instant, crossed his mind.

The cacophony of noise, the hissing of the steam, the shrill whistles of the guards, the shunting thunder of the trains had departed Pons' range of consciousness. He might as well have been solitarily confined in a cell, so occupied was he with his thoughts and the direction of his actions.

For a moment he felt dizzy with a confusion completely foreign to his experience. His palms became wet with a cold sweat and he felt his heartbeat soar uncomfortably. He took several deep breaths and pulled himself together, considering such panic intolerable.

The anxiety having receded, he took one more deep breath and removed a notebook and pencil from his inside jacket pocket. He bent down and from the tag on the trunk took a note of the details. The names of the owners, destination and their current address which caused Pons some inexplicable comfort.

He returned to his office, shut the door, sat at his desk and from the drawer removed his pipe, filled and lit it. Momentarily he relaxed in his chair, then began to mull over what he perceived as his two immediate choices. He must, he realised, bite the bullet.

He could contact the owners. What would they say? That the trunk contained fresh meat or slaughtered poultry. He laughed inwardly at an explanation so outlandish that he would have to instantly ignore it. Of course he would be offered a bribe which he would also not countenance. There was no one that could not do with more money. People could have enough of sex, drink and food but never of money. And Pons of all people, given his character and behaviour, believed that any unlimited need leads to destruction. He was happy with his salary and his legitimate percentage of his porters' tips, on account of which he smoothed their daily passage. He kept them happy and the favour reaped a double return, cash and loyalty. A fair bargain. No whiff of corruption. Bribery was different in his book. Being bought meant being owned and Pons valued his independence. His employers acknowledged it as did his workers.

Too much to lose for too little. Because as sure as tobacco was in his pipe, the owners would try to buy him off.

He had only one choice. No other.

He picked up the phone and rang a valued friend but strictly on official business.

∽◡∽

◄○►

If you enjoyed these chapters from
Game, Set, Murder by Michael Sheridan,
why not order the full book online
@ www.poolbeg.com

◄○►